365 Ways to Cook Chicken

Simply the Best Chicken Recipes You'll Find Anywhere!

Cheryl Sedaker

A JOHN BOSWELL ASSOCIATES BOOK

WILLIAM MORROW
An Imprint of *HarperCollins*Publishers

365 WAYS TO COOK CHICKEN. Copyright © 1986 by John Boswell Management, Inc. All rights reserved. Printed in the United States of America. No part of this book may be used or reproduced in any manner whatsoever without written permission except in the case of brief quotations embodied in critical articles and reviews. For information address HarperCollins Publishers Inc., 10 East 53rd Street, New York, NY 10022.

HarperCollins books may be purchased for educational, business, or sales promotional use. For information please write: Special Markets Department, HarperCollins Publishers Inc., 10 East 53rd Street, New York, NY 10022.

First Quill edition published 2004.

Design: Nigel Rollings
Index: Maro Riofrancos

The Library of Congress has catalogued the hardcover edition as follows:
Sedaker, Cheryl.
   365 ways to cook chicken.
   "A John Boswell Associates book."
   Includes index.
   1. Cookery (Chicken). I. Title. II. Title: Three hundred sixty-five ways to cook chicken.
TX750.S43
1986   641.6'65   85-45231
ISBN 0-06-015539-6

ISBN 0-06-057889-0 (pbk.)

11 12 13 14   RRD   10 9 8 7 6 5 4 3

Acknowledgments

I would like to thank the following people and organizations for their help and encouragement during the writing of this book: Pat Porto Schmidt; Norma and Norman Webster; Ceci Abbruzzese; Jane Ashley; the Delmarva Poultry Association; the National Broiler Council; and all my friends at Reynolds Aluminum.

I owe a particular debt of gratitude to Perdue Farms of Salisbury, Maryland, for their enthusiastic cooperation and generous support. Thanks especially to Rita Morgan in Maryland and to Anne Salisbury of R.C. Auletta & Co., Perdue's public relations agency in New York.

Finally, thanks to all my family and friends who acted as my unofficial taste panel and did a great job of pretending they never grew tired of eating chicken.

About The Author

Cheryl Sedaker graduated from Cornell University with a degree in Home Economics. Her lifelong passion for good food and its preparation led her to become a professional home economist for Reynolds Aluminum, for whom she appears regularly on radio and television to discuss consumer affairs, and food trends and to share new recipes developed by the Reynolds Wrap Kitchens.

She lives, works—and cooks—in Riverside, Connecticut.

Contents

Chicken's Delight

America's love of chicken is hardly a well-kept secret. Last year we consumed over 18 *billion* pounds of this succulent bird—an amount equal to twenty-five whole "oven roasters" for every man, woman, and child in the United States.

Why has chicken obtained such extraordinary popularity in this country? Because it's quick, it's easy, it's economical, it tastes good, and it's good for you. In other words, chicken is just about the perfect American food.

Chicken is nutritious. Any way you slice it chicken is healthful. One 3½-ounce all-meat (skinless) portion contains 31 grams of protein, about half the daily adult requirement. Chicken is also a source of Vitamin A, thiamine, riboflavin, niacin, iron, phosphorus, and calcium.

And chicken, of course is the dieter's delight. That same 3½-ounce portion of white meat contains only about 150 calories (10% more for dark meat). And even the skin is not as "bad" for you as most people believe, containing only 17% fat, two-thirds of which is unsaturated. The amount of protein-per-calorie makes chicken the most efficient protein source of all meats.

Chicken is a bargain. Because of vastly improved production techniques, chicken is your greatest edible hedge against inflation. In fact, were it not for inflation, chicken would now sell for about *half* of what it did twenty years ago.

Chicken tastes good. While some may find beef too heavy and fish too "fishy," chicken's light, moist, tender meat appeals to almost every taste. Moreover, its subtle flavor provides a marvelous foil for any number of other flavors.

Chicken is easy. Chicken, a short-fibered meat, is easy to eat and even easier to make. The ways in which it can be seasoned are virtually limitless, and when you're in a hurry —and these days who isn't—it can be cooked in a flash. Diced into bite-size pieces, chicken can be stir-fried in five minutes. Skinless, boneless breasts can be sautéed in no more than 10 minutes. A cut-up chicken bakes with no attention needed in roughly 45 minutes. And a whole 3 pounder will roast in little over an hour.

Since you probably already know how good, and good for you, chicken is, and since you probably eat or serve it at least once a week, this book is dedicated to the humble proposition that you can never have too many good chicken recipes. Of the 365 that follow, some are elegant, some are homespun, some are elaborate, others are quick and easy. There are international preparations and traditional American dishes, chicken with pasta, and chicken with fruit. Whatever your mood, whatever's in the pantry, you'll find plenty of recipes to suit your taste and to suit your individual needs.

In addition to this year's-worth of recipes, here are a few buying and cooking tips that will help make your chicken the talk of the table:

     —When buying chicken, look for intact, unblemished skin, with no obvious bruises. The color of the skin may vary from white to yellow, depending on the type of chicken and what it was fed. Any blood in the package should be bright red, and the meat should smell fresh. Before cooking, all chicken should be rinsed under cold running water and patted dry. Pull off any feathers and trim off extra fat.

     —Unlike red meats, chicken should never be served rare. Always cook until the meat is opaque and white throughout, with no trace of pink. Temperature should range from 175° to 185° At this stage, the juices will run clear or golden when the thigh or thickest part of the meat is pricked with a knife. Do not overcook, however, or the chicken will lose its wonderful flavor and texture. Properly cooked chicken is tender, moist, and bursting with juices. Overcooked chicken is dry and leathery.

     —All recipes that follow include short notations of estimated preparation times ("PREP:"), cooking times ("COOK:"), and number of servings ("SERVES:"). As a general rule, however, when chicken is served on the bone, allow ¾ to 1 pound per person. Boneless, one breast half (about 4 to 5 ounces) is considered an appropriate serving portion. However, if your family is made up of hearty eaters, make sure you've allowed for seconds. Any leftovers can be used in many of the recipes included here that call for precooked chicken.

     Bon appetit!

Chapter 1

American Classics

American cooking has finally come into its own. As young American-born and American-trained chefs are experimenting with native ingredients and traditional culinary techniques, home cooks are returning to good solid cooking, revitalizing their grandmothers' recipes and making the most out of America's bountiful supply of produce. This chapter celebrates some of the all-time chicken favorites that are serving as inspiration.

From country southern-fried chicken to the elegant 21 Club's chicken hash, to old-fashioned chicken and dumplings, this is comfort food—homey, tasty, satisfying.

1 SOUTHERN-FRIED CHICKEN
Prep: 10 minutes   Cook: 25 minutes   Serves: 4

You can substitute peanut or corn oil for frying, but lard will give that true southern-fried flavor.

⅓ cup buttermilk	¼ teaspoon freshly ground
½ cup flour	pepper
1 teaspoon salt	1 chicken (3 pounds), cut up
	⅔ cup lard or vegetable oil

1. Place buttermilk in a shallow dish. Combine flour, salt, and pepper in a plastic or paper bag. Dip chicken pieces in buttermilk. Place one or two pieces at a time in the bag; shake to coat.

2. In a large deep frying pan, melt lard over medium-high heat to 375°. Add chicken pieces and cook, turning frequently, until brown and crisp, 20 to 25 minutes. Drain on paper towels before serving.

2 FRIED CHICKEN WITH CREAM GRAVY
Prep: 15 minutes   Marinate: 1 hour   Cook: 30 minutes   Serves: 4

⅓ cup plus 2 tablespoons corn or peanut oil	¾ cup bread crumbs
2 tablespoons lemon juice	2 tablespoons butter or margarine
¼ teaspoon salt	1½ cups milk
Freshly ground pepper	½ cup light cream or half-and-half
1 chicken (3 pounds), cut up	¼ teaspoon paprika
½ cup plus ⅓ cup flour	¼ teaspoon cayenne pepper
2 eggs	
2 tablespoons milk	

1. In a small bowl, combine ⅓ cup oil, lemon juice, salt and pepper. Place chicken pieces in a shallow baking dish and pour marinade mixture over. Cover and marinate for 30 to 60 minutes.

2. Dry chicken pieces on paper towels. Place ½ cup flour in a plastic or paper bag. In a small bowl, combine eggs and milk; place bread crumbs in a shallow bowl. Put several pieces of chicken in the bag and shake to coat thoroughly. Dip in egg mixture then roll in bread crumbs.

3. In a large frying pan, heat remaining oil and the butter over medium heat. Add chicken pieces and cook, turning frequently, until browned all over, 20 to 25 minutes. Remove and drain on paper towels.

4. Whisk remaining ⅓ cup flour into frying pan. Reduce heat to low and cook, stirring, 3 minutes. Whisk in milk and cream. Season with paprika, cayenne, and additional salt and pepper to taste.

3   MICHAEL STERN'S MOM'S OVEN-FRIED CORNFLAKE CHICKEN

Prep: 10 minutes   Cook: 1 hour   Serves: 4

Michael Stern and his wife, Jane, are the coauthors of the best-selling American cookbook *Square Meals*.

Like many Americans—and for that matter like many of the world's great chefs and food experts—Michael came by his love of good simple food at his mother's table. Regarding this recipe he writes:

Cornflake chicken is the playful side of American home cooking. Of course, it is no replacement for chicken pan-fried in lard; but it is easy, it is delicious in its own right, and it is fun. Such culinary fun, which involves making something new from unlikely off-the-shelf supermarket products, is as American as mock apple pie.

2 eggs, slightly beaten	2 teaspoons salt
¼ cup milk	½ teaspoon freshly ground
2½ cups cornflake crumbs	pepper
(crushed but not	1 chicken (3 pounds), cut up
pulverized)	5 tablespoons butter, melted

1. Preheat oven to 350°. Mix together eggs and milk in a shallow dish. Mix cornflake crumbs, salt, and pepper in a separate dish.

2. Dip chicken pieces first in the egg mixture, then dredge in crumbs to coat evenly.

3. Arrange chicken pieces in a greased 13 x 9 x 2-inch baking dish. Drizzle with melted butter. Bake uncovered for 1 hour.

4   ROAST CHICKEN WITH POTATOES AND PAN GRAVY

Prep: 15 minutes   Cook: 1¼ hours   Serves: 4

1 whole chicken, about 3	2 tablespoons olive oil
pounds, rinsed and dried	1 medium carrot, thickly
Salt and freshly ground	sliced
pepper	4 medium-size red potatoes,
1 medium onion, thickly	peeled and quartered
sliced, and 1 small onion,	1 tablespoon flour
quartered	1 cup chicken stock or water
½ teaspoon dried thyme	
2 tablespoons butter, softened	

1. Preheat oven to 350°. Season chicken liberally with salt and pepper inside and out. Put small quartered onion and thyme inside cavity and tie legs together. Rub butter all over chicken.

2. Put oil in a large oval gratin dish or shallow roasting pan. Scatter sliced onion and carrot around center of dish. Place chicken on top. Arrange potatoes around chicken, turning to coat with oil. Season with salt and pepper to taste.

3. Roast chicken in oven, turning potatoes and basting with pan drippings, for 1 hour 15 minutes, until chicken is golden brown and potatoes are tender.

Remove to a serving platter and cover with foil to keep warm.

4. Remove all but 2 tablespoons fat from pan. Place over medium heat, add flour, and cook, stirring, for 2 minutes. Whisk in stock and bring to a boil, stirring, until thickened. Season with salt and pepper to taste. Strain into a gravy boat and pass with chicken.

5 DEEP-DISH CHICKEN POT PIE
Prep: 40 minutes   Cook: 1 hour   Serves: 6

Every region of America has its own chicken pot pie. This deep-dish version uses whole wheat, which produces a browner, more flavorful crust.

Filling:
4 tablespoons butter or margarine
½ cup chopped celery
¼ cup chopped onion
¼ cup all-purpose flour
2 cups chicken stock or canned broth
Salt and freshly ground pepper
2 cups chopped cooked chicken
¼ cup chopped parsley
½ teaspoon crumbled sage

Pastry:
1 cup whole wheat pastry flour
1 cup all-purpose flour
½ teaspoon salt
6 tablespoons chilled shortening
3 to 5 tablespoons ice water

1. Make filling: In a medium-size saucepan, melt butter over medium heat. Cook celery and onion until tender. Add flour and cook, stirring, for 1 minute without browning. Gradually add stock and cook, stirring, until sauce thickens. Season to taste with salt and pepper. Stir in chicken, parsley, and sage. Set aside.

2. Make pastry: Preheat oven to 350°. In a large bowl, stir together whole wheat flour, all-purpose flour, and salt. With a pastry blender or two knives, cut in shortening until mixture resembles cornmeal. Sprinkle with ice water until dough stays together. Roll into a ball and divide into two parts.

3. To assemble pie: On floured board, roll out one part of dough ¼ inch thick. Line a 2-quart round baking dish with pastry, allowing edges to extend over the sides; moisten top edge with a little water. Add chicken filling.

4. Roll out second half of dough and place over top of baking dish. (Handle pastry carefully to avoid holes.) Trim excess crust around edge of dish. Press edges together to seal and crimp together. Make several slashes in top. Bake for 1 hour, until golden brown and bubbly.

6   CHICKEN À LA KING
Prep: 10 minutes   Cook: 20 minutes   Serves: 6

Serve this luncheon classic over toast points, egg noodles, or pastry shells.

4 **tablespoons butter or margarine**	1/4 **teaspoon nutmeg**
1/4 **pound mushrooms, sliced**	1 **cup chicken broth**
1 **green bell pepper, sliced**	1 **cup light cream or half-and-half**
1 **small onion, sliced**	1 **egg yolk, beaten**
3 **tablespoons flour**	1 **tablespoon lemon juice**
1/2 **teaspoon salt**	1 **tablespoon sherry**
1/4 **teaspoon freshly ground pepper**	3 **cups diced cooked chicken**
	2 **tablespoons diced pimiento**

1. In a large frying pan, melt 2 tablespoons of the butter over medium heat. Add mushrooms, bell pepper, and onion. Cook 5 minutes, until vegetables are tender. Remove with a slotted spoon and set aside.

2. Melt remaining 2 tablespoons butter in the same pan. Add flour, salt, pepper, and nutmeg. Cook, stirring, for 1 minute without browning.

3. In a small bowl, combine broth and cream. Gradually stir cream mixture into pan. Bring to a boil, and cook, stirring, until sauce is smooth and thickened, 3 to 5 minutes.

4. Gradually whisk 1 cup of sauce into egg yolk. Stir back into pan until well blended. Add vegetable mixture, lemon juice, sherry, and chicken. Cook until heated through, about 5 minutes. Garnish with pimiento.

7   CHICKEN LIVERS AND MUSHROOMS WITH RICE
Prep: 10 minutes   Cook: 25 minutes   Serves: 6

Chicken livers are a great value and a nutritional bonanza. Here they're presented beautifully in a simple ring of white rice.

3 **cups chicken broth**	1/2 **cup sliced mushrooms**
1 1/2 **cups rice**	**Freshly ground pepper**
4 **tablespoons butter or margarine**	3 **tablespoons dry white wine**
6 **chicken livers, cut into 1/2-inch pieces**	2 **tablespoons chopped fresh parsley**
1/2 **cup chopped onion**	1/2 **cup grated Parmesan cheese**

1. In a medium-size saucepan, bring chicken broth to a boil. Add rice, reduce heat to low, and cook, covered, until broth is absorbed by rice, about 15 minutes.

2. Meanwhile, in a large frying pan, melt butter over medium-low heat. Sauté livers, onions, and mushrooms for 5 to 8 minutes. Season with pepper. Add wine and simmer 2 minutes.

3. Pack rice into a 5-cup ring mold; unmold onto a platter. Spoon liver mixture into center. Sprinkle with parsley and Parmesan cheese.

8   DELI CHOPPED LIVER
Prep: 10 minutes   Cook: 10 minutes   Serves: makes about 2 cups

If you can't find rendered chicken fat, use butter or margarine.

1 pound chicken livers, trimmed	1 teaspoon salt
2 medium onions, chopped	½ teaspoon freshly ground pepper
¼ cup rendered chicken fat	2 hard-cooked eggs, halved

1. Broil chicken livers about 4 inches from heat, turning frequently, until browned outside and no longer pink inside, 5 to 10 minutes.

2. Meanwhile, in a large skillet, cook onions in chicken fat over medium heat until golden brown, about 10 minutes. Scrape onions and fat into a food processor.

3. Add livers, salt, and pepper and pulse until coarsely chopped. Add eggs and chop to desired consistency.

9   KENTUCKY BURGOO
Prep: 20 minutes   Cook: 3 to 4 hours   Serves: 8

Burgoo is both a delicious winter stew and a revered Kentucky tradition, having originated in that state over a century ago. Freely translated it means "if you've got it, throw it in," and as such is one of the least intimidating of all recipes: short of forgetting the chicken, it is almost impossible to make a "bad" burgoo.

1 chicken (3½ pounds) cut up	1 cup fresh lima beans, or 1 package (10 ounces) frozen
1 teaspoon salt	
1 teaspoon cayenne pepper	1 can (16 ounces) whole or stewed tomatoes, undrained and chopped
1 garlic clove, minced	
1 large unpeeled potato, cubed	
1 large onion, chopped	1 can (17 ounces) whole kernel corn, undrained
1 medium green bell pepper, chopped	
1 cup sliced carrots	Worcestershire and hot pepper sauce to taste
1 cup fresh okra, or 1 package (10 ounces) frozen	1 jigger bourbon (optional) Fresh parsely, for garnish

1. In large stockpot, combine chicken, salt, cayenne, garlic, and 2 quarts water; bring to a boil. Cover and simmer for 1 to 2 hours, until chicken barely clings to its bones. (While chicken simmers, chop and prepare vegetables.)

2. Remove chicken from broth. Remove and discard bones. Cut chicken into pieces and return to broth.

3. Add vegetables and simmer, uncovered, for 1½ to 2 hours, until stew thickens and vegetables, save for the corn kernels, are barely recognizable.

4. Season to taste with Worcestershire and hot pepper sauce. For an extra kick, add a jigger of bourbon. Add parsley for garnish.

10   CHICKEN HASH "21"
Prep: 5 minutes   Cook: 15 minutes   Serves: 4

A natural for leftover chicken. At the 21 Club, one of New York's most exclusive restaurants, this hash is often served in an omelet or crêpes.

2 tablespoons butter
2 tablespoons flour
1 cup milk, heated
¼ teaspoon white pepper
¼ teaspoon salt
Dash of hot pepper sauce

Dash of Worcestershire sauce
½ cup light cream or half-and-half
2 tablespoons dry sherry
2 cups diced cooked chicken
2 egg yolks, beaten

1. Melt butter in a saucepan over medium heat. Stir in flour and cook about 2 minutes, stirring constantly, without browning.

2. Gradually whisk in milk and bring to a boil, stirring constantly, until mixture thickens. Reduce heat to low. Add white pepper, salt, hot pepper sauce, and Worcestershire sauce.

3. Whisk in cream. Add sherry and chicken. Season with additional salt and white pepper to taste. Cook until hot. Remove from heat. Whisk in egg yolks, blending well, and serve.

11   CHICKEN POPOVERS
Prep: 25 minutes   Cook: 40 minutes   Serves: 8

Popovers:
1 cup sifted flour
¼ teaspoon salt
¾ cup milk
¼ cup cold chicken broth
2 eggs
Filling:
4 tablespoons butter or margarine
⅓ cup flour
¼ teaspoon ground thyme
⅛ teaspoon freshly ground pepper

1 cup chicken broth
1 cup evaporated milk
2 tablespoons white wine
½ pound mushrooms, quartered and sautéed in 2 tablespoons butter until lightly browned
1 cup frozen peas, thawed
¼ cup chopped red bell pepper or pimientos
3 cups chopped cooked chicken

1. Make popovers: Preheat oven to 450°. In a blender or food processor, combine flour, salt, milk, broth, and eggs. Process until smooth. Spoon into well-greased preheated popover pan or muffin tin, filling two-thirds full. Bake 40 minutes, until well browned, puffed, and firm.

2. Make filling: Meanwhile, melt butter in a large saucepan over medium-low heat. Whisk in flour, thyme, and pepper. Cook, stirring, 1 to 2 minutes without browning. Gradually whisk in chicken broth, milk, and wine. Cook, stirring until thickened, about 5 minutes.

3. Add mushrooms, peas, red pepper, and chicken. Cook another 5 minutes, until heated through.

4. Split hot popovers and spoon in chicken filling.

12   CHICKEN AND SAUSAGE GUMBO
Prep: 20 minutes   Cook: 1 hour   Serves: 8

A spicy Louisiana hodgepodge that's a cross between a soup and a stew, gumbo can be thickened with okra or filé powder.

2 teaspoons freshly ground black pepper
1½ teaspoons cayenne pepper
1½ teaspoons paprika
1 teaspoon dry mustard
1 teaspoon filé powder
1 teaspoon garlic powder
1 teaspoon salt
1 chicken (3 pounds), cut up
1 cup vegetable oil
½ cup flour
¾ cup chopped onion
¾ cup chopped celery
¾ cup chopped green bell pepper
1½ quarts Rich Chicken Stock (p. 30)
1¾ cups thinly sliced smoked sausage (andouille or kielbasa)
1 bay leaf
2 garlic cloves, finely chopped
2 tablespoons hot pepper sauce
Cooked rice

1. In a small bowl, blend together black pepper, cayenne pepper, paprika, mustard, filé powder, garlic powder, and salt. Rub about 4 teaspoons of the spice on the chicken pieces.

2. In a large frying pan, heat oil over medium-high heat. Combine flour and 2 teaspoons of the spice mixture in a plastic bag. Add chicken pieces a few at a time; shake to coat. Brown chicken in oil on one side for 2 minutes, then turn and cook for another 3 minutes. Drain on paper towels.

3. Add remaining flour mixture used for coating to the oil. Reduce heat to medium and cook, stirring constantly with a whisk, until mixture turns nut brown. Add the onion, celery, and green pepper to the roux. Remove from heat.

4. In a large Dutch oven, bring broth to a boil. Whisk ½ cup of stock into roux mixture. Gradually add to remaining broth, stirring with a whisk. Add sausage. Cook for 15 minutes, stirring often.

5. Add chicken, bay leaf, garlic, and pepper sauce. Cook 40 minutes. Remove the chicken and pull meat from bones; discard bones. Cut chicken into bite-size pieces and return to gumbo. Serve with rice.

13 DELMONICO DEVILED CHICKEN
Prep: 5 minutes   Cook: 30 minutes   Serves: 4

3 pounds chicken drumsticks, thighs, and/or breasts
Salt and freshly ground pepper
4 tablespoons unsalted butter, at room temperature

1 teaspoon Dijon mustard
1 teaspoon red wine vinegar
½ teaspoon paprika
¾ cup fresh bread crumbs

1. Season chicken liberally with salt and pepper. Broil 6 to 8 inches from heat for 5 to 7 minutes a side, until skin is browned. Remove from broiler and reduce oven to 350 degrees.

2. In a small bowl, blend butter, mustard, vinegar, paprika, and ½ teaspoon salt.

3. Place chicken, skin side up, in a large baking dish. Brush with seasoned butter. Sprinkle bread crumbs over chicken. Bake 15 to 20 minutes, until coating is browned and crisp and chicken is tender.

14 CHICKEN WITH DUMPLINGS
Prep: 30 minutes   Cook: 1½ hours   Serves: 4

1 chicken (3 pounds), cut up
1 medium onion
4 whole cloves
3 medium carrots, cut into 2-inch chunks
2 celery ribs, finely chopped
2 sprigs of parsley
1 teaspoon salt
¼ teaspoon freshly ground pepper

1¾ cups milk
1 cup plus 3 tablespoons sifted flour
1½ teaspoons baking powder
Dash of salt
2 tablespoons chilled shortening
Chopped parsley, for garnish

1. In a large Dutch oven, combine chicken, onion pierced with cloves, carrots, celery, parsley, salt, pepper, 1 cup of the milk, and 4 cups water. Bring to a boil over medium heat, reduce heat to low, and simmer, covered, 1 hour.

2. Sift 1 cup flour, baking powder, and salt together in a medium-size bowl. Cut in shortening until mixture resembles coarse meal. Add ½ cup milk all at once and mix lightly just until dough holds together.

3. Remove onion and parsley from stew. Drain off liquid, reserving 3 cups. Skim fat off reserved liquid and pour back into pot. Bring to a simmer and drop dumpling mixture by rounded tablespoonfuls on top of liquid. Simmer uncovered 10 minutes; then cover and simmer 10 minutes longer.

4. Remove dumplings and chicken to a heated serving bowl. Stir remaining 3 tablespoons flour into remaining ¼ cup milk until smooth. Stir into sauce in pan and bring to a boil, stirring until thickened. Pour sauce over chicken and dumplings. Sprinkle with chopped parsley.

Chapter 2

Appetizers

If there is a bird that offers a more delectable variety of nibbling possibilities than the chicken, it has yet to appear on my table. From the drumstick to the liver, every tender part can be transformed into some flavorful snack, hors d'oeuvre, or first course.

But the champion of all finger foods has to be the chicken wing. The wing needs only a small napkin and maybe a bowl of dipping sauce to ensure a successful cocktail party. It has a built-in handle and can be served with any variety of seasonings.

For grilling, all three segments of the wing should be left intact, with the small tip folded akimbo in a neat, triangular package. For frying and dipping, the wing tip should be discarded and the larger joints separated into two "mini-drumsticks." Either way, the little nib on top of the wing tip is usually removed.

Though I've included a selection of ideas for chicken wings along with dipping sauces, several other recipes are also accompanied by sauces (Honey Mustard, Orange Mustard Mayonnaise, Plum Sauce, Blue Cheese). Feel free to mix and match, according to your own preferences.

15 CHICKEN-CHEESE CANAPÉS
Prep: 20 minutes   Cook: 10 minutes   Serves: makes about 32

2 cups chopped cooked
   chicken
¾ cup mayonnaise
2 scallions, minced
½ teaspoon dried basil
¼ teaspoon dried thyme

¼ teaspoon freshly ground
   pepper
½ cup grated Swiss cheese
½ cup grated Parmesan cheese
4 English muffins, split

1. Preheat oven to 350°. In a medium-size bowl, combine chicken, mayonnaise, and scallions. Blend in basil, thyme, and pepper. Add Swiss cheese and 2 tablespoons of the Parmesan; blend well.

2. Spread chicken mixture over English muffin halves, dividing evenly. Sprinkle with remaining Parmesan cheese. Arrange on a foil-lined baking sheet and bake about 10 minutes, until lightly browned on top.

3. Cut muffins into quarters and serve hot.

16 CHINESE CHICKEN TOASTS
*Prep: 25 minutes   Cook: 5 to 10 minutes   Serves: makes about 5
dozen*

Crunchy with water chestnuts, these tempting triangles are a variation on Chinese shrimp toast. They are prepared ahead, but must be served piping hot. Fry at the last moment before guests arrive, or cook an hour ahead and reheat for 10 minutes in a 325-degree oven.

1½ pounds skinless, boneless
   chicken breasts
1 cup coarsely chopped
   scallion
2 eggs, well beaten
¼ cup cornstarch
1 teaspoon Oriental sesame
   oil

½ teaspoon salt
1 can (8 ounces) water
   chestnuts, drained and
   chopped
16 slices firm white bread,
   crusts removed
   Vegetable oil, for frying

1. Cut chicken into chunks and put in a food processor. Add scallion, eggs, cornstarch, sesame oil, and salt; purée to a paste. Transfer to a bowl and stir in water chestnuts.

2. Spread chicken paste over bread slices, cover, and refrigerate until ready to cook.

3. In a large frying pan, heat ¾ inch of oil over medium heat. Add bread, chicken side down, and fry until golden brown, 1 to 2 minutes. Drain on paper towels. Cut into triangles and serve hot.

17   LEMON CHICKEN KEBABS
Prep: 20 minutes   Cook: 12 to 15 minutes   Serves: makes about 10

For garlic lovers only. Best charcoal grilled, these skewered appetizers can also be prepared under a hot broiler. You'll need small bamboo skewers, available in many supermarkets and in Oriental groceries.

¼ cup olive oil
2 tablespoons fresh lemon
   juice
3 garlic cloves, crushed

½ teaspoon coarsely cracked
   pepper
1¼ pounds skinless, boneless
   chicken breasts, cut into
   bite-size pieces

1. Light charcoal grill or preheat broiler. Soak wooden skewers in water for about 20 minutes to prevent burning.

2. Meanwhile, in a small bowl, combine oil, lemon juice, garlic, and pepper. Add chicken and toss to coat; marinate 15 minutes. Thread three or four chicken pieces onto each wooden skewer; reserve marinade.

3. Grill chicken over moderately hot coals, basting frequently with marinade and turning after 6 minutes, until chicken is no longer pink, but still juicy, 12 to 15 minutes. Or broil, turning frequently, for about 5 minutes.

18   CHICKEN AND SAUSAGE KEBABS
Prep: 45 minutes   Marinate: 2 hours   Cook: 15 minutes
Serves: makes 12 to 16

Great as an appetizer or serve as a main course with rice pilaf, roasted peppers, and a mixed green salad. The kebabs are better if they marinate for at least two hours, so plan accordingly.

1½ pounds Italian sausage (use
   sweet or hot or a
   combination of the two,
   according to your taste)
2 pounds skinless, boneless
   chicken breasts, cut into
   1-inch cubes

About 16 bay leaves, broken
   into thirds
2 tablespoons olive oil
1 garlic clove, crushed
½ teaspoon salt
½ teaspoon paprika

1. Preheat oven to 350°. Place sausage on heavy-duty aluminum foil, drizzle with 2 tablespoons water, and wrap loosely. Place on a baking sheet and bake for 30 minutes to precook the sausage. Let stand until cool enough to handle. Slice into ½-inch-thick rounds.

2. Soak about 15 bamboo skewers in water for 20 minutes. On each skewer, thread a piece of chicken, a piece of bay leaf, and a round of sausage; repeat and end with another bay leaf and a piece of chicken. Place kebabs in a large shallow pan. Combine oil, garlic, salt, and paprika. Brush all over kebabs. Cover and marinate in refrigerator for at least 2 hours.

3. Light charcoal grill or preheat broiler. Grill kebabs over moderately hot coals, turning every 5 minutes, until chicken is cooked through but still moist, 12 to 15 minutes. To broil, cook, turning frequently, for about 5 minutes.

19 HOT CHICKEN AND ARTICHOKE SPREAD
Prep: 10 minutes   Cook: 20 minutes   Serves: 8 to 10

2 cups chopped cooked
   chicken
1 can (14 ounces) artichoke
   hearts, drained and
   chopped

1 cup mayonnaise
1 cup grated Parmesan cheese
1 garlic clove, crushed
   Dash of cayenne pepper

Preheat oven to 350°. Mix all ingredients together. Spoon into a buttered gratin dish. Bake until mixture is hot and bubbling. Serve with corn or tortilla chips for dipping.

20 CHICKEN COCKTAIL LOG
Prep: 5 minutes   Chill: 4 hours   Serves: 12

2 packages (8 ounces each)
   cream cheese, at room
   temperature
1 tablespoon bottled steak
   sauce
1 teaspoon curry powder

1½ cups minced cooked chicken
⅓ cup minced celery
¼ cup chopped parsley
¼ cup chopped blanched
   almonds

1. In a medium-size mixing bowl, beat together cream cheese, steak sauce, and curry powder until well blended. Blend in chicken, celery, and 2 tablespoons of the parsley.

2. Turn out onto plastic wrap and mold into a 9-inch log. Wrap and chill until firm, at least 4 hours.

3. To garnish log, toss together almonds and remaining parsley in a baking dish. Roll chicken log in parsley and almonds to coat. Serve with crackers or toasted French bread.

NOTE: To make in a food processor, chop almonds with 2 tablespoons parsley and set aside. Without washing bowl, chop celery, then chicken. Add cream cheese, steak sauce, and curry powder and process until blended.

21 CRISPY CHICKEN NUGGETS
Prep: 10 minutes   Cook: 20 minutes   Serves: makes about 4 dozen

   Vegetable oil, for frying
½ cup milk
¼ cup flour
¼ cup freshly grated Parmesan
   cheese
1 teaspoon paprika

½ teaspoon oregano
¼ teaspoon dry mustard
2½ pounds skinless, boneless
   chicken breasts, cut into
   1-inch pieces

1. In a large frying pan or deep-fat fryer, heat 1 inch of oil to 350°.

2. Meanwhile, put milk in a bowl. In a paper bag, mix together flour, Parmesan cheese, paprika, oregano, and mustard. First dip chicken pieces in milk, then place about a dozen pieces of chicken at a time in bag and shake to coat.

3. Fry chicken in hot oil in batches without crowding, turning occasionally, for about 5 minutes, until crisp and golden brown. Drain on paper towels. Serve hot.

22 DEVILED CHICKEN BALLS
Prep: 15 minutes   Cook: 25 minutes   Serves: makes about 2 dozen

3 tablespoons butter or
    margarine
3 tablespoons flour
2 cups chicken broth
1 tablespoon grated onion
¾ teaspoon salt
½ teaspoon dry mustard
¼ teaspoon cayenne pepper
⅛ teaspoon freshly ground
    black pepper

2 cups chopped cooked
    chicken
¼ cup chopped slivered
    almonds
1 egg
2 cups seasoned bread crumbs
    Vegetable oil, for deep-
    frying

1. In a medium-size saucepan, melt butter over moderately low heat. Add flour and cook, stirring, for 1 minute without browning. Whisk in the broth. Add the onion, salt, mustard, cayenne, and black pepper. Bring to a boil, stirring, and cook until thick and smooth.

2. Remove from the heat and stir in the chicken and almonds. Spread the mixture in a pie plate and let cool; then cover and refrigerate for several hours until firm.

3. At least 45 minutes before serving, beat the egg in a shallow bowl. Spread the bread crumbs out on a sheet of wax paper. Scoop up spoonfuls of the cold chicken mixture and roll into ½-inch balls. Roll in the egg, then dredge in the bread crumbs to coat. Set aside on a baking sheet and refrigerate for at least 30 minutes (or up to several hours) before serving time.

4. Heat 3 inches of oil in a deep-fat fryer or large saucepan to 375°. Fry the balls in batches without crowding until golden brown, 3 to 5 minutes. Serve hot, with dipping sauces on the side.

23 HONEY CHICKEN WINGS
*Prep: 15 minutes   Cook: 45 minutes   Serves: makes 24 mini-
drumsticks*

2 pounds chicken wings,
    disjointed and tips
    discarded
    Freshly ground pepper
1 cup honey

½ cup soy sauce
2 tablespoons vegetable oil
2 tablespoons ketchup
1 garlic clove, crushed

1. Preheat oven to 350°. Season chicken liberally with pepper. Place wings in a large baking dish.

2. In a small bowl, mix together honey, soy sauce, oil, ketchup, and garlic until well blended. Pour over chicken. Bake for 45 minutes, until chicken is well done and sauce is thick.

24 BARBECUED CHICKEN WINGS

Prep: 10 minutes   Marinate: 1 hour   Cook: 30 minutes
Serves: makes 12

½ cup ketchup
2 tablespoons brown sugar
2 tablespoons red wine
  vinegar
1 tablespoon lime juice
2 teaspoons cornstarch
2 teaspoons Dijon mustard

1½ teaspoons chili powder
1 teaspoon Worcestershire
  sauce
1 garlic clove, crushed
  through a press
2 pounds chicken wings

1. In a large bowl, combine all the ingredients except the chicken. Mix to blend well. Add the chicken wings and toss to coat. Marinate at room temperature for a minimum of 1 hour, or overnight in the refrigerator.

2. Preheat the oven to 425° or light the grill. Arrange the wings in a single layer in a large baking dish and bake, turning once, for 30 minutes. Or grill, turning, for 30 to 35 minutes. Serve hot, warm, or cold.

25 MEXICAN CHICKEN WINGS

Prep: 15 minutes   Cook: 45 minutes   Serves: makes about 12 mini-
drumsticks

½ cup corn oil
¼ cup chili powder
1 teaspoon oregano
1 teaspoon ground cumin

12 ounces tortilla corn chips
1 pound chicken wings,
  disjointed and tips
  discarded

1. Preheat oven to 350°. In a small bowl, whisk together the oil, chili powder, oregano, and cumin to blend well.

2. Pulverize the tortilla chips in a food processor. Pour into a shallow bowl.

3. Dip the chicken pieces in the seasoned oil; then dredge in the ground chips until coated. Set on a foil-lined baking sheet and bake for 45 minutes, until browned and crisp outside and tender inside. Serve hot.

26 PARMESAN CHICKEN WINGS OREGANATA

Prep: 15 minutes   Cook: 45 minutes   Serves: makes about 12 mini-
drumsticks

1 cup grated Parmesan cheese
  (about 4 ounces)
2 tablespoons chopped parsley
2 teaspoons paprika
1 teaspoon dried oregano
½ teaspoon dried basil
¼ teaspoon salt

¼ teaspoon freshly ground
  pepper
1 stick (½ cup) butter or
  margarine, melted
1 pound chicken wings,
  disjointed and tips
  removed

1. Preheat oven to 350°. In a paper bag, combine cheese, parsley, paprika, oregano, basil, salt, and pepper. Toss to mix. Pour melted butter into a shallow bowl.

2. Dip chicken pieces into butter, then place in paper bag and shake to coat. Place chicken on foil-lined baking sheet and bake for 45 minutes. Serve hot.

27 BUFFALO CHICKEN WINGS WITH BLUE CHEESE DIPPING SAUCE

Prep: 10 minutes   Cook: 35 minutes   Serves: makes 36 mini-drumsticks

These spicy hot wings with cool, creamy dip are all the rage. Serve with plenty of ice-cold beer.

6 tablespoons butter or
   margarine
¼ cup hot pepper sauce
   Vegetable oil, for frying

18 chicken wings (about
   3 pounds), disjointed,
   with the tips discarded
   Blue Cheese Dipping Sauce
   (recipe follows)

1. Melt butter in a small saucepan. Add hot sauce and remove from the heat.

2. In large frying pan or deep-fat fryer, heat 1 inch of oil to 375°. Fry wings in batches without crowding until golden brown, 10 to 15 minutes. Drain on paper towels.

3. Brush wings with spicy butter and serve warm, with blue cheese dipping sauce.

BLUE CHEESE DIPPING SAUCE

¼ pound blue cheese,
   Roquefort or Gorgonzola
½ cup mayonnaise
½ cup sour cream

1 tablespoon lemon juice
1 tablespoon wine vinegar
   Several dashes of hot pepper
   sauce, to taste

In a small bowl, mash the blue cheese, leaving some small lumps. Whisk in the mayonnaise until blended. Add the remaining ingredients and whisk to blend well. Cover and refrigerate until serving time.

28 CHICKEN DEVILED EGGS

Prep: 20 minutes   Serves: makes 12

6 hard-cooked eggs
½ cup finely chopped cooked
   chicken
3 tablespoons mayonnaise
1 tablespoon grated onion
1 teaspoon Dijon mustard

½ teaspoon dry mustard
¼ to ½ teaspoon hot pepper
   sauce, to taste
1 tablespoon minced parsley
   Paprika, for garnish

1. Cut eggs lengthwise in half. Remove yolks and place in a small bowl.

2. Mash yolks with a fork. Add chicken, mayonnaise, onion, Dijon mustard, dry mustard, hot sauce, and parsley. Blend well. Stuff egg whites with yolk mixture. Sprinkle tops with paprika to garnish. Cover and refrigerate until serving time.

29 SESAME CHICKEN WITH HONEY DIP

Prep: 30 minutes   Cook: 10 minutes   Serves: makes about 12

1½ cups mayonnaise
 1 teaspoon dry mustard
 1 tablespoon minced onion
 1 pound skinless, boneless
   chicken breasts, poached,
   and cut crosswise into ½-
   inch strips

½ cup seasoned bread crumbs
¼ cup sesame seeds
 2 tablespoons honey
 1 tablespoon Dijon mustard

1. Preheat oven to 425°. In a medium-size bowl, combine ½ cup of the mayonnaise, dry mustard, and onion; mix to blend well. Add chicken and toss to coat.

2. In a shallow bowl, toss bread crumbs and sesame seeds to mix. Roll chicken cubes in bread crumbs to coat. Place in a single layer on a baking sheet and bake for 10 minutes, until lightly browned and crisped.

3. Meanwhile, blend remaining 1 cup mayonnaise with honey and Dijon mustard. Serve as a dipping sauce with chicken.

30 SESAME CHICKEN FINGERS WITH PLUM SAUCE

*Prep: 20 minutes   Marinate: 1 hour   Cook: 35 minutes
Serves: makes about 36*

 3 pounds skinless, boneless
   chicken breasts
1½ cups buttermilk
 2 tablespoons lemon juice
 2 teaspoons Worcestershire
   sauce
 1 teaspoon soy sauce
 1 teaspoon paprika
 1 teaspoon freshly ground
   pepper

 1 garlic clove, minced
 4 cups seasoned bread crumbs
 ½ cup sesame seeds
 4 tablespoons butter or
   margarine, melted
 1 jar (12 ounces) plum
   preserves
1½ tablespoons dry mustard
1½ tablespoons prepared white
   horseradish

1. If the breasts are whole, split them. Cut each chicken breast half crosswise into ½-inch strips. In a large bowl, combine buttermilk, 1 tablespoon of the lemon juice, Worcestershire, soy sauce, paprika, pepper, and garlic. Add chicken strips and toss to coat. Cover and marinate at room temperature for 1 hour, or refrigerate overnight.

2. Preheat oven to 350°. Drain chicken well. In a large shallow bowl, toss bread crumbs with sesame seeds to mix. Roll chicken in crumbs to coat. Arrange in a single layer on a greased baking sheet. Drizzle melted butter over chicken fingers. Bake for 35 minutes.

3. Meanwhile, in a nonaluminum saucepan, combine plum preserves, mustard, horseradish, and remaining 1 tablespoon lemon juice. Melt over low heat, stirring, until smooth.

4. Serve chicken fingers hot or warm, with plum sauce for dipping on the side.

31 CHICKEN FRITTERS
Prep: 20 minutes   Cook: 10 minutes   Serves: 6

2 cups finely chopped, cooked
   chicken
1 teaspoon salt
2 teaspoons minced fresh
   parsley
1 tablespoon lemon juice
1¼ cups flour

2 teaspoons baking powder
1 egg, beaten
⅔ cup milk
   Vegetable oil, for frying
   Honey Mustard (recipe
   follows)

1. In a large bowl, toss chicken with salt, parsley, and lemon juice. Set aside for 15 minutes. In another large bowl, combine flour, baking powder, egg, and milk. Stir to blend well.

2. Add flour mixture to chicken and mix well.

3. In a large frying pan, heat 1 inch of oil to 375°. Drop batter by tablespoons into hot oil and fry in batches without crowding for 2 minutes, until golden brown. Drain on paper towels and serve with honey mustard for dipping.

HOT HONEY MUSTARD SAUCE

1 cup dry mustard
1 cup white wine vinegar
2 eggs, beaten

¾ cup honey
¼ teaspoon salt

1. Combine mustard and vinegar in a small bowl and set aside for 30 minutes or overnight.

2. In a double boiler over medium heat, stir together mustard-vinegar mixture, eggs, honey, and salt. Cook about 20 minutes until thickened, stirring often.

32 CURRIED COCONUT CHICKEN BALLS
Prep: 25 minutes   Cook: 15 minutes   Chill: 2 hours
Serves: makes about 12

¾ cup flaked coconut
1 small package (3 ounces)
   cream cheese, at room
   temperature
2 tablespoons mayonnaise
1 cup chopped cooked chicken

1 cup (about 4 ounces) chopped
   walnuts
2 tablespoons minced onion
1 to 2 tablespoons curry
   powder, to taste
½ teaspoon salt

1. Preheat oven to 350°. Spread out coconut on a small baking sheet and toast in oven until light brown, 10 to 15 minutes. Let cool slightly.

2. In a small bowl, blend together cream cheese and mayonnaise until smooth. Add chicken, walnuts, onion, curry powder, and salt. Mix well.

3. Form chicken mixture into 1-inch balls. Roll in toasted coconut to coat. Cover and refrigerate until chilled.

33   CHICKEN-PECAN CHEESE SPREAD
Prep: 10 minutes   Chill: 2 hours   Serves: makes 2 cups

1   package (8 ounces)
        Neufchâtel cheese,
        softened
1   cup chopped cooked chicken
¾   cup chopped pecans, toasted
⅓   cup mayonnaise

2   tablespoons chopped
        chutney
1   tablespoon curry powder
2   tablespoons coarsely
        chopped parsley
    Chopped pecans, for garnish

1. In a food processor, combine cheese, chicken, toasted pecans, mayonnaise, chutney, curry, and parsley. Process just until combined.

2. Place in a serving dish and garnish with chopped pecans. Refrigerate 2 hours, or until chilled. Serve with crackers and sliced apples.

34   RASPBERRY-PINEAPPLE CHICKEN NIBBLES
Prep: 15 minutes   Cook: 15 minutes   Serves: makes about 4 dozen

2   pounds skinless, boneless
        chicken breasts, cut into
        1-inch cubes
½   teaspoon freshly ground
        pepper
2   tablespoons vegetable oil

1   jar (12 ounces) seedless
        raspberry preserves (see
        note)
1   cup chili sauce
1   can (20 ounces) pineapple
        chunks, drained

1. Season chicken with pepper. In a large frying pan or chafing dish, heat oil over medium-high heat. Add chicken and sauté, tossing, until lightly browned, about 5 minutes.

2. Add raspberry preserves and chili sauce, reduce heat to medium and cook for 10 minutes. Add pineapple and cook for 1 to 2 minutes, to heat through. Serve with toothpicks and cocktail napkins.

NOTE: If you can't find seedless preserves, heat ordinary raspberry jam over low heat, stirring, until melted and smooth. Strain through a sieve to remove seeds.

35   PARTY PICK-UP CHICKEN LIVERS
Prep: 10 minutes   Cook: 15 minutes   Serves: makes 24

These crisp-coated livers are baked, so there's no messy frying involved. Serve on toothpicks, with the zesty barbecue-style dipping sauce on the side.

⅔   cup fine dry bread crumbs
1   pound chicken livers,
        trimmed and halved
4   tablespoons butter or
        margarine, melted

¼   cup ketchup
2   tablespoons brown sugar
2   tablespoons Dijon mustard
1½ tablespoons Worcestershire
        sauce

1. Preheat oven to 400°. Place bread crumbs in a small dish. Dip chicken livers in melted butter, then in bread crumbs to coat. Place on a lightly greased baking sheet.

2. Bake livers for 15 to 20 minutes, until they are cooked through and crispy on the outside.

3. Meanwhile, in a small saucepan, combine ketchup, brown sugar, mustard, and Worcestershire. Heat sauce to boiling, stirring to dissolve sugar. Serve the warm livers with the hot sauce for dipping.

36   CHICKEN LIVER PÂTÉ
Prep: 10 minutes   Cook: 10 minutes   Chill: 3 hours   Serves: 8

An easy party spread. Serve with melba rounds or crisp toast points.

6 tablespoons butter	¼ teaspoon dried thyme
2 medium onions, finely chopped	¼ teaspoon dried tarragon
1 garlic clove, crushed	⅛ teaspoon freshly ground pepper
1 pound chicken livers, trimmed and halved	2 tablespoons Cognac or brandy
½ teaspoon salt	

1. In a large frying pan, melt 2 tablespoons of the butter over moderately low heat. Add onions and cook until onion is soft, about 5 minutes. Add garlic and cook for 1 minute longer. Transfer to a food processor or blender.

2. Melt remaining 4 tablespoons butter in the same pan. Add livers and sauté over medium-high heat, tossing, until browned outside but still rosy inside, 3 to 5 minutes. Sprinkle with salt, thyme, tarragon, pepper, and Cognac. Cook, scraping up any browned bits from the bottom of the pan, for 1 minute. Scrape liver and pan juices into food processor. Purée until smooth. Scrape into a serving bowl or crock. Let cool to room temperature. Cover and refrigerate until cool, several hours or overnight.

37   CHICKEN AND HAM MOUSSE
Prep: 10 minutes   Cook: 3 minutes   Chill: 2 hours   Serves: 8 to 12

Serve as a first course or as part of a cold buffet.

1 tablespoon butter or margarine	1 cup chopped cooked chicken
4 scallions, chopped	1 cup chopped cooked ham
2 cups chicken stock	1 tablespoon Madeira
1 envelope (¼ ounce) unflavored gelatin	1 cup heavy cream

1. In a medium-size saucepan, melt butter over medium heat. Add scallions and cook 2 minutes. Stir in stock and gelatin. Simmer, stirring, until gelatin dissolves. Pour into a food processor.

2. Add chicken, ham and Madeira to processor. Process until smooth. Pour into a bowl, cover, and chill until almost set.

3. Meanwhile, beat cream until stiff. Fold whipped cream into chicken and ham mixture and pack into a lightly greased 6-cup mold. Cover and refrigerate at least 2 hours, or overnight, until set.

38 RUMAKI

Prep: 15 minutes   Marinate: 15 minutes   Cook: 15 minutes
Serves: makes about 16

This Polynesian hors d'oeuvre combines the best of the East and the West. Guests will gobble them up.

3 tablespoons soy sauce
1 tablespoon dry sherry
   (optional)
1 teaspoon sugar
1/8 teaspoon ground ginger
4 chicken livers (about
   1/4 pound), cut into
   1-inch pieces

8 water chestnuts, cut in half
2 scallions (green part only),
   cut into 2-inch lengths
8 slices of bacon, cut in half

1. In a small bowl, mix together soy sauce, sherry, sugar, and ginger. Add chicken livers and marinate, tossing occasionally, for at least 15 minutes at room temperature, or up to 4 hours in the refrigerator.

2. Remove livers from marinade and drain. Press a piece of liver around a piece of water chestnut. Wrap with a piece of scallion and bacon and secure with a wooden toothpick.

3. Preheat the broiler. Broil the rumaki about 5 inches from the heat, turning once, until the bacon is crisp, 10 to 15 minutes.

Chapter 3

Soups

The elixir that is chicken soup—at its most humble no more than chicken, water, carrots, onion, and perhaps a few sprigs of parsley—testifies most notably to the bird's versatility. Grandmother used the hot chicken broth as a tonic. The French enriched it with egg yolks and cream, and created elegant *potages.* Italians loaded the pot with pasta, beans, and aromatic herbs. Americans added corn and potatoes, producing chowders hearty enough to satisfy Paul Bunyan's appetite. Virtually every cuisine in the world has its distinctive soups based upon our favorite bird.

Most chicken soup recipes begin by calling for a chicken stock. I prefer to make my own; it's easy enough to prepare and can be kept in the freezer for up to several months. But if you're pressed for time, canned chicken broth can be substituted for the homemade version. (Conversely, whenever a recipe in this book calls for canned broth, feel free to use "the real thing.")

When using a canned chicken broth, dilute with water to taste or to the approximate consistency of a stock (about half-and-half). Also, since most canned broths are a little on the salty side, you may want to cut back on a recipe's other salt requirements.

The following two recipes are for a simple chicken stock and, for the more adventurous, an enriched variation.

SIMPLE CHICKEN STOCK

4 pounds chicken backs, bones, necks, wings, and giblets (without liver), broken up
2 medium onions, quartered
2 medium carrots, quartered
1 large celery rib with leaves, quartered

2 garlic cloves, unpeeled
4 sprigs parsley
2 sprigs fresh thyme, or ¼ teaspoon dried
1 bay leaf
10 black peppercorns

1. Place chicken in a large saucepan or stockpot. Add 2 quarts cold water, or more if necessary, to cover chicken by at least 1 inch. Bring to a boil over medium heat, skimming off foam as it forms.

2. Add remaining ingredients, reduce heat, and simmer, partly covered, for approximately 2 hours. Add more water, if necessary, to keep ingredients covered.

3. Strain stock through a sieve lined with cheesecloth.

RICH CHICKEN STOCK

Chicken stock can be frozen either in freezer jars or in ice cube trays. If frozen in trays, remove when solid and place in freezer bags; you can use as much or as little as needed.

3 pounds chicken bones, backs, and wing tips	2 scallions, cut into 1-inch pieces
1 celery rib, quartered	2 garlic cloves
1 carrot, quartered	½ cup dry white wine or vermouth
2 sprigs of parsley	
1 onion (with skin on), quartered	10 black peppercorns
	1 bay leaf

1. Preheat oven to 375°. Place chicken bones in a roasting pan. Roast for about 40 minutes, until nicely browned.

2. Place bones in a large stockpot. Add 1 cup water to the roasting pan. Bring to a boil on top of the stove, scraping up any browned bits from bottom of pan. Pour into stockpot. Add remaining ingredients and enough water to cover (about 2 quarts). Bring to a boil over moderate heat, skimming frequently. Reduce heat to low and simmer uncovered 2 to 3 hours, adding water to cover as needed. Strain and cool stock. Skim off fat.

39   HOMEMADE CREAM OF CHICKEN SOUP WITH RICE
Prep: 5 minutes   Cook: 20 minutes   Serves: 4

4 cups chicken stock or canned broth	1 teaspoon salt
¼ cup white rice	¼ teaspoon white pepper
1 cup heavy cream	¼ teaspoon nutmeg
	1 tablespoon chopped parsley

In a large saucepan, bring broth to a simmer over low heat. Add rice and cream. Season with salt, pepper, and nutmeg. Cover and cook 20 minutes, until rice is tender. Serve hot sprinkled with parsley.

40   CHICKEN, CORN, AND TOMATO CHOWDER
Prep: 10 minutes   Cook: 1¼ hours   Serves: 8

In summer, make this soup with garden-fresh corn and tomatoes, for a seasonal authentically American treat.

1 chicken (3 pounds), cut up	1 can (16 ounces) whole tomatoes, drained and cut up
1 medium onion, chopped	
1 teaspoon poultry seasoning	1 teaspoon lemon juice
1 can (16 ounces) corn kernels, with liquid	Salt and freshly ground pepper

1. In a large saucepan, simmer chicken in 4 cups of water with onion and poultry seasoning for 45 minutes. Remove chicken and let cool; reserve broth.

2. Skim fat from chicken broth. Remove meat from chicken, discarding skin and bones. Cut meat into bite-size pieces.

3. In a large nonaluminum saucepan, combine chicken, chicken broth, corn, tomatoes, and lemon juice. Simmer for 30 minutes. Season with salt and pepper to taste.

41 CHICKEN, BLACK BEAN, AND BARLEY SOUP
Prep: 1 hour   Cook: 1½ hours   Serves: 4

This substantial soup, a real warmer in cold weather, needs no accompaniment. But I love it with warm squares of buttermilk cornbread.

1 cup dried black beans	½ cup barley
4 chicken legs (thighs and drumsticks)	Freshly ground black pepper
1 onion, quartered	½ teaspoon dry mustard
2 celery ribs, chopped	⅛ teaspoon cayenne pepper
	Salt

1. In a large saucepan, cover beans with water. Bring to a boil and cook 3 minutes. Remove from heat, cover, and let stand 1 hour.

2. Return pan to low heat and add chicken, onion, and celery. Add water to cover. Cook 1 hour.

3. Remove chicken. Add barley; season with pepper, mustard, and cayenne. Cook 30 minutes, until beans and barley are tender. Remove chicken from bones and shred. Return meat to soup. Season with salt to taste.

42 CHICKEN, ESCAROLE, AND VERMICELLI SOUP
Prep: 5 minutes   Cook: 25 minutes   Serves: 4

Easy and Italian. Especially for garlic lovers. Add the chicken for a heartier soup. Leave it out for a delicious, lighter vegetable soup.

3 garlic cloves, chopped	1 ounce spaghetti, broken into pieces (about ½ cup)
2 tablespoons olive oil	1 cup chopped cooked chicken (optional)
6 cups chicken stock or canned broth	
1 head of young escarole, broken into 2-inch pieces	Salt and freshly ground pepper
	Grated Parmesan cheese

1. In a large saucepan, cook garlic in oil over moderate heat until golden, about 3 minutes. Add stock and bring to a boil. Strain.

2. Add escarole to stock and simmer 10 minutes. Add spaghetti and simmer until tender, 10 to 12 minutes. Add chicken, if using, and heat through. Season with salt and pepper to taste. Ladle into bowls and pass cheese separately.

43   MEXICAN CORN CHOWDER
Prep: 10 minutes   Cook: 35 minutes   Serves: 8

A zesty chowder with just enough zing to delight. Adjust the hotness of the soup by your choice of canned chilies and taco sauce.

3 tablespoons butter or margarine
1 large onion, chopped
1 medium green bell pepper, chopped
1 garlic clove, crushed
1 can (4 ounces) chopped green chilies (mild or medium-hot)
1 can (16 ounces) whole tomatoes, drained and broken up

2 cans (16 ounces each) cream-style corn
1 can (16 ounces) corn kernels, drained
2 cups chicken stock or canned broth
1 cup milk
2 cups chopped cooked chicken
1 tablespoon taco sauce
1/2 cup shredded Monterey Jack cheese

1. In a large flameproof casserole, melt butter over medium heat. Add onion, bell pepper, and garlic; cook 3 to 5 minutes, until onion is tender. Add chilies and tomatoes and blend well. Stir in remaining ingredients except cheese. Bring to a boil, reduce heat, and simmer 30 minutes.

2. Stir in cheese just before serving. Heat until melted.

44   HEARTY CHICKEN CHOWDER
Prep: 15 minutes   Cook: 1 1/4 hours   Serves: 6

1 leftover chicken carcass
1 bouquet garni (4 parsley stems, 1/4 teaspoon dried thyme, 1 bay leaf, and 10 peppercorns tied in cheesecloth)
2 garlic cloves
3 medium potatoes, peeled and diced
3 carrots, sliced
2 celery ribs, chopped
1 medium onion, chopped

1/2 teaspoon salt
1/2 teaspoon dried marjoram
1/4 teaspoon freshly ground pepper
2 cups scalded milk
2 egg yolks
2 tablespoons dry sherry
1 cup chopped cooked chicken
2 eggs, hard-cooked and chopped (optional)
2 tablespoons chopped fresh parsley

1. In a large saucepan, combine chicken carcass, bouquet garni, and garlic in 2 quarts of water. Bring to a boil, reduce heat, and simmer, covered, 1 hour. Strain broth, refrigerate, and skim off fat.

2. In a large saucepan, bring broth to a boil over medium heat. Add potatoes, carrots, celery, onion, salt, marjoram, and pepper. Cook until vegetables are tender, about 10 minutes.

3. Beat milk into egg yolks in a small bowl. Gradually whisk in 1/2 cup of the hot broth. Stir into soup. Add sherry, chicken, and chopped eggs. Heat through.

4. Pour into bowls. Garnish with parsley and serve with cheese biscuits or cornbread.

45   CLASSIC JEWISH CHICKEN SOUP
Prep: 5 minutes   Cook: 1½ hours   Chill: 30 minutes   Serves: 8

Grandma's cure-all broth. Add sliced carrots, rice, noodles, matzoh balls, and/or shredded cooked chicken for a more substantial soup.

1 chicken (3 pounds), cut up	2 carrots, scrubbed and quartered
2 onions, quartered	1 teaspoon salt
3 stalks celery, scrubbed and halved	3 sprigs of parsley with stems
	Freshly ground pepper

1. In a large stockpot, combine chicken, onions, celery, carrots, salt, and parsley with 3 quarts water. Bring to a boil, reduce heat, and simmer, partly covered, for 1½ hours.

2. Remove chicken and reserve for another use; strain soup. Let cool, then refrigerate until chilled. Remove congealed fat. Return to a boil and season with salt and pepper to taste.

46   MULLIGATAWNY SOUP
Prep: 20 minutes   Cook: 40 minutes   Serves: 4

An unusual Indian soup that makes a great starter.

3 tablespoons butter or margarine	1 tablespoon curry powder
1 medium onion, sliced	3 sprigs of parsley, finely chopped
1 medium carrot, diced	¼ teaspoon nutmeg
1 green bell pepper, chopped	4 cups chicken broth
1 celery rib, chopped	1 cup chopped cooked chicken
1 apple, peeled, cored, and chopped	1 cup chopped tomatoes
2 tablespoons flour	Salt and freshly ground pepper
3 whole cloves	2 tablespoons lemon juice

1. In a large saucepan, melt butter over medium heat. Add onion and cook until soft. Add carrot, green pepper, celery, and apple. Cook until vegetables are tender, about 10 minutes.

2. Stir in flour. Add cloves, curry, parsley, and nutmeg. Blend in broth. Add chicken and tomatoes. Season with salt and pepper to taste. Reduce heat, cover, and simmer until heated through, about 10 minutes. Add lemon juice and serve.

47   GREEK LEMON CHICKEN SOUP

Prep: 10 minutes   Cook: 30 minutes   Serves: 8

The charm of this soup is the contrast between the tartness of the fresh lemon juice and the creaminess of the egg yolks, which thicken the broth slightly. It goes beautifully before almost any roasted or grilled meat and with chicken or fish.

8 cups chicken broth
½ cup fresh lemon juice
¼ teaspoon freshly ground
    pepper
½ cup white rice

1 medium carrot, shredded
4 egg yolks
1 cup chopped cooked chicken
1 lemon, thinly sliced, for
    garnish

1. In a large saucepan, combine chicken broth, lemon juice, and pepper. Bring to a boil, and add rice and carrot. Reduce heat, cover, and simmer 25 minutes, until rice and carrots are tender.

2. Remove ½ cup soup and gradually whisk into egg yolks. Stir back into soup. Add chicken and heat through, but do not let boil, or eggs will curdle.

3. To serve, ladle into bowls and garnish with lemon slices.

48   CHICKEN IN HOTPOT

Prep: 20 minutes   Cook: 25 minutes   Serves: 4

If you have a Sterno burner, this meal-in-a-bowl can be cooked at table for an informal supper.

4 ounces cellophane noodles
4 cups chicken stock or canned
    broth
¼ cup dry sherry
3 tablespoons soy sauce
2 teaspoons finely chopped
    fresh ginger
2 garlic cloves, crushed
    through a press
3 scallions, cut into ½-inch
    pieces

¼ pound mushrooms, sliced
2 medium carrots, sliced
2 cups shredded cabbage
¾ pound skinless, boneless
    chicken breast, partly
    frozen and cut crosswise
    on the diagonal into
    paper-thin slices
1 teaspoon Oriental sesame
    oil

1. In a medium-size bowl, cover cellophane noodles with warm water. Let soak until soft, about 15 minutes, and drain.

2. Meanwhile, in a large saucepan, combine chicken stock, sherry, soy sauce, ginger, garlic, and scallions. Bring to a boil, reduce heat, and simmer 5 minutes.

3. Add mushrooms, carrots, and cabbage. Simmer 10 minutes, until tender. Add chicken strips and cellophane noodles and cook until chicken is tender and opaque, 3 to 5 minutes. Stir in sesame oil and ladle into bowls.

49 CHICK-PEA CHICKEN SOUP, TUSCAN STYLE
Prep: 10 minutes   Cook: 25 minutes   Serves: 6 to 8

Pasta and beans make for a substantial soup that's literally a meal in a bowl. Follow with a green salad, some cheese, and crusty bread for a perfect Sunday night supper.

2 tablespoons olive oil
1 garlic clove, chopped
2 tomatoes, peeled, seeded, and chopped
1 cup chopped cooked chicken
8 cups chicken stock or canned broth

1 teaspoon dried rosemary
Salt and freshly ground pepper
½ cup tiny pasta shells
2 cans (16 ounces each) chick-peas, rinsed and drained

1. In a large saucepan, heat oil over low heat and cook garlic 2 minutes. Stir in tomatoes, chicken, chicken stock, rosemary, and salt and pepper to taste. Simmer 20 minutes.

2. Meanwhile, cook pasta shells according to package directions. Drain.

3. Put chick-peas in a food processor. Ladle in 1 cup of chicken broth. Process until smooth. Return to soup and add cooked shells. Simmer 5 minutes.

50 POTAGE SENEGALESE
Prep: 5 to 10 minutes   Cook: 10 minutes   Serves: 6

Apple and curry add the distinctive flavors to this unusual soup.

2 tablespoons butter or margarine
1 onion, finely chopped
1 small apple, peeled, cored, and sliced
2 teaspoons curry powder
3 cups chicken stock or canned broth

1 cup finely chopped cooked chicken
2 cups heavy cream or half-and-half
4 egg yolks
1 can (8 ounces) water chestnuts, drained and sliced (optional)

1. In a large saucepan, melt butter over moderate heat. Add onion and apple. Cook until onion is tender, about 3 minutes. Stir in curry powder. Add chicken stock and chicken. Bring to a boil and reduce heat.

2. In a small bowl, whisk cream into egg yolks. Gradually beat in ½ cup hot soup. Stir into remaining soup in saucepan; do not boil or eggs will curdle. Add water chestnuts for crunchiness, if desired. Serve hot or cold.

51   COCK-A-LEEKIE
Prep: 30 minutes   Cook: 1⅓ hours   Serves: 6

As its name implies, this Scottish soup was originally made from an old rooster. For a thicker soup, add ¼ cup pearl barley when the stock is poured over the leeks.

1 chicken (3 pounds), cut up	½ teaspoon freshly ground
2 carrots, coarsely chopped	pepper
1 onion, quartered	2 tablespoons butter
1 bouquet garni (4 parsley	5 to 6 medium leeks (white
sprigs, ¼ teaspoon dried	part only), well rinsed and
thyme, 1 bay leaf, and 8	cut into ½-inch pieces
peppercorns tied in	6 to 8 prunes (optional)
cheesecloth)	1 tablespoon chopped fresh
1 teaspoon salt	parsley

1. Place chicken in a large Dutch oven or stockpot. Pour in 2 quarts water and bring to a boil over high heat; skim off foam as it collects. Add carrots, onion, bouquet garni, salt, and pepper. Reduce heat and simmer 45 minutes, until chicken is falling off the bones. Remove chicken and let cool; remove skin and bones; cut meat into bite-size pieces.

2. Strain stock into a large bowl; discard vegetables and bouquet garni. Skim off fat.

2. In a large saucepan, melt butter over medium heat. Add leeks, cover, and cook 10 minutes, until soft.

4. Pour reserved stock over leeks. Bring to a boil, reduce heat, and cook 15 minutes. Add chicken and prunes; simmer 15 minutes. Season with additional salt and pepper to taste. Add parsley and serve.

Chapter 4

Salads

Of all the myriad preparations to which chicken so beautifully adapts, perhaps none is as simple or as popular as the salad. Certainly no other can so easily wear so many different disguises. Chicken provides a light but flavorful foil for any number of other flavors: chicken with apples; chicken with olives; curried chicken with chutney; chicken with avocados; chicken with spicy sesame noodles; chicken with pesto.

Salad can be the familiar mélange of tossed cubed ingredients bound with a dressing, or it can be an artfully arranged composed platter of colorful ingredients. With the coming of age of the new American cuisine, salads are served in any number of ways: as an hors d'oeuvre, first course, or entrée.

Undoubtedly, chicken salads were invented as the perfect way to use leftover cooked chicken. But if the salad, not the chicken, comes first, you'll have to begin by poaching chicken breasts.

The trick to poaching chicken breasts successfully is to cook them gently, so that the protein in the meat doesn't contract and make them tough, and to cook them until they are just done, so that they remain juicy.

Chicken breasts for salads, whether cut up or served whole, must obviously be skinless and boneless. To poach:

1. Place in a saucepan and cover with cold water. Add salt to the water if you wish, but it is not necessary.

2. Bring slowly to a simmer over moderately low heat. Simmer skinless, boneless breasts for 10 to 15 minutes; chicken on the bone with skin for 15 to 20 minutes. The chicken breasts are done when they are slightly opaque, no longer pink in the center, but still moist and juicy.

52   COLD POACHED CHICKEN BREASTS WITH CUCUMBER DILL SAUCE

Prep: 20 minutes   Serves: 4

1 medium cucumber, peeled,
   seeded, and grated
1 teaspoon coarse salt
1 cup plain yogurt
1 tablespoon grated onion
¼ cup minced fresh dill
¼ teaspoon freshly ground
   pepper
4 chicken breasts, poached
   and chilled

1. Place grated cucumber in a strainer and sprinkle with salt. Let drain 15 to 30 minutes. Rinse under cold water and squeeze dry.

2. In a medium-size bowl, combine cucumber with remaining ingredients except chicken. Stir to mix well. Season with additional salt to taste. Cover and refrigerate until serving time. Serve over chicken breasts.

53   POACHED CHICKEN BREASTS WITH TARRAGON CHAUDFROID SAUCE

Prep: 5 minutes   Cook: 35 minutes   Serves: 8

This white aspic creates a professional-looking presentation for a knock-out cold buffet.

3 cups chicken stock, or 1½
   cups canned broth diluted
   with 1½ cups water
3 large sprigs of fresh
   tarragon, or 2 teaspoons
   dried
2 tablespoons butter
2 tablespoons flour
1 envelope (¼ ounce)
   unflavored gelatin,
   softened in ¼ cup cold
   water
1 egg yolk
⅓ cup heavy cream
8 skinless, boneless chicken
   breast halves, poached

1. In a medium-size saucepan, simmer chicken stock with tarragon until reduced to 3 cups, about 30 minutes. Strain to remove tarragon.

2. In a medium-size heavy saucepan, melt butter over medium heat. Add flour and cook, stirring, for 1 to 2 minutes without browning. Whisk in stock and bring to a boil. Cook, stirring, until thickened. Reduce to a simmer. Stir gelatin into sauce and cook, stirring, until dissolved.

4. In a small bowl, whisk together egg yolk and cream. Whisk in ½ cup hot sauce and stir back into sauce in pan. Cook until hot; do not boil. Remove from heat and let cool until sauce is of coating consistency.

5. Spoon chaudfroid sauce over chicken breasts set on a rack and refrigerate until set. Repeat, if necessary, to coat well. Decorate with tarragon leaves, slivers of scallion, decoratively cut pimiento, sliced black olives, and/or chopped hard-cooked egg yolk.

54   CHINESE HACKED CHICKEN
Prep: 30 minutes   Serves: 8

Fresh ginger is now available in most supermarkets. A "piece" here refers to the finger-like extensions that grow out of the ginger root.

1   2-inch piece fresh ginger, peeled and quartered
1   garlic clove, peeled
1/4 cup Chinese sesame paste or tahini
2   tablespoons soy sauce
2   tablespoons cider vinegar
1   tablespoon Szechuan chili paste with garlic

1   teaspoon Oriental sesame oil
1/2 teaspoon salt
1/2 teaspoon sugar
2   pounds skinless, boneless chicken breasts, poached and shredded
1/2 head iceberg lettuce, shredded
3   to 4 scallions, sliced

1. In a blender, chop ginger and garlic. Add sesame paste, soy sauce, vinegar, chili paste, sesame oil, salt, and sugar and puree.

2. Put chicken in a large bowl. Add sesame dressing and toss to mix well.

3. Cover a large platter with shredded lettuce. Arrange chicken on top and garnish with scallions. Serve at room temperature or slightly chilled.

55   HOT CASHEW CHICKEN SALAD
Prep: 25 minutes   Cook: 5 minutes   Serves: 4

1/2 small head romaine lettuce, torn into bite-size pieces (to yield 2 cups)
1/2 pound spinach, well rinsed, stemmed, and torn into bite-size pieces
1   can (11 ounces) mandarin oranges, drained
3   tablespoons soy sauce
1   tablespoon honey

1/4 teaspoon ground ginger
3   tablespoons vegetable oil
1 1/4 pounds skinless, boneless chicken breasts, cut into 1-inch pieces
3   tablespoons chopped scallions
1   garlic clove, minced
1/4 cup cashews

1. In a large salad bowl, combine lettuce, spinach, and oranges.

2. In a small bowl, combine soy sauce, honey, ginger, and 3 tablespoons water. Set sauce aside.

3. In a wok or large frying pan, heat oil over medium-high heat. Add chicken and stir-fry until barely opaque throughout, about 5 minutes. Add scallions and garlic and cook 1 more minute. Add sauce and cook, tossing, for 30 seconds.

4. Pour chicken and sauce over greens and oranges and toss. Sprinkle cashews on top.

56 CHICKEN WALDORF SALAD
Prep: 25 minutes   Serves: 4

With the addition of cooked chicken, a familiar side salad is updated to an entrée of the eighties. For an elegant luncheon, serve on a bed of red leaf lettuce, with croissants and a glass of buttery rich Chardonnay.

2 cups diced cooked chicken	¼ cup mayonnaise
1 large tart apple, cored and diced	2 teaspoons lime juice
1 cup chopped celery	2 teaspoons honey
½ cup chopped walnuts	Salt and pepper

1. In a medium-size bowl, combine chicken, apple, celery, and walnuts.

2. In a small bowl, combine mayonnaise, lime juice, and honey; stir to blend well. Season to taste with salt and pepper. Spoon dressing over chicken salad and toss to coat.

57 ANTIPASTO CHEF'S SALAD
Prep: 20 minutes   Marinate: 2 hours, or overnight   Serves: 4 as a main course; 6 as a first course

This zippy salad combines the julienned meats and cheese and crisp greens of a classic chef's salad with the marinated peppers, onions, and olives of an antipasto.

1 cup canned chicken broth	¼ pound sliced smoked ham, julienned
½ cup olive oil	1 medium green bell pepper, julienned
¼ cup red wine vinegar	1 medium red bell pepper, julienned
1 teaspoon marjoram	1 medium onion, halved and thinly sliced
½ teaspoon dried oregano	1 head of Romaine lettuce, rinsed, dried, and torn into bite-size pieces
¼ teaspoon dried thyme	
½ teaspoon sugar	
½ teaspoon coarsely cracked black pepper	¼ pound sliced Swiss cheese, julienned
Dash of cayenne pepper	12 Kalamata or oil-cured Mediterranean olives
1 pound skinless, boneless chicken breasts, poached and julienned (cut into 2 x ¼-inch strips)	

1. In a shallow dish, combine chicken broth, oil, vinegar, marjoram, oregano, thyme, sugar, black pepper, and cayenne. Add chicken, ham, green and red peppers, and onion. Toss to coat with marinade. Cover and marinate at room temperature 2 hours, or refrigerate overnight, tossing occasionally.

2. To serve, drain marinated ingredients, reserving ⅓ cup of marinade. Toss lettuce with reserved marinade. Arrange lettuce in large salad bowls or on plates. Add cheese to marinated ingredients and toss gently to mix. With a slotted spoon, arrange some of the marinated ingredients on top of each salad. Garnish with olives.

58   CHICKEN WITH WALNUT MAYONNAISE AND RADICCHIO

Prep: 25 minutes   Serves: 8

Admittedly walnut oil, available in specialty food shops and in the fine oil section of some supermarkets, is an extravagance, but this is a special dish. The salad is a gorgeous composition of white chicken, red tomatoes, purple radicchio, fresh green beans, and bright yellow egg yolk.

2 eggs
1 tablespoon fresh lemon juice
2 teaspoons white wine vinegar
1 teaspoon Dijon mustard
½ teaspoon salt
¼ cup walnut oil
1¼ cups vegetable oil
¾ cup walnuts, chopped

¾ pound green beans, trimmed
8 skinless, boneless chicken breast halves, poached
1 head of radicchio, separated into leaves
2 medium tomatoes, cut into wedges
4 hard-cooked eggs, cut into wedges (optional)

1. In a blender or food processor, combine eggs, lemon juice, vinegar, mustard, and salt. Blend well. With machine on, slowly drizzle in walnut oil and vegetable oil to make a mayonnaise. Taste and add additional lemon juice or salt to taste. Stir in chopped walnuts.

2. In a large pot of boiling salted water, cook green beans until bright colored and crisp-tender, 3 to 5 minutes. Drain and rinse under cold water until cool; drain well.

3. On a large serving platter or individual dinner plates, decoratively arrange radicchio, chicken breasts (whole or cut crosswise into 1-inch slices), green beans, tomatoes, and eggs. Spoon mayonnaise over chicken.

59   CHICKEN SALAD WITH MANDARIN ORANGES AND PECANS

Prep: 15 minutes   Serves: 4

½ cup coarsely chopped pecans
2 cups diced (½-inch) cooked chicken
1 bunch of watercress, tough stems removed
1 can (11 ounces) mandarin oranges, chilled and drained

2 scallions, sliced
6 tablespoons olive oil
2 tablespoons raspberry or red wine vinegar
½ teaspoon salt
¼ teaspoon freshly ground pepper

1. Preheat oven to 325 degrees. Spread out pecans on a small baking sheet. Bake for 10 to 15 minutes, until lightly toasted.

2. In a salad bowl, combine chicken, watercress, oranges, scallions, and toasted pecans. Drizzle on oil, vinegar, salt, and pepper. Toss to coat.

60 CHICKEN AND PASTA SALAD WITH PESTO
Prep: 15 minutes   Cook: 10 minutes   Serves: 4 to 6

Pesto has traditionally been a summer favorite, when garden fresh basil is in season. Now fresh basil, grown hydroponically in greenhouses, is available in many markets all year. Here pesto is combined with pasta and chicken for an Italianate salad that's loaded with flavor.

½ pound penne or pasta shells
2 cups diced cooked chicken

1 cup Pesto Sauce (recipe follows)
12 cherry tomatoes, halved

1. In a large saucepan of boiling salted water, cook the pasta until just tender, about 10 minutes. Drain and rinse under cold water until cool; drain well.

2. In a large serving bowl, combine pasta, chicken, and pesto sauce. Toss to coat with sauce. Garnish with tomatoes. Serve at room temperature or slightly chilled.

PESTO SAUCE

½ cup olive oil, preferably
    extra virgin
¼ cup pine nuts or walnuts
2 garlic cloves
½ teaspoon salt

2 cups fresh basil leaves
¾ cup grated imported
    Parmesan cheese
¼ cup grated Romano cheese

Place oil, nuts, garlic, and salt in a blender or food processor. Process until nuts and garlic are finely chopped. Add basil and process until finely chopped. Stir in Parmesan and Romano cheeses.

61 DILLED CHICKEN AND POTATO SALAD
Prep: 15 minutes   Cook: 10 minutes   Serves: 4

A lovely light luncheon dish, this salad is particularly tempting served in avocado halves. Because it is made with no mayonnaise, it travels well—for picnics and tailgate parties.

2 medium red potatoes, cut
    into bite-size pieces
6 tablespoons olive oil
2 tablespoons white wine
    vinegar
1¼ pounds skinless, boneless
    chicken breasts, poached
    and cut into bite-size
    pieces

2 tablespoons minced fresh
    dill, or 1½ teaspoons
    dried dill weed
2 scallions, finely sliced
2 tablespoons lemon juice
½ teaspoon salt
¼ teaspoon freshly ground
    black pepper
Dash of cayenne pepper

1. In a medium-size saucepan with boiling water, cook potatoes until just tender, about 10 minutes; drain. Toss warm potatoes with oil and vinegar. Let cool for 15 to 20 minutes, tossing several times.

2. Add chicken, dill, scallions, lemon juice, salt, black pepper, and cayenne. Toss to mix well. Cover and refrigerate until serving time. Serve slightly chilled or at room temperature.

62 COBB SALAD
Prep: 30 minutes   Serves: 6

A stylish layered salad served in a glass bowl.

½ head of iceberg lettuce, shredded
½ bunch of chicory, coarsely chopped
2 cups diced cooked chicken
1 medium red onion, diced
6 strips of bacon, cooked and crumbled
3 ounces Roquefort or other blue cheese, crumbled
3 hard-cooked eggs, chopped
2 large tomatoes, peeled, seeded, and diced
1 large avocado, peeled and diced
2 teaspoons lemon juice
3 tablespoons white wine vinegar
½ teaspoon salt
½ teaspoon dry mustard
⅔ cup olive or vegetable oil

1. Toss together lettuce and chicory and place in the bottom of a large glass bowl or dish. On top of lettuce, arrange strips of chicken, onion, bacon, cheese, eggs, tomatoes, and finally, avocado tossed with the lemon juice.

2. Whisk together vinegar, salt, and mustard. Whisk in oil to make a vinaigrette. At table, pour dressing over salad.

63 CURRIED CHICKEN AND RICE SALAD
Prep: 20 minutes   Cook time: 25 minutes   Serves: 8 to 10

This is one of my favorite buffet salads for a party. It is easy, quick, and delicious, with dark and golden raisins, red and green peppers, and the pleasant crunch of almonds.

3½ cups canned chicken broth
2 teaspoons curry powder
½ teaspoon ground ginger
½ teaspoon turmeric
2 cups converted rice
¼ cup olive oil
¼ cup lemon juice
2 cups chopped cooked chicken
½ cup dark raisins
½ cup golden raisins
½ cup chopped green bell pepper
½ cup chopped red bell pepper
½ cup mayonnaise
½ cup sour cream
½ cup slivered almonds, toasted
Salt and freshly ground pepper

1. In a medium-size saucepan, bring chicken stock, curry powder, ginger, turmeric, and 1 cup of water to a boil. Add rice, cover tight, reduce heat, and simmer until rice is tender and all the liquid is absorbed, about 25 minutes.

2. Transfer rice to a large serving bowl. Pour on oil and lemon juice and toss to mix. Cover and refrigerate until cool.

3. Add all remaining ingredients and mix well. Serve slightly chilled.

64   CHICKEN AND PASTA SALAD WITH BALSAMIC DRESSING

Prep: 20 minutes   Cook: 10 minutes   Serves: 6 to 8

1 pound ziti or pasta shells
1 medium yellow squash, sliced into ½-inch-thick rounds
½ head of broccoli, separated into 1-inch florets
1½ cups diced (1-inch) cooked chicken
8 medium-size fresh mushrooms, sliced
8 cherry tomatoes, cut in half
1 small red bell pepper, cut into thin strips

¼ cup extra virgin olive oil
2 tablespoons balsamic or red wine vinegar
2 tablespoons chopped fresh basil, or ½ teaspoon dried
1 tablespoon chopped fresh parsley
1 garlic clove, crushed
1 teaspoon salt
½ teaspoon coarsely cracked pepper

1. Bring a large pot of salted water to a boil for the pasta, and a large saucepan of salted water for the vegetables. While they are heating, cut up all the vegetables and the chicken.

2. Cook the pasta in the large pot of boiling water until it is tender but still firm to the bite, 10 to 12 minutes. Drain and rinse under cold running water to cool; drain well.

3. While the pasta is cooking, add the squash to the saucepan of boiling water and cook until just beginning to soften, about 2 minutes. Remove with a slotted spoon or skimmer and rinse under cold water; drain well. Add broccoli to the same pan and cook until bright green and crisp-tender, about 3 minutes. Remove with a slotted spoon, rinse until cool, and drain. Add beans to the same pan and cook until crisp-tender, about 3 minutes. Drain, rinse until cool, and drain well.

4. In a large salad bowl, combine the pasta, chicken, and vegetables. Toss lightly to mix. In a small bowl, combine oil, vinegar, basil, parsley, garlic, salt, and black pepper. Whisk to blend well. Pour dressing over salad and toss. Serve slightly chilled or at room temperature.

65   COLD CHICKEN AND RICE SALAD WITH OLIVES

Prep: 25 minutes   Serves: 6 to 8

You can serve this sprightly salad informally, or present it molded, "frosted," and decorated for a buffet or party. To mold, line a 1½-quart bowl with plastic wrap, pack the salad into the bowl, cover, and refrigerate for about 2 hours. Shortly before serving, unmold onto a bed of leaf lettuce, pulling on the edges of the plastic wrap to help, if necessary. Frost the molded salad with more mayonnaise and sour cream and garnish the top with sieved hard-cooked egg yolk. This salad keeps well and can be made a day ahead.

2 cups finely diced cooked chicken

3 cups cold cooked rice (made from 1 cup converted rice and 2¼ cups water)

1 jar (2½ ounces) pimiento-stuffed olives, drained and coarsely chopped

1½ cups chopped celery

2 pimientos, drained and diced

2 tablespoons chopped fresh parsley

½ cup mayonnaise

½ cup sour cream

2 tablespoons lemon juice

Salt and freshly ground pepper

Dash of hot pepper sauce

1. In a large bowl, combine chicken, rice, olives, celery, pimientos, and parsley. Toss to mix.

2. In a small bowl, combine all remaining ingredients. Stir to blend well. Spoon dressing over salad and toss to coat. Cover and refrigerate until serving time, or mold and decorate as described above.

---

66 NINE TREASURES PASTA SALAD
Prep: 40 minutes   Cook time: 10 minutes   Serves: 8

It is a typical Chinese custom to name the number of goodies in a dish, and the dressing for this salad, which combines rice wine vinegar, soy sauce, and fresh ginger, has a distinctly Oriental flavor. If that seems surprising in a pasta salad, remember it is claimed that Marco Polo brought spaghetti back to Italy from his travels in the Far East.

½ pound rotini or pasta shells

¼ cup vegetable oil

1 cup thinly sliced carrots

½ pound mushrooms, quartered

½ small bunch of broccoli, separated into florets

½ small head of cauliflower, separated into florets

¼ pound snow peas

1 red bell pepper, cut into thin strips

5 scallions, cut into 1-inch lengths

2 pounds skinless, boneless chicken breasts, poached and cut into 1-inch pieces

3 tablespoons soy sauce

2 tablespoons rice wine vinegar or cider vinegar

2 teaspoons sugar

2 teaspoons minced fresh ginger

1. In a large saucepan of boiling salted water, cook pasta until just tender, 10 to 12 minutes. Drain into a colander and rinse under cold water until cool; drain well.

2. In a wok or large Dutch oven, heat 2 tablespoons of the oil. Add carrots and stir-fry over medium-high heat for 2 minutes. Add mushrooms and stir-fry 1 minute longer. With a slotted spoon or Chinese strainer, remove to a large bowl.

3. Heat remaining oil in wok. Add broccoli, cauliflower, snow peas, bell pepper, and scallions. Stir-fry until vegetables are crisp-tender, about 4 minutes. Add vegetables to carrots and mushrooms. Add chicken and pasta.

4. In a small bowl, combine, soy sauce, vinegar, sugar, and ginger. Stir to dissolve sugar. Pour sauce over salad and toss gently to mix. Cover and refrigerate until serving time. Serve slightly chilled or at room temperature.

67 BOMBAY SALAD
Prep: 20 minutes   Serves: 4

A delightful salad for summer, when peaches and plums are at the height of their season. Serve on lettuce leaves, if desired.

1 cup sour cream
1/3 cup mango chutney, such as Major Grey's, finely chopped
1 tablespoon lime juice
1 teaspoon curry powder
1/3 cup shredded coconut, toasted (see note)
1/4 cup slivered almonds, toasted (see note)

2 cups diced (1/2-inch) cooked chicken
1 bunch of watercress, large stems removed
3 medium peaches, peeled and sliced
4 plums, sliced
1 kiwi, peeled and sliced

1. Combine sour cream, chutney, lime juice, curry powder, 1/4 cup of the coconut, and the almonds. In a medium-size bowl, toss chicken with 3/4 cup of the curry dressing. Cover and refrigerate chicken mixture and remaining dressing separately for about 30 minutes to develop the flavors, or longer if desired.

2. To serve, arrange watercress around edge of platter. Mound chicken salad in center. Arrange peaches, plums, and kiwi around chicken. Sprinkle remaining toasted coconut on top. Serve extra dressing on side.

Note: To toast coconut or almonds, spread on a baking sheet and toast in a 325-degree oven, shaking pan once or twice, for 10 to 15 minutes, until light brown.

68 RAINBOW CHICKEN SALAD WITH ORANGE-MUSTARD MAYONNAISE
Prep: 30 minutes   Serves: 4

1 head of romaine lettuce, separated into leaves
2 avocados, peeled and sliced lengthwise
1 tablespoon lemon juice
2 seedless grapefruit, peeled and separated into sections
4 navel oranges, peeled and separated into sections

1 medium red onion, halved and sliced
4 skinless, boneless chicken breast halves, poached and cut crosswise into thin slices
Orange-Mustard Mayonnaise (recipe follows)

1. On a large platter, arrange lettuce leaves, stems toward the center. Brush avocado with lemon juice to prevent discoloration. Arrange alternating ring of avocado and grapefruit around edge of platter. Arrange alternating ring of orange and red onion inside.

2. Toss chicken with 1/3 cup of mayonnaise and mound in center of platter. Pass remaining mayonnaise separately.

ORANGE-MUSTARD MAYONNAISE

2 egg yolks, at room
   temperature
2 teaspoons Dijon mustard
2 teaspoons lemon juice
1 cup vegetable oil

Grated peel from 1 orange
2 tablespoons fresh orange
   juice
Salt and freshly ground
   pepper

In a medium-size bowl, whisk together egg yolks, mustard, and lemon juice. Slowly whisk in oil, drop by drop, until mayonnaise begins to thicken. Gradually whisk in remaining oil in a thin stream. Blend in orange peel and juice. Season to taste with salt and pepper. Cover and refrigerate until serving time.

69 COLD SESAME NOODLES WITH CHICKEN AND BROCCOLI

Prep: 40 minutes   Serves: 4

Ideally, the chicken should be marinated for 2 hours.

1 bunch of broccoli, cut into
   1-inch florets
½ cup smooth peanut butter
½ cup hot water
¼ cup soy sauce
2 tablespoons red wine
   vinegar
2 tablespoons Oriental
   sesame oil
2 teaspoons sugar

2 garlic cloves, crushed
½ to 1 teaspoon crushed hot
   red pepper, to taste
2 skinless, boneless chicken
   breast halves, poached
   and shredded, or cut into
   ½-inch pieces
½ pound linguine
1 tablespoon vegetable oil
½ cup chopped scallions

1. In a large saucepan of boiling water, cook broccoli until bright green and crisp-tender, about 3 minutes. Drain into colander and rinse until cool; drain well.

2. Combine peanut butter and water in a blender or food processor; mix until smooth. Add soy sauce, vinegar, sesame oil, sugar, garlic, and red pepper; blend.

3. Put cooked chicken in a medium bowl, add peanut-sesame sauce and toss to coat. If you have time, cover and let marinate in the refrigerator for 2 hours.

4. In a large pot of boiling salted water, cook linguine until tender but still firm to the bite, about 10 minutes. Drain and rinse under cold running water; drain well.

5. In a large bowl, toss linguine with vegetable oil. Add chicken with sauce, broccoli, and scallions. Toss and serve slightly chilled or at room temperature.

70   CHICKEN SALAD NIÇOISE
Prep: 20 minutes   Cook: 10 to 15 minutes   Serves: 4

Traditionally, this Mediterranean salad is made with tuna fish, but chicken provides a delightful alternative.

¾ **pound green beans, trimmed**
4 **skinless, boneless chicken breast halves, poached and cut into 1-inch-wide slices**
1 **large cucumber, peeled, seeded, and cut into 1½ x ½-inch sticks**
2 **large tomatoes, cut into wedges**
1 **can (2 ounces) flat anchovy fillets, rinsed and drained**
12 **to 16 niçoise or Mediterranean black olives**

2 **tablespoons red wine vinegar**
1 **teaspoon Dijon mustard**
¼ **teaspoon salt**
¼ **teaspoon coarsely cracked pepper**
5 **tablespoons olive oil**
2 **tablespoons coarsely chopped flat-leaf parsley**
1 **tablespoon minced fresh basil, or ½ teaspoon dried**

1. In a large saucepan of boiling, salted water, cook greenbeans until just tender. 3 to 5 minutes. Drain and rinse under cold water until cool; drain well.

2. Arrange chicken in the center of a large platter. Surround with bundles of green beans, cucumber, and tomato wedges. Arrange anchovy fillets over chicken in a lattice pattern. Put an olive in the center of each lattice diamond.

3. In a small bowl, whisk together the vinegar, mustard, salt, and pepper. Gradually whisk in the oil until well blended. Mix in the parsley and basil. Drizzle the dressing over the salad shortly before serving.

71   GRAPEFRUIT AND CHICKEN SALAD
Prep: 30 minutes   Serves: 4

2 **medium grapefruit**
½ **cup plain yogurt**
¼ **cup mayonnaise**
1 **tablespoon minced fresh dill, or 1 teaspoon dried dill weed**
Salt and freshly ground pepper

1¼ **pounds skinless, boneless chicken breasts, poached and cut into ½-inch pieces**
½ **cup chopped celery**
2 **scallions, chopped**
2 **tablespoons chopped pimiento (optional)**
Sprigs of fresh dill for garnish

1. Cut each grapefruit in half crosswise. With a curved, serrated grapefruit knife, cut around each section to separate the fruit from the membrane. Remove the grapefruit sections and cut into bite-size pieces; set aside to drain. Scrape the remaining membrane from the shells and discard; reserve shells.

2. In a medium-size bowl, combine yogurt, mayonnaise, dill, and salt and pepper to taste. Stir to blend well. Add grapefruit, chicken, celery, scallions, and pimiento; toss lightly to blend. Cover and refrigerate until serving time. Wrap the grapefruit shells and refrigerate separately.

3. To serve, scoop about ¾ cup of chicken salad into each grapefruit shell. Garnish with a sprig of dill.

---

72 CHICKEN SALAD WITH CASHEWS AND ORANGE-MUSTARD DRESSING
Prep: 25 minutes   Serves: 4

1¼ pounds skinless, boneless chicken breasts, poached and shredded
3 celery ribs, cut into thin strips
1 large red bell pepper, cut into thin strips
3 scallions, sliced
½ cup cashews
   Orange-Mustard Dressing (recipe follows)
3 cups shredded Romaine lettuce

1. In a large bowl, combine chicken, celery, pepper, scallions, and cashews. Add ½ cup dressing and toss to coat.

2. Divide lettuce among four plates. Spoon chicken salad into center of plate. Pass remaining dressing separately.

ORANGE-MUSTARD DRESSING

1 egg
¼ cup orange juice, preferably fresh
¼ cup olive oil
1½ teaspoons red wine vinegar
1½ teaspoons Dijon mustard
1 teaspoon salt
½ teaspoon sugar
¼ teaspoon freshly ground pepper
   Dash of hot pepper sauce
½ cup parsley sprigs, lightly packed

In a blender or food processor, combine all ingredients except parsley. Process until well blended. Add parsley and process until finely chopped.

Chapter 5

The Well-Traveled Chicken

Chicken has been all over the world, and wherever it's landed, it's made a lot of friends. In many Latin countries, chicken is a festive dish, reserved for large Sunday dinners. In China, special chicken preparations are served at banquets. The French perfected the art of chicken cookery while we were still out in the woods shooting squirrels.

Wherever it's been, chicken has acquired a new seasoning, a distinctive form of preparation, a different way of cooking. This chapter does not contain a recipe from every country, but it does introduce a wide sampling of ethnic classics and exotic recipes from many far-off lands.

73   KUNG PAO CHICKEN
Prep: 10 minutes   Cook: 10 minutes   Serves: 4

This Chinese stir-fried chicken with peanuts bears the name of a high-ranking officer of the Ching dynasty, in whose honor it was created. It's a very popular Szechwan dish and, typically, flaming hot.

1¼ **pounds skinless, boneless**
    chicken breasts, cut into
    ½-inch pieces
1 **egg white**
1 **tablespoon plus 1 teaspoon**
    cornstarch
1 **teaspoon Szechwan chili**
    paste with garlic
2 **tablespoons soy sauce**
1 **teaspoon dry sherry**
1 **teaspoon red wine vinegar**

¼ **cup chicken broth**
1 **teaspoon Oriental sesame**
    oil
3 **tablespoons vegetable oil**
½ **cup raw peanuts**
4 **scallions, cut into ½-inch**
    lengths
2 **garlic cloves, chopped**
½ **to 1 teaspoon crushed hot**
    pepper, to taste

1. In a small bowl, combine chicken pieces with egg white and 1 tablespoon cornstarch. Toss to coat and set aside.

2. In another small bowl, blend chili paste with soy sauce, sherry, vinegar, broth, 1 teaspoon cornstarch, and sesame oil. Set sauce aside.

3. Heat oil in a wok or large frying pan over medium-high heat. Add chicken and stir-fry until it separates and turns white, about 4 minutes. Remove with a slotted spoon and drain on paper towels. Deep-fry peanuts in oil over medium heat until they are golden brown, about 3 minutes. Remove and drain.

4. Remove all but 2 tablespoons oil from the wok. Stir-fry scallions, garlic, and hot pepper for 30 seconds. Add chicken. Stir-fry over high heat for 1 minute.

5. Add sauce. Stir-fry until heated through and thickened. Add peanuts; stir to mix. Serve over rice.

74   POULET VALLÉE D'AUGE
Prep: 15 minutes   Cook: 30 minutes   Serves: 4

1 **chicken (3 pounds), cut up**
    Salt and freshly ground
    pepper
3 **tablespoons butter**

2 **large tart apples, peeled,**
    cored, and chopped
1 **large onion, chopped**
¼ **cup Calvados or applejack**
1 **cup heavy cream**

1. Season chicken pieces with salt and pepper. In a large frying pan, melt butter over medium heat. Add chicken and cook until brown on all sides, about 10 minutes. Remove and set aside.

2. Add apples and onions to pan. Cook until onion is tender, 3 to 5 minutes. Return chicken to pan. Add Calvados, reduce heat to a simmer, cover, and cook 20 minutes. Stir in cream and cook, covered, 10 minutes longer, until chicken is tender. Season sauce with salt and pepper to taste.

75 CHICKEN TEMPURA
Prep: 15 minutes   Cook: 15 minutes   Serves: 4

The secret of a light, crisp tempura is in not overmixing the batter—it should remain lumpy—and in making sure the oil is efficiently hot.

3 eggs
1 cup ice water
½ teaspoon baking powder
1½ cups flour
½ teaspoon salt
 Vegetable oil, for frying
¾ pound skinless, boneless
  chicken breasts, cut into
  2-inch pieces

½ small eggplant, sliced
  ½-inch thick and cut into
  2 x ½-inch sticks
¼ pound green beans, trimmed
1 sweet potato, peeled and
  thickly sliced
1 cup broccoli florets
 Lemon wedges

1. In a large bowl, beat eggs and water with a whisk until blended; stir in baking powder, flour, and salt. Mixture should remain lumpy.

2. In a large saucepan or deep-fat fryer, heat 2 inches of oil to 375° over medium-high heat. Dip chicken pieces in batter and fry in batches without crowding in hot oil until coating is brown and crisp, 5 to 7 minutes. Remove and drain on paper towels; keep warm. Repeat with vegetables. Serve with lemon wedges.

76 CHINESE STIR-FRIED CHICKEN WITH PEPPERS
*Prep: 10 minutes   Marinate: 20 minutes   Cook: 15 minutes
Serves: 4*

2 garlic cloves, finely chopped
3 tablespoons peanut oil
2 tablespoons soy sauce
¼ teaspoon freshly ground
  pepper
2 teaspoons cornstarch
1¼ pounds skinless, boneless
  chicken breasts, cut into
  1-inch pieces

3 red and/or green bell
  peppers, cut into ½-inch
  cubes
8 scallions, chopped
½ head Chinese celery
  cabbage, sliced into
  ½-inch pieces

1. In a medium-size bowl, combine garlic, 1 tablespoon of the oil, 1 tablespoon of the soy sauce, pepper, and 1 teaspoon of the cornstarch. Add chicken and toss to coat; let stand at least 20 minutes.

2. Heat remaining 2 tablespoons oil in a wok or large frying pan over medium-high heat. Add peppers and scallions and stir-fry 2 minutes. Add cabbage and cook 2 minutes, until tender but not limp. Remove vegetables with a slotted spoon.

3. Heat oil remaining in wok. Add chicken and stir-fry 3 minutes, until opaque. Mix remaining soy sauce and cornstarch with ¼ cup cold water. Add to pan.

4. Return vegetables and cook, stirring, 3 minutes, until sauce thickens.

77 TOKYO CHICKEN
Prep: 20 minutes   Cook: 10 minutes   Serves: 4

Toasted sesame seeds make this easy stir-fry irresistible.

2 **tablespoons hot water**	2 **tablespoons vegetable oil**
3 **tablespoons dry mustard**	1¼ **pounds skinless, boneless**
½ **cup soy sauce**	**chicken breasts, cut into**
2 **tablespoons plus 2 teaspoons**	**1-inch cubes**
toasted sesame seeds	**Freshly ground pepper**
1 **garlic glove**	1 **tablespoon lemon juice**

1. Place water and mustard in a blender and process to mix. Add soy sauce, 2 tablespoons sesame seeds, and garlic. Process about 1 minute. Set aside.

2. Heat oil in a large nonstick frying pan or wok over medium-high heat. Add chicken cubes; season with pepper to taste. Cook 5 to 8 minutes, until chicken is opaque and firm to the touch.

3. Sprinkle with lemon juice and remaining 2 teaspoons sesame seeds; cook 2 minutes more and serve with mustard-sesame mixture for dipping.

78 RED CHICKEN ENCHILADAS
Prep: 20 minutes   Cook: 25 minutes   Serves: 6

To save time, you can substitute a can of red enchilada sauce for the version in Step 1.

¼ **cup plus 2 tablespoons**	12 **corn tortillas**
vegetable oil	1 **medium onion, chopped**
2 **tablespoons flour**	2 **cups chopped cooked**
⅓ **to ½ cup ground chilies, to**	**chicken**
taste (not chili powder)	1¼ **cups (5 ounces) grated sharp**
2 **cups chicken broth**	**Cheddar cheese**
2 **garlic cloves, crushed**	**Sour cream, shredded**
through a press	**lettuce, and chopped**
½ **teaspoon cumin**	**tomatoes**
½ **teaspoon salt**	

1. In a medium-size saucepan, heat 2 tablespoons oil over medium heat. Add flour and cook, stirring, for 1 minute without browning. Add ground chilies and cook, stirring, for 30 seconds. Gradually whisk in broth. Season with garlic, cumin, and salt, reduce heat to low, and cook 10 minutes.

2. Preheat oven to 325°. Line up chicken, onions, and cheese next to a 13 x 9 x 2-inch baking dish. Heat remaining oil in a small frying pan. For each enchilada, fry one tortilla, turning once, for several seconds on each side, until softened. Place about 3 tablespoons of chicken down the middle, followed by about 1 heaping tablespoon each onion and cheese. Roll and place seam side down in the baking dish. Repeat with remaining tortillas.

3. Pour enchilada sauce over rolled tortillas and top with remaining cheese. Bake 15 minutes, until enchiladas are hot and cheese is melted. Top with sour cream and serve with shredded lettuce and chopped tomatoes.

79 CHICKEN BRAZIL
Prep: 45 minutes   Cook: 30 minutes   Serves: 6

This is a marvelous party dish with a dramatic presentation. If you have any trouble unmolding, don't despair. Simply scrape casserole onto platter and garnish with some of the bell pepper and olives.

3 tablespoons butter or margarine	1 can (3½ ounces) pitted black olives, sliced
1 small onion, chopped	1 package (10 ounces) frozen peas, thawed
2 garlic cloves, crushed	
1½ cups rice	2 hard-cooked eggs, chopped
1 can (14 ounces) Italian peeled tomatoes, coarsely chopped, juices reserved	3 tablespoons grated Parmesan cheese
	3 cups chopped cooked chicken
½ teaspoon salt	2 egg yolks, beaten
¼ teaspoon freshly ground pepper	½ cup chicken broth (optional)
1 red bell pepper, sliced into rings	½ cup bread crumbs

1. In a Dutch oven, melt 2 tablespoons of the butter over medium heat. Add onion and garlic; cook 2 minutes. Add rice and cook, stirring, until translucent. Add tomatoes, salt, and pepper.

2. Add enough hot water to reserved tomato juices to measure 3 cups. Stir into rice, cover, and simmer 25 minutes, until liquid is absorbed.

3. Preheat oven to 350°. Grease a 2½-quart round baking dish. Layer bottom with a design of sliced red pepper and half the olives. Add 1 cup rice mixture, spreading it over design.

4. Combine remaining rice and olives with peas, eggs, Parmesan cheese, chicken, and egg yolks. Mix well. Add chicken broth if mixture is dry. Press into baking dish. Sprinkle with bread crumbs. Dot with remaining 1 tablespoon butter. Bake 30 minutes.

5. Let casserole cool for 15 minutes. Run a knife around the edges to loosen and invert to unmold onto a platter.

80 CHICKEN PERUVIAN
Prep: 5 minutes   Cook: 45 minutes   Serves: 4

The zest of raisins, spices, and wine combined with the richness of almonds, egg yolks, and cream make this a special dish indeed.

2 tablespoons butter or magarine	1¼ cups dry white wine
1 chicken (3 pounds), cut up	½ cup golden raisins
1 small onion, chopped	½ cup sliced, blanched almonds
4 whole cloves	½ cup heavy cream
1 bay leaf	2 egg yolks
½ teaspoon cumin	Salt and freshly ground pepper
1 cup chicken broth	

1. In a large frying pan, melt butter over medium heat. Brown chicken

lightly, about 4 minutes on each side. Add onion, cloves, bay leaf, cumin, and broth. Cover and cook over low heat 15 minutes.

2. Add 1 cup of the wine, raisins, and almonds and increase heat to moderately low. Cook, partly covered, another 20 to 25 minutes, until chicken is tender but still juicy.

3. In a small bowl, whisk together cream, egg yolks, and remaining ¼ cup wine. Stir small amount of sauce into cream sauce and return to pan. Stir until thickened, but do not boil. Season to taste with salt and pepper.

---

81 CHICKEN JAKARTA
Prep: 20 minutes   Cook: 1 hour   Serves: 4

This recipe combines typical flavors of Southeast Asia. If kale is not available, fresh spinach can be substituted.

1 chicken (3 pounds), cut up	2 teaspoons ground ginger
½ teaspoon dry mustard	2½ tablespoons sugar
½ teaspoon ground cumin	3 tablespoons soy sauce
½ teaspoon ground coriander	2 tablespoons vegetable oil
¾ teaspoon crushed hot red pepper	¾ pound fresh kale, stemmed and coarsely chopped
1 medium onion, chopped	3 tablespoons red wine vinegar
1 tablespoon olive oil	2 teaspoons cornstarch dissolved in 2 teaspoons water
2 tablespoons butter or margarine	
1 cup walnut pieces	

1. Preheat oven to 375°. Oil a 13 x 9 x 2-inch baking dish. Arrange chicken pieces in dish and sprinkle with mustard, cumin, coriander, and ½ teaspoon of the hot pepper. Mix onion with oil; spoon around chicken. Bake uncovered 50 minutes, until chicken is browned, stirring onions occasionally to prevent excess browning.

2. Meanwhile, melt butter in a large frying pan over medium heat. Add walnuts and cook 2 to 3 minutes, stirring constantly, until nuts are lightly toasted. Sprinkle with ginger and 1½ teaspoons sugar. Cook, stirring, until sugar melts. Add 1 tablespoon of the soy sauce and cook, stirring, until liquid evaporates to a glaze. Remove from heat and let cool.

3. Heat vegetable oil in the same pan over medium heat. Add kale and remaining 1 tablespoon soy sauce. Stir-fry until wilted and tender; set aside.

4. In a small saucepan, combine vinegar, remaining 2 tablespoons sugar, ¼ teaspoon hot pepper, 1 tablespoon soy sauce, and 3 tablespoons water. Bring to a boil. Stir dissolved cornstarch slowly into hot sauce. Return to a boil, stirring, until thickened. Remove from heat, cover, and set aside.

5. When chicken is done, stir sauce and kale into pan juices. Scatter walnuts on top. Return to oven for 5 to 10 minutes to heat through.

82 THE COMMISSARY'S THAI CHICKEN WITH PAPAYA AND LIME

Prep: 10 to 15 minutes   Cook: 30 minutes   Serves: 6

Authenticaly seasoned and colorful—perfect party fare.

4 tablespoons vegetable oil	1½ cups chopped fresh papaya
1 large onion, chopped	1 pound boneless, skinless,
2 packages (½ ounce each)	chicken breasts, cut into
green Thai curry paste*	½-inch cubes
2 tablespoons curry powder	1 large green bell pepper, cut
1 garlic clove, crushed	into ¼-inch wide strips
2 teaspoons grated fresh	16 snow peas
ginger	2 tablespoons fresh lime juice
1 teaspoon salt	1 cup (8 ounces) plain yogurt
½ teaspoon cardamom	1 tablespoon minced fresh
2½ cups chopped fresh tomatoes	mint

1. In a large frying pan, heat 2 tablespoons of the vegetable oil over medium heat. Add onion and cook 5 minutes, until tender. Add curry paste, curry powder, garlic, ginger, salt, and cardamom. Cook, stirring to break up curry paste, 3 minutes. Add tomatoes and papaya and simmer 10 minutes.

2. Meanwhile, heat remaining 2 tablespoons vegetable oil in another frying pan over medium-high heat. Add chicken cubes. Stir-fry 3 to 4 minutes, until opaque and tender. With slotted spoon, transfer chicken to sauce.

3. Add pepper strips to second frying pan and cook 2 minutes. Add snow peas and cook 30 seconds. Remove vegetables with a slotted spoon to sauce.

4. Sprinkle lime juice over chicken mixture. Mix well. Heat through. Serve over rice. Combine yogurt and mint in a small serving container and pass separately.

*Available at Asian groceries.

83 CHICKEN TERIYAKI

Prep: 5 minutes   Marinate: 2 hours   Cook: 10 minutes   Serves: 4

A classic Japanese grill. For a light summer supper, serve with your favorite salad. Although the instructions below are for a broiler, the chicken is even better cooked over a charcoal grill. Cooking time may vary slightly.

2 whole chicken breasts, split	1 tablespoon sugar
in half	1 garlic clove, chopped
½ cup soy sauce	½ teaspoon ground ginger
¼ cup dry sherry	

1. Arrange chicken, skin side up, in a single layer in a shallow dish.

2. Combine soy sauce, sherry, sugar, garlic, and ginger; pour over chicken. Marinate in refrigerator, turning once or twice, for 2 hours.

3. Preheat broiler. Remove chicken from marinade. Spray rack in broiler pan with vegetable spray; place chicken on rack. Broil 5 to 6 inches from heat, turning once and basting with marinade, about 10 minutes.

84   COQ AU VIN
Prep: 25 minutes   Cook: 1 hour   Serves: 4

This is a classic French dish, which gets its flavor and color from a good strong red wine.

4 slices of bacon, diced	2 garlic cloves, chopped
1 tablespoon butter or margarine	2 tablespoons flour
	1/4 cup brandy
1 chicken (3 pounds), cut up	1 3/4 cups fruity red wine, such as hearty burgundy
Salt and freshly ground pepper	
	1/3 cup chopped parsley
18 to 20 very small white onions, peeled	1 bay leaf
	1/4 teaspoon dried thyme
2 cups thickly sliced mushrooms	

1. In a large frying pan, cook bacon over low heat until brown and crisp. Remove with a slotted spoon and drain on paper towels. Melt butter in bacon drippings. Season chicken pieces with salt and pepper and brown in skillet over medium-high heat, turning, about 5 minutes on each side. Transfer to a 5½-quart heatproof casserole.

2. Add whole onions to frying pan and cook, turning until browned. Transfer to pot with chicken. Add mushrooms and garlic to frying pan and brown slightly. Place in casserole with chicken.

3. Preheat oven to 325°. Add flour to fat in skillet. Cook, stirring, for 1 to 2 minutes without browning. Stir in brandy and red wine and bring to a boil. Pour into casserole. Sprinkle with 3 tablespoons parsley, the bay leaf, and thyme. Add bacon.

4. Bake covered for 1 hour. Remove bay leaf and garnish with the remaining chopped parsley.

85   MOROCCAN CHICKEN
Prep: 15 minutes   Cook: 30 minutes   Serves: 4

3 tablespoons vegetable oil	1 pound small white onions, peeled
1 chicken (3 pounds), cut up	
1 garlic clove, crushed	1/4 pound blanched almonds
1/2 cinnamon stick	2 tablespoons chopped parsley
1/4 teaspoon ground saffron	1/2 teaspoon salt
1/4 teaspoon freshly ground pepper	

1. In a large flameproof casserole, heat oil over moderate heat. Add chicken. Cook, turning, until brown on all sides, about 10 minutes. Add garlic, cinnamon, saffron, and pepper; cook for 1 minute.

2. Add onions, almonds, parsley, salt, and 2 cups of water. Partly cover and simmer 30 minutes, until chicken is tender. Remove chicken to a serving platter.

3. Spoon onions, almonds, and some sauce over chicken. Pass remaining sauce separately.

86 SPANISH PAELLA
Prep: 10 to 15 minutes   Cook: 1¼ hours   Serves: 6

2 tablespoons vegetable oil
1 chicken (3 pounds), cut up
1 large onion, chopped
1 garlic clove, finely chopped
1½ cups long-grain white rice
3 cups chicken broth
¼ teaspoon ground saffron
 Salt
½ pound chorizo or hot Italian sausage, cut into ½-inch rounds

1 pound shrimp, shelled and deveined
2 large red bell peppers, cut into 1-inch squares
1 package (10 ounces) frozen peas
12 to 18 littleneck clams
1 jar (2 ounces) pimientos, drained and cut into strips

1. Preheat over to 375°. In a large frying pan, heat oil over medium-high heat. Add chicken and sauté, turning, until browned, about 10 minutes. Remove chicken to a plate.

2. Reduce heat to medium. Cook onion and garlic in pan drippings until tender, about 3 minutes; push to one side. Sprinkle rice into pan and cook, stirring constantly, until translucent. Add chicken broth, 1 cup water, saffron, and salt to taste; bring to a boil. Pour into a paella pan or large shallow casserole. Add browned chicken and chorizo; cover.

3. Bake 45 minutes. Remove from oven and mix in shrimp, red peppers, and peas; arrange clams on top. Cover and bake 15 minutes longer, until shrimp and rice are tender and cooking liquid is absorbed. Discard any clams that do not open. Garnish with pimiento strips.

87 CHICKEN RATATOUILLE
Prep: 30 minutes   Cook: 40 minutes   Serves: 4

In this Moroccan variation of the classic French vegetable stew, the chicken soaks up all the wonderful flavors of the ratatouille: peppers, garlic, tomatoes, and Mediterranean herbs.

1 medium eggplant, cut into 1-inch cubes
1 teaspoon salt
3 tablespoons olive oil
1 chicken (3 pounds), cut up
1 large onion, chopped
2 garlic cloves, finely chopped
1 green bell pepper, cut into 1-inch pieces
1 red bell pepper, cut into 1-inch pieces

1 medium zucchini, cut into 1-inch cubes
2 tomatoes, quartered
1 tablespoon lemon juice
1 tablespoon chopped parsley
½ teaspoon dried oregano
½ teaspoon dried basil
¼ teaspoon freshly ground pepper

1. Lay eggplant cubes on paper towels. Sprinkle with salt and let sit about 15 minutes. Blot excess water with additional paper towels.

2. Heat oil in a large Dutch oven over medium heat. Brown chicken pieces in a single layer, in two batches, about 5 minutes a side. Remove chicken and set aside.

3. Add onion and garlic to oil in Dutch oven. Sauté until onion is tender, about 2 minutes. Add green and red bell peppers and cook 2 minutes, stirring constantly. Add eggplant, zucchini, tomatoes, lemon juice, parsley, oregano, basil, and pepper; mix well.

4. Return chicken to Dutch oven; cover with vegetables. Season ratatouille with additional salt to taste. Surround chicken with ratatouille, and simmer uncovered for 30 minutes, until vegetables and chicken are tender. Remove chicken to a heated platter and smother with ratatouille.

88 CHINESE LEMON CHICKEN
Prep: 40 minutes   Marinate: 30 minutes   Cook: 20 minutes
Serves: 4

Everyone has his favorite recipe for lemon chicken. This is mine. Serve over white rice.

4 tablespoons plus 1 teaspoon vegetable oil	¼ cup fresh lemon juice
2 teaspoons soy sauce	1 teaspoon vegetable oil
½ teaspoon dry sherry	½ teaspoon salt
¼ teaspooon freshly ground pepper	1 teaspoon cornstarch dissolved in 2 tablespoons water
4 skinless, boneless chicken breast halves, flattened to ½-inch	2 ounces (about ⅔ cup) snow peas
1 tablespoon cornstarch	⅔ cup thinly sliced bamboo shoots
1 tablespoon sugar	½ cup thinly sliced water chestnuts
2 tablespoons ketchup	

1. For marinade, combine 1 tablespoon of the oil, the soy sauce, sherry, and pepper in a small bowl. Place chicken in a shallow dish. Rub marinade over chicken. Coat lightly with cornstarch. Refrigerate at least 30 minutes.

2. For lemon sauce, in a small saucepan over medium-high heat, combine sugar, ketchup, lemon juice, 1 teaspoon oil, salt, and ¾ cup water, bring to a boil, stirring occasionally. Add dissolved cornstarch and stir until slightly thickened. Keep warm.

3. In a wok or a large frying pan, heat remaining oil. Add chicken and stir-fry over medium-high heat until golden brown on each side, about 8 minutes. Remove with tongs and cut into ¾-inch-wide strips. Set aside and cover with foil to keep warm.

4. Add snow peas, bamboo shoots, and water chestnuts to wok and stir-fry 2 minutes; transfer to heated serving platter. Top with chicken and spoon lemon sauce over all.

89   SPICY BOLIVIAN CHICKEN
Prep: 20 minutes   Cook: 20 minutes   Serves: 6

A spicy peanut butter sauce makes this a hot food lover's favorite.

1½ pounds skinless, boneless
     chicken breasts, cut into
     ½-inch strips
Salt and freshly ground
     pepper
2 tablespoons vegetable oil
2 large onions, chopped
2 red bell peppers, cut into
     ¼-inch strips

2 garlic cloves, finely chopped
1 teaspoon crushed hot red
     pepper
3 cups chicken broth
¾ cup peanut butter
1 package (10 ounces) frozen
     peas, thawed
¼ cup bread crumbs

1. Season chicken with salt and pepper. In a large frying pan, heat oil over medium heat. Add chicken strips and sauté, stirring, for 3 minutes, until chicken turns opaque. Remove chicken and set aside.

2. Add onions, bell peppers, and garlic to pan. Sauté 3 minutes, until onions are tender. Stir in hot pepper. Add broth and peanut butter. Simmer, stirring occasionally, for 10 minutes.

3. Stir in chicken, peas, and bread crumbs. Cook 5 to 10 minutes, stirring occasionally, until sauce is thickened and mixture is heated through. Serve over rice.

90   ARROZ CON POLLO
Prep: 20 minutes   Cook: 25 minutes   Serves: 4

Spanish rice with chicken—a favorite Sunday dish. Serve with plenty of ice cold beer.

1 chicken (3 pounds), cut up
Salt and freshly ground
     pepper
2 tablespoons olive oil
1 teaspoon minced garlic
1 large onion, chopped
1 medium-size green bell
     pepper, cut into strips
1 medium-size red bell
     pepper, cut into strips
1 cup rice
½ pound cooked smoked
     sausage, cut into ½-inch
     pieces

¼ teaspoon ground saffron
1 can (16 ounces) whole
     tomatoes, drained and cut
     up, or 2 fresh tomatoes,
     chopped
½ cup dry white wine
½ teaspoon dried oregano
¼ teaspoon cayenne pepper
1½ cups chicken broth
½ cup frozen peas, thawed
½ cup pitted black olives, sliced

1. Season chicken with salt and pepper. In a large frying pan, heat olive oil over medium heat. Add chicken and cook, turning, until brown all over, about 10 minutes. Transfer with tongs to a large flameproof casserole.

2. Add onion and bell peppers to skillet and cook until onions and peppers are soft. Transfer to casserole; add rice and sausage.

3. Add saffron, tomatoes, wine, oregano, cayenne, and chicken broth to skillet. Bring to a boil, scraping up brown bits from bottom of pan. Pour into casserole. Stir to distribute rice evenly. Bring to boil, reduce heat, cover, and simmer for 25 minutes, until chicken is tender.

4. Stir in peas and olives and heat through. Serve immediately.

91 POACHED CHICKEN PORTUGUESE
Prep: 15 minutes   Cook: 30 minutes   Serves: 4

2 tablespoons olive oil
1 cup sliced scallions
2 garlic cloves, crushed
⅛ teaspoon hot pepper sauce
4 medium tomatoes, peeled, seeded, and chopped
1 tablespoon red wine vinegar
1 bay leaf
½ teaspoon ground cloves

½ teaspoon Worcestershire sauce
⅛ teaspoon ground saffron (optional)
⅛ teaspoon freshly ground pepper
2 pounds skinless, boneless chicken breast halves

1. In a large frying pan, heat oil over medium heat. Add scallions and cook until lightly browned, about 3 minutes. Add garlic and hot pepper sauce; cook 1 minute. Add tomatoes, vinegar, bay leaf, cloves, Worcestershire, saffron, and pepper. Bring to a boil, reduce heat, and simmer uncovered for 15 minutes.

2. Place chicken on top of sauce, cover, and simmer 15 to 20 minutes, until chicken is tender and opaque.

92 CHICKEN KIEV
Prep: 20 minutes   Chill: 2 hours   Cook: 20 minutes   Serves: 4

This is a classic recipe for tender moist chicken bursting with chives and parsley butter. Experiment with different fresh herbs for different tastes.

6 tablespoons butter or margarine, softened
2 tablespoons minced chives
2 tablespoons chopped parsley
4 skinless, boneless chicken breast halves

Freshly ground pepper
2 eggs, lightly beaten
1 cup bread crumbs
Vegetable oil, for frying
Lemon wedges

1. Blend together butter, chives, and parsley. Form into a roll the size of a stick of butter, wrap, and place in freezer until firm, about 1 hour.

2. Pound chicken breasts to ¼-inch thickness between two pieces of plastic wrap or wax paper. Season with pepper.

3. Remove butter from freezer and cut into 4 equal portions. Place one cube on each breast and roll, tucking in all sides; secure with wooden toothpicks. Dip each piece in beaten eggs, then roll in bread crumbs. Refrigerate at least 1 hour.

4. In a deep-fat fryer or large heavy saucepan, heat 3 inches of oil to 350°. Add chicken and fry for 15 to 20 minutes, until golden brown. Remove wooden picks and serve with lemon wedges.

Chapter 6

American (and Oven) Fried

America's No. 1 favorite fast food is fried chicken. In recent years we've consumed over 1½ billion pounds annually. With the recipes in this chapter, you can enjoy this all-time favorite anytime you want in your own home. What's more, you can tailor it to your personal tastes and specifications.

The secret to great fried chicken is to make sure the frying oil is heated to the proper temperature (around 375°), and not to cook too many pieces at one time, which reduces the temperature and results in soggy chicken.

If you don't have a deep-fat thermometer, here is a test to tell if the oil is the correct temperature: drop a cube of white bread into the hot oil. The oil should bubble up around the bread, and the bread should brown in 1 minute. If it browns sooner, the oil is too hot and the outside of the chicken will overcook before the inside is done. If the bread takes much longer to brown, the oil is not hot enough; the chicken will take too long to cook, and the crust will be greasy.

For those who eschew frying to avoid fats, a selection of oven-fried recipes is also included.

93 BASIC FRIED CHICKEN
Prep: 10 minutes   Chill: up to 12 hours   Cook: 20 minutes
Serves: 4

Refrigerating floured chicken gives the coating a chance to set, which produces a crisp crust that adheres to the skin.

⅓ cup flour
1 teaspoon paprika
1 teaspoon dry mustard
½ teaspoon onion salt

Freshly ground pepper
1 broiler-fryer chicken (3 pounds), cut up
Vegetable oil, for frying

1. In a plastic or paper bag, combine flour, paprika, mustard, onion salt, and pepper. Moisten chicken pieces with water. Place in bag, several pieces at a time, and shake to coat thoroughly. Repeat with remaining chicken. Place chicken on a wire rack on a baking sheet, cover, and refrigerate for at least 30 minutes and up to 12 hours.

2. In a large saucepan or deep-fat fryer, heat 3 inches of oil over medium heat to 375°. Fry chicken in batches without crowding, turning once, for 15 to 20 minutes, until chicken is tender and golden brown. Drain on paper towels.

94 CINNAMON-FRIED CHICKEN
Prep: 5 minutes   Chill: 1 hour   Cook: 25 minutes   Serves: 4

1 chicken (3 pounds), cut up
1 tablespoon cinnamon
2 tablespoons sugar
1 teaspoon freshly ground pepper

¾ teaspoon dried oregano
1½ teaspoons salt
1½ cups flour
Vegetable oil, for frying

1. Place chicken pieces in a large baking dish. Mix cinnamon, sugar, pepper, oregano, and salt in a small bowl. Sprinkle evenly over chicken, coating both sides. Cover chicken and refrigerate for at least 1 hour.

2. Dredge chicken in flour; shake off excess. In a large saucepan or deep-fat fryer, heat 2 inches of oil to 375°. Fry chicken in batches without crowding, turning, until browned outside and tender and cooked through, about 25 minutes.

95   SOUTHERN CRACKER-FRIED CHICKEN
Prep: 15 minutes   Cook: 20 minutes   Serves: 4

This is really two recipes in one, depending on the type of crackers you use. Both produce a lighter crust and a distinctively different flavor from flour. To pulverize the crackers, I've recommended using a food processor to save time. But there is also something wonderfully tactile—and soothing—about crushing them by hand.

⅓ cup buttermilk
30 Saltines or Ritz-style
    crackers, pulverized in a
    food processor or by hand
½ teaspoon garlic powder
½ teaspoon sage

½ teaspoon salt
1 teaspoon freshly ground
    pepper
3 pounds chicken drumsticks,
    thighs, or breasts
1 cup lard or vegetable oil

1. Place buttermilk in a shallow dish. Combine crackers, garlic powder, sage, salt, and pepper in a plastic bag, and shake to mix thoroughly. Dip chicken pieces in buttermilk. Place one or two pieces at a time in bag; shake to coat.

2. In a large deep frying pan, melt lard over medium-high heat to 375°. Add chicken pieces and cook, turning frequently, until brown and crispy, about 20 minutes. Drain on paper towels before serving.

96   OVEN-FRIED COCONUT CHICKEN
Prep: 5 to 10 minutes   Cook: 50 minutes   Serves: 4

1½ cups (loosely packed) flaked
    coconut
1 cup seasoned bread crumbs
2 eggs

4 tablespoons butter or
    margarine, melted
1 chicken (3 pounds), cut up

1. Preheat oven to 350°. Mix coconut and bread crumbs in a shallow dish. Beat eggs until foamy in a separate dish.

2. Pour melted butter into a large baking pan. Dip chicken in egg, one piece at a time, then roll in coconut mixture. Arrange chicken skin side down in pan.

3. Bake for 25 minutes. Turn chicken, bake 25 minutes longer, until tender and lightly browned outside.

97   OVEN-FRIED GARLIC CHICKEN
Prep: 15 minutes   Cook: 1 hour   Serves: 4

⅔ cup bread crumbs
⅔ cup grated Parmesan cheese
¼ cup minced fresh parsley
¼ teaspoon salt
⅛ teaspoon freshly ground
    pepper

5 tablespoons butter or
    margarine
3 garlic cloves, minced
1 chicken (3 pounds), cut up

1. Preheat oven to 350°. In a shallow bowl, blend together bread crumbs,

Parmesan cheese, parsley, salt, and pepper.

2. In a small saucepan, heat butter and garlic over very low heat until butter melts. Remove from heat. Brush chicken pieces with garlic butter, then roll in bread crumb mixture to coat.

3. Place chicken skin side up on a large foil-lined baking sheet. Mix together any remaining crumb mixture and butter and sprinkle over chicken. Bake 1 hour.

98 CORNFLAKE-FRIED CHICKEN BREASTS
Prep: 10 minutes   Chill: 1 hour   Cook: 10 to 20 minutes
Serves: 4 to 8

3 eggs
1 cup milk
1 teaspoon poultry seasoning
¼ teaspoon salt
   Freshly ground pepper
8 chicken breast halves with
   bone

1 box (12 ounces) cornflakes,
   finely crushed
½ of a 10-ounce box biscuit mix
   Vegetable oil, for frying
   Juice of 1 lemon

1. In a large bowl, beat eggs with milk, poultry seasoning, salt, and pepper. Add chicken pieces and refrigerate 1 hour.

2. In a plastic or paper bag, combine crushed cornflakes and biscuit mix. Add chicken, a few pieces at a time, and shake to coat well. Place on a baking sheet and refrigerate chicken for 2 hours.

3. Heat 1½ to 2 inches oil in a large saucepan or deep-fat fryer to 375°. Fry chicken in batches without crowding, turning, 5 minutes a side, until browned and crisp. Remove chicken and drain on paper towels. Sprinkle lemon juice over chicken before serving.

99 BACON-FRIED CHICKEN
Prep: 10 minutes   Chill: 1 hour   Cook: 50 minutes   Serves: 8

1 cup milk
1 egg
2 chickens (3 pounds each), cut
   up
½ cup flour

¼ teaspoon salt
   Freshly ground black pepper
   Pinch of cayenne pepper
½ pound lean slab bacon,
   chopped

1. Combine milk and egg in a large bowl. Place chicken pieces in mixture and refrigerate 1 hour.

2. In a medium-size bowl, mix flour, salt, black pepper, and cayenne. Dredge chicken pieces in flour mixture; shake off excess.

3. Spread bacon over bottom of a large, heavy frying pan. Arrange chicken pieces on top of bacon in a single layer. Cook uncovered over medium-low heat, turning as chicken browns, 50 minutes, until chicken is tender. Remove chicken from the skillet and drain on paper towels. Sprinkle any loose bacon pieces over chicken before serving.

100 OVEN CRISP CHICKEN
Prep: 10 minutes   Cook: 1 hour   Serves: 4

This can also be used for chicken wings to be served as an appetizer.

1 cup sour cream
2 tablespoons lemon juice
2 tablespoons Worcestershire
   sauce
1 teaspoon paprika
½ teaspoon celery salt
½ teaspoon garlic powder

½ teaspoon freshly ground
   pepper
1 package (8 ounces) herb-
   seasoned stuffing mix
1 chicken (3 pounds), cut up
2 to 3 tablespoons butter or
   margarine, melted

1. Preheat oven to 350°. In a small bowl, mix together sour cream, lemon juice, Worcestershire sauce, paprika, celery salt, garlic powder, and pepper.

2. Place stuffing mix in a blender or food processor. Process until it resembles fine crumbs. Coat the chicken pieces with the sour cream mixture, then roll in the crumbs. Place in a greased 13 x 9 x 2-inch baking dish. Drizzle with melted butter and bake 1 hour.

101 HOMEMADE SHAKE-AND-BAKE CHICKEN
Prep: 10 minutes   Cook: 40 minutes   Serves: 4

½ cup flour
1 teaspoon paprika
½ teaspoon salt
½ teaspoon garlic powder
½ teaspoon dried thyme

¼ teaspoon freshly ground
   pepper
4 chicken legs and thighs
½ cup milk

1. Preheat oven to 375°. Combine flour, paprika, salt, garlic powder, thyme, and pepper in a plastic bag.

2. Dip chicken legs in milk; shake off excess. Add to bag and shake to coat evenly. Place chicken on a greased baking sheet. Bake 40 minutes, until chicken is tender and coating crisp.

102 BATTER-DIPPED CRUNCHY FRIED CHICKEN
Prep: 10 minutes   Cook: 1 hour   Serves: 8

Here's a different way to have fried chicken. Poaching chicken ahead in water reduces fat and allows for less frying time later.

2 chickens (3 pounds each), cut
   up
2 bay leaves
2 whole cloves
1 garlic clove, finely chopped
1 tablespoon celery seed
1½ quarts vegetable oil

2 cups pancake mix
1 teaspoon paprika
¼ teaspoon salt
⅛ teaspoon freshly ground
   pepper
2 eggs, well beaten

1. Place chicken pieces in a large saucepan or flameproof casserole. Add 2 cups water, bay leaves, cloves, garlic, and celery seed. Cover and bring to a boil. Reduce heat and simmer 45 minutes, until chicken is tender. Remove chicken from stock. Strain and reserve 1⅓ cups of stock. Refrigerate chicken for 15 to 20 minutes. Meanwhile, in a large saucepan or deep-fat fryer, heat all but 2 tablespoons vegetable oil over medium heat.

2. In a large bowl, combine pancake mix, paprika, salt, pepper, 2 tablespoons vegetable oil, eggs, and reserved chicken stock. Generously coat each piece of chicken with batter.

3. Fry chicken in batches without crowding 7 to 10 minutes, turning once, until golden brown and crisp. Remove and drain on paper towels.

---

103   OVEN-FRIED CHICKEN WITH BISCUITS AND PEACHES

Prep: 10 minutes   Cook: 1 hour 5 minutes   Serves: 4

Here's a down-home southern meal in a pan. Try cream of broccoli soup as a starter and chocolate ice cream with a splash of dark rum for dessert.

¼ cup vegetable shortening	1 chicken (3 pounds), cut up
4 tablespoons butter or margarine	1 can (6 ounces) refrigerator biscuits
1 cup plus 2 tablespoons flour	1 can (30 ounces) cling peach halves, drained
2 teaspoons paprika	Whole cloves
¼ teaspoon salt	1½ cups hot milk
Freshly ground pepper	

1. Preheat oven to 425°. Place shortening and butter in a 13 x 9 x 2-inch baking dish and set in oven until melted. In a plastic or paper bag, combine 1 cup flour, paprika, salt, and pepper. Add chicken, a few pieces at a time, and shake to coat thoroughly. Place chicken skin side down in hot shortening. Bake 45 minutes, then turn.

2. Push chicken to one end of pan. At the other end, arrange uncooked biscuits in a single layer, without draining off shortening. Stick each peach half with a clove and place on top of chicken. Bake 15 minutes.

3. To make gravy, remove chicken, biscuits, and peaches to a serving platter. Pour pan drippings into a medium-size saucepan and place over medium heat. Whisk in 2 tablespoons flour and cook for 1 minute without browning. Whisk in milk, bring to a boil, and cook, stirring, until thick and smooth. Serve with chicken and biscuits.

104 OVEN-FRIED WHOLE WHEAT CHICKEN
Prep: 15 minutes   Cook: 45 minutes   Serves: 4

Whole wheat flour produces a darker, nutty-flavored crust.

1 stick (½ cup) butter or
   margarine
1 chicken (3 pounds), cut up
1 cup whole wheat flour

2 teaspoons paprika
¼ teaspoon salt
⅛ teaspoon freshly ground
   pepper

1. Preheat oven to 400°. Put butter in a 13 x 9 x 2-inch baking dish and place in oven until melted.

2. In a plastic or paper bag, combine whole wheat flour, paprika, salt, and pepper. Add chicken pieces, a few at a time, and shake to coat.

3. Roll chicken in melted butter in baking dish. Bake for 30 minutes. Turn and bake another 10 to 15 minutes, until lightly browned and crisp.

Chapter 7

Could Be Veal

Veal and chicken share many of the same positive attributes. Both are light, "white" meats, relatively low in calories and fat. Both are delicately flavored and lend themselves to a variety of tastes and cooking techniques. Skinless, boneless chicken breasts, in fact, lend themselves very well to many of the same quick, elegant recipes used for veal scaloppine.

There are, however, two major differences. Veal scallops cost three to four times more than skinless, boneless chicken breasts, and white meat chicken still beats veal nutritionally. It has roughly two-thirds the calories and less than half the fat.

To turn skinless, boneless chicken breasts into cutlets or scaloppine, lay the chicken flat, smooth side down. Fold out the small strip of "fillet," so that the breast is of roughly even thickness. There is a small tendon in this fillet piece, which can tighten during cooking, shrinking the breast. To remove it, grasp the end of this small, tough white string and pull gently, while scraping against the tendon with the dull side of a knife to separate it from the meat; it should come out neatly. Place the breast between sheets of wax paper or plastic wrap and pound with a heavy rolling pin to flatten evenly to about ¼ inch.

These chicken cutlets, or scaloppine, or paillards, as they are sometimes called, can be sautéed in a flash, about 4 minutes in a hot pan. Be sure to keep them moist for maximum flavor and tenderness.

Following are some fabulous recipes for chicken posing as veal. Pound your scaloppine ahead of time and they are ready for a quick after-work supper or for hassle-free elegant entertaining.

Note: A whole chicken breast is two breast halves joined in the center by cartilage, and is sold either "whole" or "split." When sold skinless and boneless, however, each breast piece is actually one breast half. Since a breast half equals a single serving of 4 to 5 ounces, recipe portions throughout this chapter are described as "breast halves."

105   CHICKEN PICCATA
Prep: 10 minutes   Cook: 10 minutes   Serves: 4

½ cup flour
1 teaspoon salt
¼ teaspoon freshly ground
   pepper
2 pounds skinless, boneless
   chicken breast halves,
   pounded to ¼-inch
   thickness
2 tablespoons butter or
   margarine

1 tablespoon vegetable oil
3 tablespoons dry white wine
   or water
3 tablespoons lemon juice
1 lemon, thinly sliced
3 tablespoons capers
   (optional)
3 tablespoons chopped fresh
   parsley

1. Combine flour, salt, and pepper in a shallow dish. Dredge chicken breasts in flour mixture; shake off excess.

2. In a large frying pan, heat butter and vegetable oil over medium heat. Add chicken breasts. Cook about 3 minutes a side, until tender and opaque. Remove and keep warm.

3. Add wine to pan juices. Cook 1 minute, scraping up brown bits from bottom of pan. Add lemon juice and heat to boiling. Return chicken to pan, cover with lemon slices, and cook until sauce thickens slightly, about 3 minutes. Serve garnished with capers and parsley.

106   CHICKEN MARSALA WITH MUSHROOMS
Prep: 10 minutes   Cook: 25 minutes   Serves: 4

3 tablespoons flour
½ teaspoon freshly ground
   pepper
4 skinless, boneless chicken
   breast halves, pounded to
   ¼-inch thickness
4 tablespoons butter or
   margarine

1 tablespoon vegetable oil
½ cup chopped onion
2 garlic cloves, chopped
½ pound mushrooms, sliced
3 tablespoons dry Marsala
⅔ cup beef stock
   Salt to taste

1. Mix flour and pepper in a shallow dish. Dredge chicken in flour mixture to coat; shake off excess.

2. In a large frying pan, heat 2 tablespoons of the butter in oil over medium heat. Add chicken and cook until lightly brown, about 3 minutes a side. Remove and keep warm. Add onion and garlic and sauté until onion is tender, about 3 minutes. Add mushrooms and cook until they are lightly browned, 3 to 5 minutes.

3. Return chicken to pan, stir in Marsala and beef stock. Bring to a boil, reduce heat, and simmer until liquid reduces by one-third. Whisk in remaining butter. Season with salt and additional pepper to taste. Serve with buttered, parsleyed noodles.

107 LEMON CHICKEN SCALOPPINE WITH ARTICHOKES

Prep: 10 minutes   Cook: 25 minutes   Serves: 4

¼ cup flour
　　Salt and freshly ground
　　　pepper
4 skinless, boneless chicken
　　breast halves, pounded to
　　¼-inch thickness
2 tablespoons butter or
　　margarine
1 tablespoon vegetable oil

1 garlic clove, minced
1 cup chicken broth
¼ cup dry vermouth
¼ teaspoon dried marjoram
1 bay leaf
1 can artichoke hearts,
　　drained and quartered
8 thin lemon slices

1. Combine flour, salt, and pepper in a shallow dish. Dredge chicken breasts in flour to coat; shake off excess.

2. In a large frying pan, melt butter in oil over medium heat. Add chicken and cook until lightly browned, about 4 minutes a side. Remove and keep warm.

3. Add garlic to pan and cook for 1 minute, until translucent. Add broth, vermouth, marjoram, and bay leaf to pan. Bring to a boil, stirring constantly. Return chicken to pan; add artichoke hearts and 4 lemon slices. Cover and simmer 10 to 15 minutes, until liquid begins to thicken and flavors are blended. Discard bay leaf and lemon slices.

4. Arrange chicken and artichokes on a platter. Pour sauce over chicken. Garnish with remaining lemon slices.

108 CHICKEN SALTIMBOCCA

Prep: 15 minutes   Cook: 40 minutes   Serves: 6

Prosciutto and sage are the classic flavorings in a saltimbocca, literally "jump into the mouth."

1½ teaspoons crumbled sage
　½ teaspoon freshly ground
　　pepper
6 skinless, boneless chicken
　　breast halves, pounded to
　　¼-inch thickness
6 thin slices prosciutto

4 tablespoons butter or
　　margarine, melted
⅓ cup fine dry bread crumbs
2 tablespoons grated
　　Parmesan cheese
2 tablespoons chopped parsley

1. Preheat oven to 350°. Sprinkle the sage and pepper over the chicken. Place a slice of prosciutto on top. Roll up jelly-roll style and secure with wooden toothpicks.

2. Place butter in a shallow dish. In another shallow dish combine bread crumbs, Parmesan cheese, and parsley. Dip chicken first in melted butter, then roll in crumb mixture.

3. Place chicken in shallow baking dish. Bake 40 minutes, until tender. Remove picks and serve.

109 CHICKEN CUTLET PARMESAN WITH FRESH TOMATO SAUCE

Prep: 35 minutes   Cook: 15 minutes   Serves: 4

Here's an all-time favorite that tastes just like the restaurant version. To save time, you can substitute your favorite canned tomato sauce for homemade. Serve with buttered spaghetti and a tossed salad.

¾ cup seasoned bread crumbs
¼ cup grated Parmesan cheese
1 egg, beaten
4 skinless, boneless chicken
   breast halves, pounded to
   ¼-inch thickness

2 tablespoons olive oil
  tomato sauce (recipe follows)
¼ pound mozzarella cheese,
   thinly sliced

1. Combine bread crumbs and Parmesan cheese in a shallow dish. Place egg in another shallow dish. Dip chicken first in egg, then dredge in bread crumb mixture to coat.

2. Preheat oven to 350°. In a large frying pan, heat oil over medium heat. Add coated chicken breasts. Cook, turning once, about 5 minutes a side, until lightly browned.

3. Arrange chicken cutlets in a single layer on an ovenproof serving platter or baking dish. Pour tomato sauce over chicken. Top with mozzarella cheese. Bake 15 minutes, until cheese is melted and bubbly.

TOMATO SAUCE

2 tablespoons olive oil
1 medium-size onion,
   chopped
1 garlic clove, crushed
2 cups chopped peeled fresh
   tomatoes, or 1 can
   (28 ounces) Italian peeled
   tomatoes, drained and
   chopped

2 tablespoons tomato paste
1 bay leaf
½ teaspoon sugar
¼ teaspoon dried oregano

In a medium-size saucepan, heat oil over medium heat. Add onion and garlic. Cook until onion is soft, about 3 minutes. Add tomatoes, tomato paste, bay leaf, sugar, and oregano. Simmer until sauce reduces by half.

110 MUSHROOM-GARLIC CHICKEN WITH ARTICHOKES

Prep: 30 minutes   Cook: 20 minutes   Serves: 6

6 skinless, boneless chicken breast halves, pounded to ¼-inch thickness
  Salt and freshly ground pepper
3 tablespoons butter or margarine
8 garlic cloves, crushed through a press

1 tablespoon olive oil
¼ pound mushrooms, sliced
1 can (14 ounces) artichoke hearts, drained and quartered
2 tablespoons dry Marsala
1 tablespoon lemon juice

1. Season chicken with salt and pepper. In a large frying pan, melt butter over medium heat. Add half the garlic and cook 1 minute. Add chicken and cook until lightly browned, about 3 minutes a side. Remove to a warm serving platter.

2. In the same frying pan, add olive oil and remaining garlic; cook 1 minute. Add mushrooms and cook until tender, about 3 minutes. Add artichokes and cook 1 minute, until heated through. Add Marsala and lemon juice. Bring to a boil. Stir continuously until mixture thickens, about 5 minutes. Pour over chicken. Serve with rice or pasta.

111 CHICKEN PAILLARD WITH LEMON-BRANDY SAUCE

Prep: 15 minutes   Cook: 15 minutes   Serves: 6

½ cup flour
½ teaspoon salt
¼ teaspoon freshly ground pepper
6 skinless, boneless chicken breast halves, pounded to ¼-inch thickness

2 tablespoons butter
1 tablespoon vegetable oil
2 shallots, minced
2 tablespoons lemon juice
2 tablespoons brandy
2 tablespoons chopped parsley

1. In a shallow bowl, combine flour, salt, and pepper. Dredge chicken breasts in flour mixture to coat: shake off excess.

2. In a large frying pan, heat butter and oil over medium heat. Add chicken and cook, turning, until opaque throughout, about 6 minutes. Remove and set aside. Add shallots to pan and cook until soft, about 2 minutes. Return chicken to pan with any juices that may have collected.

3. Increase heat to medium-high; add lemon juice and brandy. Ignite carefully with a match. After flames subside, transfer chicken and sauce to a serving platter. Sprinkle with chopped parsley and serve.

112   CHICKEN CORDON BLEU
Prep: 45 minutes   Cook: 40 minutes   Serves: 6

6 skinless, boneless chicken
  breast halves, pounded to
  ¼-inch thickness
6 slices Swiss cheese
6 slices prosciutto
½ cup flour
½ teaspoon salt
¾ teaspoon freshly ground
  pepper

2 eggs, beaten
¾ cup bread crumbs
5 tablespoons butter or
  margarine
2 tablespoons vegetable oil
¼ cup dry white wine
⅔ cup chicken stock

1. Cover each chicken breast with a slice of cheese. Top with a slice of ham and trim to fit. Roll up lengthwise and secure with a wooden toothpick. In a shallow dish, mix flour, salt, and ¼ teaspoon of the pepper. Dredge rolled chicken beasts in flour, dip in egg, and coat with bread crumbs.

2. In a large frying pan, heat 3 tablespoons of the butter in oil over medium heat. Add chicken and cook, turning, until browned, about 10 minutes. Remove chicken to a platter, cover loosely to keep warm.

3. Pour off fat from skillet. Add wine and bring to a boil, scraping up browned bits from bottom of pan. Boil until reduced to 2 tablespoons. Add stock and boil until reduced by half. Remove from the heat and whisk in remaining 2 tablespoons butter. Season with additional salt and pepper to taste. Pour over chicken and serve.

113   CHICKEN BREASTS WITH RED PEPPER SAUCE
Prep: 20 minutes   Cook: 30 minutes   Serves: 4

2 medium tomatoes, peeled,
  seeded, and chopped
1 small onion, chopped
1 medium red bell pepper,
  chopped
1 tablespoon chopped parsley
1 tablespoon chopped fresh
  basil, or ½ teaspoon dried
1 teaspoon salt
¼ teaspoon dried thyme

¼ teaspoon hot pepper sauce
¼ teaspoon freshly ground
  pepper
4 skinless, boneless chicken
  breast halves, pounded to
  ¼-inch thickness
2 tablespoons butter or
  margarine
½ cup white wine

1. Combine tomatoes, onion, red pepper, parsley, basil, salt, thyme, hot sauce, and pepper in a medium-size saucepan. Bring to a boil, reduce heat, and simmer 20 minutes. Transfer to a food processor or blender and purée until smooth. Pour into a small saucepan and keep warm over very low heat.

2. In a large frying pan, melt butter over medium heat. Add chicken breasts; cook 3 minutes a side, until chicken turns white. Add white wine, reduce heat, and simmer 10 minutes.

3. Spoon red pepper purée onto plates. Arrange chicken on top.

114 CHICKEN MARSALA
Prep: 5 minutes   Cook: 15 minutes   Serves: 4

Quick and company quality. Serve with buttered fettuccine. Begin with an arugula-tomato salad and end with some goat cheese or Gorgonzola, crusty bread, and fruit, for a delightfully elegant dinner.

4 tablespoons butter
4 skinless, boneless chicken
    breast halves, pounded to
    ¼-inch thickness
4 shallots, finely chopped
½ pound mushrooms, sliced

¼ cup dry Marsala
½ cup heavy cream
1 teaspoon lemon juice
  Salt and freshly ground
    pepper

1. In a large frying pan, melt 2 tablespoons of the butter over medium heat. Add chicken and sauté, turning once, until lightly browned, about 2 minutes on each side. Remove and set aside.

2. Melt remaining butter in pan. Add shallots and mushrooms. Cook until mushrooms are lightly browned, 3 to 5 minutes. Add Marsala and bring to a boil, scraping up any browned bits from bottom of pan. Add cream and lemon juice and return to a boil. Season with salt and pepper to taste.

3. Return chicken to pan and cook, turning in sauce, for about 3 minutes to reheat and finish cooking.

115 CHICKEN ROULADES WITH GOAT CHEESE AND SUN-DRIED TOMATOES
Prep: 20 minutes   Cook: 20 minutes   Serves: 6

Goat cheese and sun-dried tomatoes are two of the most popular new ingredients of recent years. Here they are used to create colorful, elegant chicken medallions.

6 ounces goat cheese
6 skinless, boneless chicken
    breast halves, pounded to
    ¼-inch thickness
¼ pound sun-dried tomatoes
    (in oil), drained and
    chopped (about ½ cup)

2 tablespoons chopped fresh
  basil
2 tablespoons butter
1 tablespoon olive oil
½ cup chicken broth

1. Spread 1 ounce of goat cheese over each chicken breast. Top each with 1 tablespoon sun-dried tomatoes and sprinkle with 1 teaspoon basil. Roll up jelly-roll style and secure with wooden toothpicks.

2. In a large frying pan, heat butter and olive oil over medium heat. Add chicken; cook, turning, until lightly browned outside and white but still moist inside, 10 to 12 minutes. Remove and set aside.

3. Pour off all but 1 tablespoon fat from pan. Add broth and remaining 2 tablespoons sun-dried tomatoes. Boil until liquid is reduced by half.

4. To serve, remove picks from chicken; cut crosswise on the diagonal into ½-inch slices. Arrange on plates and spoon about 1 tablespoon sauce over each serving.

116 LEMON CHICKEN ALMONDINE
Prep: 20 minutes   Marinate: 1 hour   Cook: 20 minutes   Serves: 6

6 skinless, boneless chicken breast halves, pounded to ¼-inch thickness	2 tablespoons butter or margarine
⅓ cup lemon juice	1 cup chicken broth
3 tablespoons Dijon mustard	1 teaspoon cornstarch, dissolved in 1 tablespoon water
2 garlic cloves, finely chopped	
¼ teaspoon freshly ground pepper	2 tablespoons chopped fresh parsley
⅓ cup olive oil	¼ teaspoon cayenne pepper
1 package (2½ ounces) sliced almonds	Lemon slices, for garnish

1. Place chicken in a large shallow baking dish. Combine lemon juice, mustard, garlic, and pepper in a small bowl. Beat in oil. Pour over chicken. Marinate 1 hour at room temperature.

2. Preheat oven to 350°. Place almonds in a small baking pan. Bake until lightly browned, about 10 minutes.

3. Drain chicken, reserving marinade. In a large frying pan, melt butter over medium heat. Add chicken and cook about 4 minutes a side, until lightly browned. Remove to a dish.

4. Add reserved marinade and chicken broth to pan. Boil over high heat, stirring, until the sauce reduces by half, about 5 minutes. Stir in cornstarch mixture and cook, stirring, until thickened and smooth. Add parsley and cayenne pepper. Reduce heat, return chicken to pan, and heat through. Transfer chicken to a serving platter and pour sauce over all. Sprinkle toasted almonds over chicken and garnish with lemon slices.

117 CHICKEN WITH BLUE CHEESE
Prep: 45 minutes   Cook: 1 hour   Serves: 8

Use any good-quality blue cheese—American Maytag, French Roquefort, or Danish blue.

4 tablespoons butter or margarine	2 teaspoons lemon juice
2 tablespoons chopped onion	3 tablespoons flour
1 package (10 ounces) frozen chopped spinach, thawed and drained	8 skinless, boneless chicken breast halves, pounded to ¼-inch thickness
½ cup bread crumbs	¾ cup chicken broth
4 ounces blue cheese, crumbled	¼ cup dry white wine
	¼ teaspoon salt
	½ teaspoon paprika

1. In a small frying pan, melt 2 tablespoons of the butter over medium heat. Add onion and cook until soft, 2 to 3 minutes. Add spinach; cook to remove excess moisture. Add bread crumbs, blue cheese, and lemon juice; blend well.

2. Preheat oven to 350°. Divide spinach mixture among chicken breasts. Roll up jelly-roll style and secure with wooden toothpicks. Place flour in a shallow dish and dredge chicken to coat.

3. In a large frying pan, melt remaining 2 tablespoons butter over medium heat. Add chicken, in batches if necessary, and brown all over, about 10 minutes. Remove chicken to a 13 x 9 x 2-inch baking dish. Add broth, wine, and salt to frying pan and bring to a boil; pour over chicken. Cover with foil and bake 35 minutes. Uncover and sprinkle with paprika. Bake 10 minutes. Transfer chicken to a serving platter; remove toothpicks. Pour pan juices over chicken.

118   CHICKEN ROULADES WITH MUSHROOM SAUCE

Prep: 30 minutes   Cook: 30 minutes   Serves: 4

Here is a chicken variation on stuffed veal "birds."

½ pound mushrooms
3 tablespoons butter or margarine
1 tablespoon vegetable oil
¾ cup chopped onion
2 tablespoons bread crumbs
Salt and freshly ground pepper
½ teaspoon crumbled sage

4 skinless, boneless chicken breast halves, pounded to ¼-inch thickness
1 tablespoon flour
½ cup light cream or half-and-half
⅓ cup dry white wine
1 tablespoon minced parsley

1. Preheat oven to 375°. Chop half the mushrooms. Slice the remainder.

2. In a medium-size frying pan, melt 2 tablespoons of the butter in 1 tablespoon oil over medium heat. Add ½ cup of the onion and sauté 3 minutes. Add chopped mushrooms and cook until beginning to brown, about 3 minutes. Remove from heat and stir in bread crumbs. Season with salt, pepper, and sage.

3. Spread filling over chicken breasts. Fold sides of chicken over stuffing and secure with wooden toothpicks. Arrange in a foil-lined 8 x 8 x 2-inch baking dish.

4. Cover dish with foil and bake 15 minutes. Uncover and bake 10 to 15 minutes, until chicken is tender but still moist.

5. Meanwhile, in a medium-size saucepan, melt remaining 1 tablespoon butter over medium heat. Add remaining ¼ cup onions; cook 2 minutes. Add sliced mushrooms to pan; cook 3 minutes. Stir in flour and cook, stirring, 1 minute. Gradually blend in cream and wine until smooth. Bring to a boil and cook, stirring, until thick. Season with salt and pepper to taste. Remove wooden picks from roulades and spoon sauce on top. Garnish with parsley.

119   ITALIAN CHICKEN ROLLS
Prep: 30 minutes   Cook: 45 minutes   Serves: 4

3 large plum tomatoes, peeled, seeded, and chopped
½ cup tomato sauce
2 garlic cloves, minced
1 medium-size green bell pepper, finely chopped
1 medium-size onion, finely chopped
¼ teaspoon dried oregano
¼ teaspoon freshly ground pepper

4 skinless, boneless chicken breast halves, pounded to ¼-inch thickness
1 egg
½ cup ricotta cheese
1 tablespoon grated Parmesan cheese
1 tablespoon chopped parsley
1 cup grated mozzarella cheese

1. Preheat oven to 350°. In a medium-size saucepan, combine tomatoes, tomato sauce, garlic, bell pepper, onion, oregano, and pepper. Bring just to a boil, reduce heat, and simmer 15 minutes, stirring occasionally.

2. Cut each chicken breast in half to make 8 pieces. In a small bowl, beat egg. Blend in Ricotta, Parmesan cheese, and parsley. Spoon one-eighth of this mixture onto each piece of chicken. Roll up chicken and secure with wooden toothpicks.

3. Spoon half the tomato sauce into an 8-inch square baking dish. Arrange chicken rolls in dish. Pour remaining sauce over chicken. Sprinkle mozzarella cheese on top. Bake 45 minutes.

Chapter 8

Other Ideas for Chicken Breasts

There is no doubt about it, the chicken breast is just about the most popular meat in the butcher's case these days. Due to consumer demand, you can buy this white-meat cut any way you want—on the bone, off the bone, skin on or skinless and boneless. Fancy meat markets even sell the skinless, boneless breasts prepounded into cutlets, or scaloppine.

Just as the size of broiler-fryer chickens is uniform these days, so is the size of chicken breasts. An average skinless, boneless chicken breast half will weigh about 5 ounces, a perfect portion size.

Recipes for chicken breasts are scattered generously throughout this book, and the previous chapter was devoted exclusively to chicken breasts, pounded thin. But because they are so popular, so versatile, and so nutritious, I decided to throw in a bonus chapter of nothing but chicken breast recipes.

Note: A whole chicken breast is two breast halves joined in the center by cartilage, and is sold either "whole" or "split." When sold skinless and boneless, however, each breast piece is actually one breast half. Since a breast half equals a single serving of 4 to 5 ounces, recipe portions throughout this chapter are described as "breast halves."

120 CHICKEN WITH MORELS IN CREAM SAUCE
Prep: 30 minutes   Cook: 20 minutes   Serves: 4

For your most elegant dinner parties. Serve with fine egg noodles and buttered asparagus.

1 **ounce dried morels**	3 **tablespoons butter**
4 **skinless, boneless chicken breast halves**	2 **shallots, finely chopped**
Salt and freshly ground pepper	½ **cup dry white wine**
	½ **cup heavy cream**
	¼ **cup Madeira**

1. In a small bowl, soak morels in warm water to cover for 30 minutes, until softened; drain. Rinse under running water to remove any sand and squeeze dry.

2. Season chicken with salt and pepper. In a large frying pan, melt 2 tablespoons of the butter over medium heat. Add chicken and cook 3 to 4 minutes a side, until lightly browned. Transfer to a platter and cover with foil to keep warm.

3. Pour off all but 1 tablespoon pan drippings. Add shallots and cook 1 minute, until soft. Add morels and wine. Boil until liquid is reduced by half. Stir in cream and Madeira and boil until sauce thickens slightly, about 2 minutes. Stir in remaining 1 tablespoon butter until melted. Pour sauce over chicken and serve.

121 CHICKEN À LA NANCY
Prep: 10 minutes   Cook: 15 minutes   Serves: 4

Frank ("it takes a tough man to make a tender chicken") Perdue is the most famous chicken purveyor on the East Coast and maybe in America. When asked for his own personal favorite chicken recipes this is one of the two he suggests.

4 **skinless, boneless chicken breast halves**	¼ **teaspoon freshly ground pepper**
¼ **cup vegetable oil**	¼ **teaspoon dried oregano**
1 **garlic clove, finely chopped**	½ **cup dry white wine**
½ **pound mushrooms, sliced**	1 **can (14 ounces) whole artichoke hearts, drained and quartered**
½ **lemon, thinly sliced**	
1 **tablespoon flour**	
1 **teaspoon salt**	

1. Pound chicken breasts to ¼-inch thickness between sheets of plastic wrap or wax paper. Cut into 2-inch squares.

2. In a large frying pan, heat oil over medium heat. Add chicken and cook 2 to 3 minutes a side, until tender and opaque. Remove chicken and keep warm.

3. Add garlic, lemon, and mushrooms to the same pan. Cook until tender, 3 to 5 minutes. Sprinkle with flour, salt, pepper, and oregano. Cook, stirring, 1 minute. Add wine and bring to a boil, stirring until mixture thickens. Add artichokes and return chicken to pan. Simmer 2 minutes, until heated through.

122 CHICKEN BREASTS IN TOMATO-CREAM SAUCE

Prep: 5 minutes   Cook: 20 minutes   Serves: 4

Easy and delicious! Serve with fine noodles and zucchini.

4 skinless, boneless chicken breast halves Salt and freshly ground pepper 3 tablespoons butter or margarine	1 shallot, chopped 1 can (14 ounces) Italian peeled tomatoes, drained and chopped ⅓ cup sweet vermouth ½ cup heavy cream

1. Season chicken breasts with salt and pepper. In a large frying pan, melt butter over medium heat. Add chicken and cook, turning once, until tender and opaque throughout, 3 to 5 minutes a side; do not brown. Remove to a platter and cover with foil to keep warm.

2. Add shallots to pan and cook until soft, 1 to 2 minutes. Add tomatoes and cook for 2 minutes. Add vermouth and boil for 5 minutes, until sauce reduces by half.

3. Pour sauce into a food processor or blender and purée until smooth. Return to pan. Add cream and simmer for 2 minutes. Pour sauce over chicken and serve.

123 PECAN-BREADED CHICKEN BREASTS WITH DIJON MUSTARD SAUCE

Prep: 15 minutes   Cook: 10 minutes   Serves: 4

Finely ground pecans are used instead of flour to coat these savory chicken breasts. The resulting flavor and texture are irresistible.

8 tablespoons (1 stick) butter 3 tablespoons Dijon mustard 6 ounces pecans, finely ground (about 1½ cups) 8 skinless, boneless chicken breast halves, pounded to ¼-inch thickness	1 tablespoon vegetable oil ⅔ cup sour cream ½ teaspoon salt ¼ teaspoon freshly ground pepper

1. In a small saucepan, melt 6 tablespoons of the butter. Whisk in 2 tablespoons of the mustard until blended; scrape into a shallow dish. Place pecans in another shallow dish.

2. Dip chicken first in butter mixture, then dredge in pecans to coat.

3. In a large frying pan, heat remaining 2 tablespoons butter in oil over medium heat. Add chicken and cook 3 minutes a side, until lightly browned and tender. Remove to a serving platter and cover with foil to keep warm.

4. Discard all but 2 tablespoons of fat from pan and reduce heat to low. Add sour cream; whisk in remaining 1 tablespoon mustard, salt, and pepper. Blend well. Cook just until heated through; do not boil. Serve over chicken.

124   PIQUANT APRICOT CHICKEN BREASTS
Prep: 5 minutes   Cook: 40 minutes   Serves: 4 to 6

2 tablespoons vegetable oil
6 chicken breast halves, with bone
¾ cup canned chicken broth
⅓ cup apricot preserves

1 tablespoon chili sauce
2 teaspoons prepared mustard
  Salt and freshly ground pepper

1. In a large frying pan, heat oil over medium heat. Add chicken and cook, turning, until browned, about 10 minutes. Pour off fat. Add stock to pan and simmer, covered, 30 minutes, until chicken is fork tender. Remove to a platter and cover with foil to keep warm.

2. In a small bowl, combine preserves, chili sauce, and mustard. Stir into liquid in pan. Bring to a boil, stirring constantly. Season with salt and pepper to taste. Pour over chicken and serve.

125   BAKED SESAME CHICKEN BREASTS
Prep: 10 minutes   Cook: 50 minutes   Serves: 6

To toast sesame seeds for this recipe, spread seeds in a small baking pan and bake in a 350-degree oven, shaking the pan occasionally, for 10 minutes, until lightly browned.

6 chicken breast halves with bone, or 12 chicken thighs
4 tablespoons butter or margarine, softened

1 teaspoon crushed sage
3 tablespoons toasted sesame seeds

1. Preheat oven to 350°. Gently separate chicken skin from meat without removing it. Leave skin attached at several points.

2. In a small bowl, blend butter and sage. Spread 3 tablespoons under skin. Place chicken, skin side up, in a 13 x 9 x 2-inch baking dish.

3. Brush chicken with remaining butter. Sprinkle toasted sesame seeds on top and bake 50 minutes, until chicken is tender.

126   SOUTHERN CHICKEN BREASTS WITH SWEET POTATOES
Prep: 20 minutes   Cook: 50 minutes   Serves: 4

Buttered lima beans or broccoli and homemade biscuits are all you'll need to complete this down-home dinner.

2 tablespoons vegetable oil
4 chicken breast halves with bone
1 cup evaporated milk
2 tablespoons honey
1 teaspoon salt
¼ teaspoon nutmeg

¼ teaspoon ground cloves
1 can (16 ounces) sweet potatoes in syrup, drained, reserving ¼ cup syrup
¼ cup raisins

1. In a large frying pan, heat oil over medium heat. Add chicken breasts and cook until lightly browned, about 5 minutes a side. Drain on paper towels.

2. Preheat oven to 350°. Arrange chicken in a 13 x 9 x 2-inch baking dish. In a small bowl, combine evaporated milk, honey, salt, nutmeg, and cloves. Pour over chicken.

3. Bake 10 minutes. Remove from oven and arrange sweet potatoes and raisins around chicken. Pour reserved ¼ cup syrup over chicken. Return to oven and bake 40 minutes, until chicken is tender.

127 CHICKEN BREASTS WITH ASPARAGUS MOUSSE
Prep: 45 minutes   Cook: 15 minutes   Serves: 8

3 egg yolks
2 tablespoons lemon juice
¼ teaspoon salt
1 stick (½ cup) butter or margarine, melted
1 pound fresh asparagus, trimmed, or 1 package (10 ounces) frozen asparagus, thawed

5 shallots, chopped
½ cup flour seasoned with salt and pepper
8 skinless, boneless chicken breast halves, pounded to ¼-inch thickness
4 tablespoons butter
⅓ cup grated Parmesan cheese

1. In a blender or food processor, combine egg yolks, lemon juice, and salt; process until smooth. With the machine on, slowly add melted butter. (Begin by adding a few drops at a time; when mixture begins to thicken, add butter in a slow steady stream.) Process until thick and smooth.

2. Cut asparagus into 1-inch pieces. Place in a small saucepan with half the shallots and enough water to cover. Cook until tender, 3 to 5 minutes. Drain well, pressing out water. Add to hollandaise sauce in blender and purée until smooth.

3. Preheat broiler. Place seasoned flour in a shallow dish. Dredge chicken in flour; shake off excess.

4. In a large frying pan, heat the 4 tablespoons butter over medium heat. Sauté remainder of shallots until soft. Add chicken breasts and cook until lightly browned, about 3 minutes a side. Remove chicken to a large flameproof baking dish or platter.

5. Spoon asparagus mousse onto each chicken breast, dividing evenly. Sprinkle with Parmesan cheese. Place under broiler until top is light brown and bubbly, 1 to 2 minutes. Serve immediately.

128   CHICKEN BREASTS CHASSEUR
Prep: 25 minutes   Cook: 35 minutes   Serves: 6

Shallots, mushrooms, fresh tomatoes, and tarragon ensure a superior sauté. Serve with rice to catch all the juices.

2   tablespoons vegetable oil
1   tablespoon butter
6   chicken breast halves with bone
2   shallots, finely chopped
½   pound mushrooms, quartered
1   garlic clove, crushed through a press
2   tomatoes, peeled, seeded, and chopped

½   teaspoon dried tarragon
½   teaspoon salt
¼   teaspoon freshly ground pepper
½   cup dry white wine
½   cup beef broth
1   tablespoon cornstarch dissolved in 2 tablespoons water

1. In a large frying pan, heat oil and butter over medium heat. Add chicken and cook, turning, until browned all over, about 10 minutes. Remove and set aside.

2. Add shallots to pan drippings. Cook 1 minute to soften. Add mushrooms; cook until lightly browned, about 3 minutes. Add garlic, tomatoes, tarragon, salt, and pepper; simmer 5 minutes.

3. Add wine and beef broth. Return chicken to pan, cover, and cook over low heat until tender, about 20 minutes. Remove chicken.

4. Stir dissolved cornstarch into sauce. Bring to a boil and cook, stirring, until thickened, 1 to 2 minutes. Return chicken to pan and turn to coat with sauce.

129   CHICKEN MANHATTAN
Prep: 15 minutes   Cook: 20 minutes   Serves: 4

¾   cup bread crumbs
1   egg, lightly beaten
4   skinless, boneless chicken breast halves, pounded to ¼-inch thickness
2   tablespoons vegetable oil
2   tablespoons butter or margarine
½   cup chopped onion

½   pound mushrooms, sliced
1   garlic clove, minced
1   package (10 ounces) frozen spinach, thawed and drained
½   teaspoon nutmeg
4   slices provolone cheese
¼   cup dry white wine

1. Place bread crumbs and egg in separate shallow dishes. Dip chicken in egg; then dredge in bread crumbs to coat.

2. In a large frying pan, heat oil over medium heat. Add chicken and cook about 4 minutes on each side, until lightly browned. Remove pan from heat; cover to keep chicken warm.

3. In another large frying pan, melt butter over medium heat. Add onion and sauté until beginning to soften, about 2 minutes. Add mushrooms and garlic; sauté until mushrooms are tender, 3 to 5 minutes. Add spinach and nutmeg. Mix well and cook until heated through.

4. Top each chicken breast with one quarter of spinach-mushroom mixture. Arrange provolone cheese slices on top. Return pan to medium heat. Add wine and cover. Cook 5 minutes, until cheese is melted and chicken is tender.

130   LEMON CHICKEN BREASTS WITH ALMONDS
Prep: 15 minutes   Marinate: 1 hour   Cook: 20 minutes   Serves: 6

⅓ cup fresh lemon juice	1 cup canned chicken broth
¼ cup olive oil	2 tablespoons butter or
3 tablespoons Dijon mustard	margarine
3 garlic cloves	½ cup slivered almonds
¼ teaspoon dried rosemary	1 teaspoon grated lemon peel
6 chicken breast halves with	Salt and freshly ground
bone	pepper
1 tablespoon cornstarch	3 tablespoons chopped parsley

1. In a food processor or blender, combine lemon juice, oil, mustard, garlic, and rosemary; process until well blended. Arrange chicken in a 13 x 9 x 2-inch baking dish. Pour marinade over chicken. Cover and marinate 1 hour. Remove chicken; reserve marinade.

2. In a small bowl, dissolve cornstarch in 2 tablespoons of the chicken broth.

3. In a large frying pan, melt butter over medium heat. Add chicken and cook until white, about 5 minutes a side. Remove chicken and set aside.

4. Scrape reserved marinade into frying pan. Whisk in remaining broth and dissolved cornstarch. Bring to a boil and cook, stirring, until thickened and smooth, about 2 minutes. Add almonds and lemon peel. Season with salt and pepper to taste. Return chicken to pan; heat through. Garnish with parsley.

131   CHICKEN CUTLETS BOLOGNESE
Prep: 15 minutes   Cook: 15 minutes   Serves: 4

This Italian version of chicken Cordon Bleu, layered with prosciutto and mozarella cheese, is both easy and quick.

3 tablespoons butter or	¼ teaspoon freshly ground
margarine	pepper
4 skinless, boneless chicken	4 thin slices prosciutto
breast halves, pounded to	4 slices mozzarella cheese
¼-inch thickness	¼ cup dry white wine
1 teaspoon dried oregano	

1. In a large frying pan, melt butter over medium heat. Add chicken breasts and cook 3 minutes on each side. Season with oregano and pepper.

2. Place a slice of prosciutto and then a slice of cheese on each breast. Drizzle the wine over all. Cover pan and cook 5 minutes, until cheese is melted and chicken is cooked through.

132   CHICKEN BREASTS WITH YOGURT AND LIME

Prep: 5 minutes   Marinate: 30 minutes   Cook: 20 minutes
Serves: 4

½ cup taco sauce
¼ cup Dijon mustard
2 tablespoons fresh lime juice
3 whole chicken breasts,
    skinned and split

2 tablespoons butter or
    margarine
6 tablespoons plain yogurt
6 slices of lime
    Fresh coriander or parsley,
    for garnish

1. In a large bowl, combine taco sauce, mustard, and lime juice. Add chicken breasts and marinate at room temperature for 30 minutes. Remove chicken; reserve marinade.

2. In a large frying pan, melt butter over medium heat. Add chicken breasts and cook 3 to 5 minutes a side, until lightly browned. Add marinade to pan and cook, turning chicken once or twice, until fork tender. Remove to a warm platter.

3. Raise heat to high and boil marinade 1 minute. Pour over chicken. Top each chicken breast with 1 tablespoon yogurt and a slice of lime. Garnish with coriander.

133   LIME CHICKEN WITH BASIL

Prep: 20 minutes   Cook: 20 minutes   Serves: 8

Fresh basil, now grown hydroponically in winter and available year-round in many areas, has a sparkling taste and aroma. In this recipe, dried basil is not an adequate substitute.

3 tablespoons vegetable oil
8 chicken breast halves with
    bone
1 large onion, chopped
1 tablespoon chopped fresh
    basil
½ cup dry white wine
¼ cup fresh lime juice
¼ teaspoon salt

⅛ teaspoon freshly ground
    pepper
1 cup light cream or half-and-
    half
2 tablespoons flour
2 egg yolks
    Fresh basil leaves and lime
    slices, for garnish

1. In a large frying pan, heat oil over medium heat. Brown chicken breasts, about 4 minutes on each side. Remove and set aside.

2. Add onion to pan drippings and sauté until tender, 3 to 5 minutes. Add basil, wine, lime juice, salt, and pepper. Bring to a boil and reduce heat. Return chicken to pan, turn to coat with sauce and simmer, covered, 15 to 20 minutes, until tender. Remove chicken to a platter.

3. In a small bowl, whisk cream and flour until smooth. Stir into pan. Bring to a boil, stirring constantly. Cook, stirring, until thickened and smooth. Whisk in egg yolks. Reduce heat and simmer 2 minutes. Spoon sauce over chicken. Garnish with basil and lime.

134 CHICKEN BREASTS WITH CHAMPAGNE SAUCE
Prep: 15 minutes   Cook: 30 minutes   Serves: 4

There are so many excellent sparkling wines available these days, feel free to substitute your favorite American, Italian, or Spanish brand for the real French product, as long as the bottle is labeled *brut*.

4 chicken breast halves with bone	2 tablespoons Cognac or brandy
Salt and freshly ground pepper	½ cup chicken broth
3 tablespoons butter	2 cups brut champagne
	1 tablespoon tomato paste
	1 cup heavy cream

1. Season chicken breasts with salt and pepper. In a large frying pan, melt butter over medium heat. Add chicken and cook, turning, until lightly browned, about 5 minutes a side. Pour off fat from pan.

2. Pour Cognac over chicken and ignite carefully with a match. When flames subside, add chicken broth, champagne, tomato paste, and ½ cup of the cream. Simmer uncovered, turning chicken occasionally, 25 to 30 minutes, until chicken is tender. Remove chicken.

3. Add remaining cream to sauce in pan. Bring to a boil and cook until slightly thickened, 3 to 5 minutes. Season with salt and pepper to taste. Pour sauce over chicken and serve.

135 SAUTÉED CHICKEN BREASTS WITH SUMMER VEGETABLES
Prep: 10 minutes   Cook: 30 minutes   Serves: 4

This dish can be made any time of year, but it is especially nice in summer, when garden fresh vegetables are available.

4 chicken breast halves with bone	1 medium zucchini, sliced
½ teaspoon salt	1 medium yellow squash, sliced
¼ teaspoon freshly ground pepper	1 red bell pepper, diced
¼ teaspoon paprika	1 tablespoon chopped fresh basil, or ½ teaspoon dried
2½ tablespoons olive oil	2 tablespoons grated Parmesan cheese
½ cup chicken broth	

1. Season chicken with salt, pepper, and paprika. In a large frying pan, heat oil over medium heat. Add chicken and cook, turning once, until browned, about 10 minutes.

2. Pour chicken broth over chicken, cover, and simmer 20 minutes. Add vegetables and basil to pan. Cover and cook 3 to 5 minutes, until vegetables are crisp-tender. Season with additional salt and pepper to taste. Transfer chicken and vegetables to a platter and sprinkle Parmesan cheese on top.

136 SAUTÉED CHICKEN BREASTS CORDIER
Prep: 15 minutes   Cook: 30 minutes   Serves: 4

Greg Cordier is a chef and caterer. This is his favorite chicken dish for a small dinner party. He recommends Lyonnaise potatoes as a winning accompaniment.

2 tablespoons butter or margarine	2 tablespoons fresh lemon juice
2 packages (10 ounces each) frozen chopped spinach, thawed and drained	1/2 cup bread crumbs
	1/2 cup grated parmesan cheese
1/2 teaspoon nutmeg	1 egg, beaten
1/2 teaspoon salt	4 skinless, boneless chicken breast halves, pounded to 1/4-inch thickness
1/4 teaspoon freshly ground pepper	2 tablespoons vegetable oil
1/4 cup heavy cream	1/2 cup dry white wine

1. In a large frying pan, melt butter over medium heat. Add spinach, nutmeg, salt, and pepper. Simmer 5 minutes. Stir in cream and lemon juice. Simmer, stirring occasionally, until spinach absorbs liquid, 5 to 10 minutes.

2. Combine bread crumbs and Parmesan cheese in a shallow dish. Place beaten egg in another shallow dish. Dip chicken breasts in egg; then dredge in crumbs to coat.

3. In a large frying pan, heat oil over medium heat. Cook chicken 1 minute a side. Reduce heat to medium-low. Add 1/4 cup of the wine. Cook 7 minutes. Turn chicken and add remaining wine; cook 7 minutes.

4. To serve, arrange spinach around edge of a large platter. Place chicken breasts in center.

137 STUFFED CHICKEN BREASTS WITH APRICOT SAUCE
Prep: 20 minutes   Cook: 45 minutes   Serves: 4

The apricot sauce made in Step 1 can also be served as a dipping sauce for chicken fritters or fried wings (see Appetizers).

1/2 cup dried apricots	1 cup grated Swiss cheese
1/4 cup cider vinegar	1/4 cup chopped toasted almonds
2 tablespoons honey	3 scallions, sliced
1/4 teaspoon salt	
4 skinless, boneless chicken breast halves	

1. In a small nonaluminum saucepan, combine dried apricots, vinegar, honey, salt, and 1/2 cup water. Bring to a boil, reduce heat, and simmer until apricots are soft, about 15 minutes. In a food processor or blender, purée until smooth. Thin with more water if desired. Set sauce aside.

2. Preheat oven to 325°. With a sharp knife, cut a pocket lengthwise in each chicken breast half.

3. In a small bowl, combine cheese, almonds, and scallions. Stuff pockets in chicken with cheese filling. Arrange chicken breasts in a 12 x 8 x 2-inch baking dish. Pour reserved sauce over chicken.

4. Cover with foil and bake 30 minutes. Uncover, baste with pan drippings, and bake for 15 minutes longer, until chicken is tender.

138 BAKED CHICKEN BREASTS WITH HORSERADISH CREAM SAUCE
Prep: 10 minutes   Cook: 45 minutes   Serves: 4

2 tablespoons butter
2 tablespoons flour
1 cup milk
3 tablespoons prepared white horseradish, drained
2 tablespoons sour cream
1 teaspoon sugar

1 teaspoon Dijon mustard
1 teaspoon white wine vinegar
Salt and freshly ground pepper
4 chicken breast halves with bone

1. Preheat oven to 350°. In a medium-size saucepan, melt butter over medium heat. Stir in flour and cook, stirring, for 1 minute without browning. Whisk in milk, bring to a boil, and cook, stirring, until sauce is thick and smooth, about 3 minutes. Stir in horseradish, sour cream, sugar, mustard, and vinegar. Season with salt and pepper to taste.

2. Arrange chicken breasts, skin side up, in a 13 x 9 x 2-inch baking dish. Spoon half the horseradish sauce over chicken. Bake 45 minutes, until chicken is tender. Reheat remaining sauce and serve over chicken.

139 CARIBBEAN CHICKEN BREASTS WITH COCONUT
Prep: 20 minutes   Cook: 30 minutes   Serves: 6

6 skinless, boneless chicken breast halves
Salt and freshly ground pepper
6 tablespoons butter or margarine
2 sweet onions, thinly sliced

1 tablespoon brown sugar
¼ cup slivered pimientos
3 tablespoons raisins
3 tablespoons lemon juice
¾ cup flaked coconut
3 tablespoons chopped parsley

1. Preheat oven to 375°. Season chicken with salt and pepper. In a large frying pan, melt 4 tablespoons of the butter over medium heat. Add chicken and cook until lightly browned, about 3 minutes a side. Transfer chicken to a 12 x 8 x 2-inch baking dish.

2. Add onions to frying pan and cook until soft, 3 to 5 minutes. Add brown sugar, pimientos, raisins, and half the lemon juice. Pour over chicken, cover with foil, and bake 10 minutes.

3. Meanwhile, melt remaining 2 tablespoons butter. In a small bowl, combine melted butter, coconut, parsley, remaining lemon juice, ½ teaspoon salt and ¼ teaspoon pepper.

4. Sprinkle topping over chicken. Return to oven and bake uncovered 10 minutes, until coconut is lightly browned.

Chapter 9

Chicken Quick

These days time seems to be everybody's scarcest commodity. Whether you're running a home, dashing to and from the office, or both, getting a tasty dinner on the table in the shortest possible time is high on everyone's list of priorities.

I've tried to consider time throughout this book (hence, the "prep time, cook time" notations on most recipes), and while there are many recipes in other chapters that do not take any longer than the ones included here, these struck me as being particularly "quick" because of their ease of preparation as well.

Chicken does cook quickly. A 3-pound chicken sautéed French fashion with an initial browning and then braised with any number of different flavorings and ingredients takes only 25 to 35 minutes. Broiled chicken will cook in 20 to 25 minutes. Poached chicken breasts take 15 to 20 minutes. Removed from the bone and skinned, white meat cutlets, or scaloppine as they are called when pounded flat, can be sautéed in 5 to 10 minutes. And diced or shredded chicken stir-fried Chinese style can be whipped up in a matter of minutes. Best of all, if you have leftover cooked chicken, you can assemble any number of varied dishes with a minimum of effort.

Here are some of my favorite ways to put good food on the table—fast and without a lot of bother. For other quick ideas, take a look at Chapter 7, "Could Be Veal."

140 VERY GINGERY CHICKEN
Prep: 15 minutes   Cook: 20 minutes   Serves: 8

½ cup flour
1 teaspoon ground ginger
½ teaspoon salt
8 skinless, boneless chicken
  breast halves, pounded to
  ¼-inch thickness
4 tablespoons butter or
  margarine

1 onion, finely chopped
1 cup chicken broth
½ cup Madeira
¾ cup heavy cream
2 tablespoons finely chopped
  crystallized ginger

1. In a shallow dish, combine flour, ground ginger, and salt. Dredge chicken breasts in flour mixture to coat. Shake off excess; reserve flour mixture.

2. In a large frying pan, melt butter over medium heat. Add chicken and cook until browned, about 3 minutes a side. Remove to a serving platter.

3. Add onion and cook until softened, about 3 minutes. Stir in reserved flour mixture. Cook, stirring, for 1 to 2 minutes without browning. Gradually whisk in chicken broth. Bring to a boil and cook, stirring, until sauce thickens, about 5 minutes. Add Madeira and cream. Add crystallized ginger and pour over chicken.

141 QUICK ITALIAN SKILLET CHICKEN
Prep: 15 minutes   Cook: 8 minutes   Serves: 4

Tomatoes, peppers, and anchovies give this colorful Mediterranean dish a distinctly Italian aspect. Since the chicken and vegetables are cut up, they cook quickly. I like to serve this tasty dish with pasta tossed with olive oil and grated Parmesan cheese.

3 tablespoons olive oil
1 garlic clove, finely chopped
1½ pounds skinless, boneless
  chicken breasts, cut into
  1-inch cubes
½ pound green beans, cut into
  2-inch pieces
1 medium red bell pepper, cut
  in thin strips

¼ cup chopped scallion
4 plum tomatoes, quartered
1 can (2 ounces) anchovies
  stuffed with capers,
  drained and coarsely
  chopped
2 tablespoons lemon juice

1. In a large frying pan, heat oil over medium-high heat. Add garlic and cook 30 seconds. Add chicken and sauté, tossing, until chicken is opaque, about 3 minutes. Remove with a slotted spoon and set aside.

2. Add green beans, red pepper, and scallion to pan. Cook, stirring, until vegetables are crisp-tender, about 2 minutes. Add tomatoes, anchovies with capers, and reserved chicken. Sprinkle with lemon juice. Cook 2 minutes, until heated through.

142 QUICK CHICKEN WITH LIME BUTTER
Prep: 2 minutes   Cook: 15 minutes   Serves: 6

6 skinless, boneless chicken
   breast halves
   Salt and freshly ground
   pepper
3 tablespoons vegetable oil
   Juice of 1 lime

6 tablespoons butter or
   margarine
1 tablespoon minced chives
1 teaspoon minced fresh dill,
   or ½ teaspoon dried dill
   weed

1. Season chicken with salt and pepper. In a large frying pan, heat oil over medium heat. Add chicken and sauté 4 minutes, until lightly browned. Turn chicken, cover, and reduce heat to low. Cook 10 minutes, until tender. Remove to a platter and keep warm.

2. Discard oil and wipe out pan. Add lime juice and cook over low heat until bubbly. Add butter, stirring until butter becomes opaque and sauce thickens. Stir in chives and dill. Season with salt and pepper to taste. Spoon over chicken and serve.

143 EASY GLAZED CHICKEN
Prep: 5 minutes   Cook: 1 hour   Serves: 8

Though this chicken bakes for an hour, it takes virtually no time to prepare.

½ cup flour
   Freshly ground pepper
2 chickens (3 pounds each),
   halved

⅔ cup mayonnaise
⅓ cup ketchup

1. Preheat oven to 375°. In a plastic or paper bag, combine flour and pepper. Add chicken and shake to coat well. Place in a lightly greased 13 x 9 x 2-inch baking dish.

2. In a small bowl, mix mayonnaise and ketchup until thoroughly blended. Pour half the mixture evenly over chicken. Bake 30 minutes. Remove from oven and turn. Cover with remaining mayonnaise mixture. Return to oven and bake for another 30 minutes.

144 ZANZIBAR CHICKEN
Prep: 5 minutes   Cook: 30 minutes   Serves: 4

3 pounds chicken thighs and/
   or drumsticks
2 teaspoons ground cinnamon
¼ teaspoon ground cloves
½ teaspoon salt
¼ teaspoon freshly ground
   pepper

2 tablespoons vegetable oil
1 medium onion, chopped
1 garlic clove, crushed
   through a press
¾ cup orange juice
3 tablespoons raisins
⅓ cup slivered almonds

1. Season chicken with cinnamon, cloves, salt, and pepper. In a large frying pan, heat oil over medium-high heat. Add chicken, in batches if necessary, and cook, turning until browned, about 10 minutes. Remove and set aside.

2. Add onion to pan. Cook until soft, about 3 minutes. Add garlic and cook 1 minute longer.

3. Return chicken to pan. Add orange juice and raisins. Cover, reduce heat, and simmer 15 minutes, until chicken is tender. Garnish with almonds.

145   QUICK AND EASY TARRAGON CHICKEN
Prep: 5 minutes   Cook: 20 minutes   Serves: 4

2 tablespoons butter or margarine
1 tablespoon vegetable oil
4 skinless, boneless chicken breast halves
¾ cup dry white wine or vermouth

2 teaspoons Dijon mustard
1 tablespoon chopped fresh tarragon, or 1 teaspoon dried
½ teaspoon salt
Freshly ground pepper
¾ cup heavy cream

1. In a large frying pan, melt butter in oil over medium-high heat. Add chicken breasts and cook, turning once, until lightly browned, about 4 minutes a side. Remove and set aside.

2. Add wine to the pan. Bring to a boil, scraping up brown bits from bottom of pan with a wooden spoon. Stir in mustard, tarragon, salt, and pepper to taste. Whisk in cream and boil until mixture thickens slightly, about 3 minutes.

3. Return chicken to pan; turn in sauce to coat, and simmer 5 to 10 minutes, until chicken is tender. Remove chicken to a serving platter; spoon sauce over all.

146   STIR-FRY CHICKEN AND BROCCOLI
Prep: 20 minutes   Cook: 20 minutes   Serves: 4

2 tablespoons vegetable oil
1¼ pounds skinless, boneless chicken breasts, cut into 1-inch pieces
2 cups broccoli florets
½ pound fresh mushrooms, sliced
4 scallions, cut into 1-inch pieces

3 tablespoons soy sauce
3 tablespoons dry sherry
½ teaspoon ground ginger
1 teaspoon cornstarch dissolved in 2 tablespoons water
1 teaspoon Oriental sesame oil

1. In a large frying pan or wok, heat oil over medium-high heat. Add chicken cubes and stir-fry 3 minutes, until chicken becomes opaque. Remove with a slotted spoon and set aside.

2. Add broccoli; stir-fry 1 to 2 minutes. Add mushrooms, scallions, soy sauce, sherry, ginger, and sesame oil. Stir-fry 2 more minutes. Add dissolved cornstarch and reserved chicken. Cook until heated through and sauce has thickened. Serve over rice.

147 STIR-FRIED CHINESE CHICKEN WITH CASHEWS

Prep: 15 minutes   Marinate: 15 minutes   Cook: 5 minutes
Serves: 6

Most of the time it takes to make this dish is devoted to slicing, chopping, and assembling. The actual cooking time is only about 5 minutes. You'll be amazed at how authentic it tastes. You may say good-by to Chinese take-out forever.

1 **egg white, lightly beaten**	²/₃ **cup unsalted cashews**
¼ **cup soy sauce**	**1-inch square of fresh**
1 **tablespoon plus 1 teaspoon**	**ginger, peeled and**
cornstarch	**quartered**
1½ **pounds skinless, boneless**	2 **scallions, sliced**
chicken breasts, cut into	1 **can (8 ounces) water**
1-inch cubes	**chestnuts, drained and**
1 **tablespoon dry sherry**	**sliced**
2 **teaspoons cider vinegar**	1 **medium green bell pepper,**
1 **teaspoon sugar**	**cut into ½-inch dice**
¼ **cup vegetable oil**	

1. In a medium-size bowl, combine egg white, 1 tablespoon of the soy sauce, and 1 tablespoon cornstarch. Add chicken cubes and toss to coat. Let stand 15 minutes.

2. Meanwhile, in a small bowl, combine remaining soy sauce, 1 teaspoon cornstarch, sherry, vinegar, and sugar; set seasoning sauce aside.

3. In a large frying pan or wok, heat oil over medium-high heat. Stir-fry cashews 1 minute; remove with a slotted spoon or Chinese strainer and drain on paper towels. Add chicken and stir-fry until opaque, 2 to 3 minutes; remove and set aside.

4. Discard all but 2 tablespoons oil. Add ginger, scallions, and water chestnuts; stir-fry 1 minute. Add chicken, bell pepper, and reserved seasoning sauce. Cook, stirring, until thickened. Discard ginger pieces; add reserved cashews. Serve over rice.

148 EASY BROILED CHICKEN THIGHS

Prep: 5 minutes   Cook: 20 to 25 minutes   Serves: 4

8 **chicken thighs (about**	2 **teaspoons mayonnaise**
3 pounds)	
¼ **cup Hot Honey Mustard**	
(p. 25) or commercially	
prepared honey mustard	

1. Preheat broiler. Place chicken thighs skin side down on broiler pan.

2. In a small bowl, combine honey mustard and mayonnaise. Brush chicken with half the sauce. Broil 8 to 10 inches from heat for 10 to 12 minutes.

3. Turn chicken and brush with remaining sauce. Broil 10 to 12 minutes, until tender.

149 HAM AND CHEESE CHICKEN TURNOVERS
Prep: 15 minutes   Cook: 15 minutes   Serves: 6

Here's an easy variation of chicken cordon bleu.

6 **thin slices prosciutto**
6 **thin slices mozzarella cheese**
6 **skinless, boneless chicken**
    breast halves, pounded to
    ¼-inch thickness

1 **tablespoon vegetable oil**
1 **tablespoon butter or**
    margarine
¼ **cup dry white wine**
2 **tablespoons chopped parsley**

1. Place 1 slice of prosciutto and 1 slice of cheese on each flattened chicken breast. Fold in half. Secure with wooden toothpicks or small skewers.

2. In a large frying pan, heat oil and butter over medium heat. Add chicken turnovers and cook 3 to 4 minutes a side, until chicken is barely opaque throughout. Add wine and simmer 5 minutes. Remove to a serving platter, discard picks, and garnish with parsley.

150 EASY ASPARAGUS CHICKEN
Prep: 20 minutes   Cook: 30 minutes   Serves: 4

Serve with parsleyed egg noodles. Substitute broccoli florets for the asparagus if desired.

1¼ **pounds skinless, boneless**
    chicken breasts, cut into
    ½-inch strips
    Salt and freshly ground
    pepper
2 **tablespoons vegetable oil**
2 **packages (10 ounces each)**
    frozen asparagus spears,
    thawed

1 **can (10¾ ounces) condensed**
    cream of mushroom soup
½ **cup mayonnaise**
1 **tablespoon lemon juice**
1 **teaspoon curry powder**
1 **cup shredded sharp Cheddar**
    cheese

1. Preheat oven to 375°. Sprinkle chicken with salt and pepper. In a large frying pan, heat oil over medium heat. Add chicken strips; cook, tossing, until meat turns opaque, about 3 minutes. Remove chicken from pan with a slotted spoon; reserve pan juices.

2. Brush a 12 x 8 x 2-inch baking dish with reserved pan juices. Arrange asparagus spears on bottom of baking dish; top with chicken strips.

3. Add soup, mayonnaise, lemon juice, and curry powder to remaining pan drippings. Stir over low heat for 1 minute, until well blended. Pour sauce over chicken and asparagus.

4. Sprinkle casserole with cheese. Cover and bake 30 minutes, until hot and bubbly.

151   POACHED CHICKEN WITH MUSTARD CREAM SAUCE

Prep: 15 minutes   Cook: 15 to 20 minutes   Serves: 4

2 pounds skinless, boneless
    chicken breast halves
½ cup dry white wine
½ pound mushrooms, sliced
2 shallots, finely chopped
1 garlic clove, crushed
½ cup heavy cream

1 tablespoon Dijon mustard
1 tablespoon capers
1 tablespoon chopped fresh
    dill, or ½ teaspoon dried
⅛ teaspoon freshly ground
    pepper
Salt

1. Poach chicken as directed on page 37.

2. In a large frying pan, combine wine, mushrooms, shallots, and garlic. Cook over medium-high heat for 5 minutes, until mushrooms are tender and wine is reduced by half.

3. In a small bowl, whisk together cream and mustard until blended. Stir into sauce and cook until slightly thickened, 3 to 5 minutes. Stir in capers, dill, and pepper. Season with salt to taste. Serve sauce over poached chicken breasts.

152   CHICKEN VÉRONIQUE

Prep: 5 minutes   Cook: 15 minutes   Serves: 4

The word *véronique* indicates green grapes. Paired with chicken, cream, and white wine, they make a surprisingly elegant dish.

2 tablespoons butter
1 tablespoon vegetable oil
4 skinless, boneless chicken
    breast halves
⅓ cup dry white wine

1 cup heavy cream
½ pound seedless green
    grapes, halved
Salt and pepper

1. Heat butter and oil in a large frying pan over medium-high heat. Add chicken and sauté, turning once, until meat turns white, about 8 minutes. Remove from pan and keep warm. Add wine to pan and bring to a boil, scraping up browned bits from bottom of pan with a wooden spoon.

2. Stir cream into pan. Boil, stirring occasionally, until sauce thickens slightly, about 5 minutes. Add chicken and grapes. Heat through.

153 CHICKEN TACOS
Prep: 10 minutes   Cook: 5 minutes   Serves: 6

12 taco shells
2 tablespoons vegetable oil
1 medium onion, chopped
1 garlic clove, chopped
2 cups chopped, cooked
  chicken
1 teaspoon cumin
½ teaspoon dried oregano

Salt and freshly ground
  pepper
1½ cups grated, sharp Cheddar
  or Monterey Jack cheese
  (about 6 ounces)
Bottled taco sauce, chopped
  tomatoes, and shredded
  lettuce

1. Preheat oven to 350°. Place taco shells in a 13 x 9 x 2-inch baking dish. Place in oven for 5 minutes to crisp.

2. Meanwhile, in a large frying pan, heat oil and cook onion until softened, 2 to 3 minutes. Add garlic and cook 1 minute. Add chicken and season with cumin, oregano, and salt and pepper to taste. Cook until heated through.

3. Fill shells halfway with filling, top each with about 2 tablespoons cheese and taco sauce, tomatoes, and lettuce to taste.

154 BAKED GARLIC-THYME CHICKEN
Prep: 5 minutes   Cook: 50 minutes   Serves: 4

4 tablespoons butter, softened
2 scallions, chopped
2 garlic cloves, crushed
  through a press
1 teaspoon lemon juice

1 teaspoon dried thyme leaves
½ teaspoon salt
¼ teaspoon freshly ground
  pepper
1 chicken (3 pounds), cut up

1. Preheat oven to 350°. In a small bowl, blend together butter, scallions, garlic, lemon juice, thyme, salt, and pepper.

2. Arrange chicken, skin side up, in a 13 x 9 x 2-inch baking dish. Spread seasoned butter over chicken. Bake 50 minutes, or until tender, basting occasionally with pan juices.

155 GINA WILSON'S LEMON CHICKEN FROM THE CHICKEN RANCH

Prep: 5 minutes   Cook: 40 minutes   Serves: 6

1 lemon, thinly sliced
6 chicken breast halves with
   bone
4 tablespoons butter or
   margarine, melted
¼ cup lemon juice

1 teaspoon lemon-pepper
   seasoning
1 tablespoon chopped parsley
1 can (4 ounces) sliced
   mushrooms, drained
   (optional)

1. Preheat oven to 375°. Arrange lemon slices in bottom of a 13 x 9 x 2-inch baking dish. Place chicken breasts in dish.

2. Combine melted butter and lemon juice. Pour over chicken. Sprinkle evenly with lemon-pepper and parsley. Bake 30 minutes. Sprinkle mushrooms around chicken. Bake 10 minutes longer, until chicken is tender.

156 CHICKEN À LA GREQUE

Prep: 5 minutes   Cook: 40 minutes   Serves: 4

1 tablespoon dried oregano
½ teaspoon salt
¼ teaspoon freshly ground
   pepper

1 chicken (3 pounds), cut up
¼ cup olive oil
2 tablespoons lemon juice

1. Preheat oven to 400°. Combine oregano, salt, and pepper in a small dish. Rub seasonings into chicken. Arrange in a 13 x 9 x 2-inch baking dish.

2. Blend together olive oil and lemon juice. Pour over chicken pieces. Bake 40 minutes, until tender.

Chapter 10

Chicken Lite

Who's counting calories these days? Almost all of us are. And chicken is truly the perfect diet food. First of all it's low in calories. A 4-ounce serving of white meat chicken, equal to one skinless, boneless chicken breast half, contains only 200 calories. What's more, it is exceedingly low in fat—only 5 grams. That's lower than an equivalent portion of veal or oily fish.

In addition, chicken cooks with little or no added fat. It can be poached in water, roasted, baked, or broiled. It combines beautifully with vegetables, themselves fat-free and high in healthy fiber.

Some recipes are naturally low in calories. To add variety, others get help from reduced-calorie products. In any recipe where the skin is left on the chicken, calories and fat can be reduced even further simply by removing the skin.

157 BLACK CHERRY CHICKEN
Prep: 15 minutes   Cook: 30 minutes   Serves: 4

4 skinless, boneless chicken
   breast halves
2 cups black cherries, canned
   or frozen, no sugar added
1 tablespoon Worcestershire
   sauce
1 teaspoon brown sugar

1 teaspoon garlic powder
1 teaspoon dry sherry
½ cup chopped onion
¼ cup raisins
2 teaspoons cornstarch
   dissolved in ¼ cup cold
   water

1. Preheat broiler. Place chicken breasts on broiler rack and broil 3 minutes a side, until browned. Transfer to an 8 x 8 x 2-inch baking dish.

2. In a blender or food processor, combine 1 cup of the cherries, Worcestershire sauce, brown sugar, garlic powder, and sherry. Process until puréed. Pour into a small saucepan; add onion, raisins, and cornstarch mixture. Cook, stirring occasionally, over medium-high heat until mixture thickens.

3. Pour cherry sauce over chicken breasts. Add remaining cherries. Turn oven heat to 350° and bake 30 minutes.

---

158 TOMATO-APPLE CHICKEN
Prep: 25 minutes   Cook: 25 minutes   Serves: 4

2 teaspoons vegetable oil
4 skinless, boneless chicken
   breast halves, pounded to
   ¼-inch thickness
1 medium onion, sliced
1 can (16 ounces) tomatoes
1 teaspoon light brown sugar
¼ teaspoon dried thyme
¼ teaspoon garlic powder
¼ teaspoon salt

¼ teaspoon Worcestershire
   sauce
½ lemon, thinly sliced
2 small apples, cored and cut
   into eighths
½ teaspoon cornstarch
   dissolved in 1 tablespoon
   water
1 tablespoon chopped fresh
   parsley

1. Heat oil in a large nonstick frying pan over medium heat. Add chicken and cook about 4 minutes a side, until lightly browned. Scatter onion slices over chicken.

2. In a medium-size bowl, combine tomatoes, brown sugar, thyme, garlic powder, salt, and Worcestershire sauce; pour over chicken. Top with lemon slices and bring to a boil. Cover and reduce heat. Simmer 10 minutes. Add apples and cook 10 minutes more, until chicken is tender. Remove chicken and apples to a platter and keep warm.

3. Stir dissolved cornstarch into liquid in pan. Cook over high heat, stirring until sauce thickens, about 5 minutes. Spoon over chicken and apples. Garnish with parsley.

159 POACHED CHICKEN AND VEGETABLE MEDLEY
Prep: 30 minutes   Cook: 25 minutes   Serves: 4

This is especially nice to do when vegetables are fresh and in season.

1 cup canned chicken broth plus ½ cup water
1 cup cauliflower florets
1 cup sliced green beans
1 cup diced sweet red bell pepper
1 cup fresh peas
1 cup pearl onions, peeled

1¼ pounds skinless, boneless chicken breast halves, cut into 1-inch cubes
Freshly ground pepper
1 tablespoon fresh lemon juice
8 large iceburg lettuce leaves, washed and drained

1. In a large frying pan, combine broth and vegetables. Arrange chicken over vegetables; sprinkle with pepper and lemon juice. Cover with lettuce. Bring to a boil. Reduce heat to low and cook, covered, until chicken is tender, about 25 minutes.

2. Discard lettuce; drain and discard liquid. Arrange vegetables with chicken on a warmed serving platter.

160 GARLIC CHICKEN WITH FRESH CORIANDER
*Prep: 15 minutes   Marinate: 2 hours   Cook: 20 minutes
Serves: 4 to 6*

7 garlic cloves, peeled
2 tablespoons cracked black peppercorns
¼ teaspoon salt
4 bunches of fresh coriander, including roots (about 8 ounces total), well washed and coarsely chopped

2 tablespoons fresh lemon juice
1 chicken (3 pounds), cut up and skinned

1. In a blender or food processor, chop garlic, peppercorns, and salt. Gradually add coriander, then lemon juice, and process to a coarse paste.

2. With a sharp heavy cleaver or with poultry shears, cut chicken through the bone into 2-inch pieces. Cut breast into sixths, thighs in half. Or chicken may be left in traditional serving pieces.

3. In a medium-size bowl, combine chicken pieces and garlic-coriander mixture, turning to coat. Cover and marinate 2 hours at room temperature or refrigerate overnight.

4. Preheat oven to broil or light a charcoal grill. Place chicken on a rack over broiler pan or on grill, patting any excess garlic mixture on chicken. Cook about 6 inches from the flame 7 to 9 minutes on each side, until outside is crisp and chicken is tender.

161 POACHED RUBY RED CHICKEN
Prep: 5 minutes   Cook: 25 minutes   Serves: 6

1 cup canned chicken broth
  plus ½ cup water
¾ cup fruity red wine, such as
  hearty burgundy
2 tablepoons tarragon
6 skinless, boneless chicken
  breast halves

2 teaspoons cornstarch
  dissolved in 2 tablespoons
  water
Salt and freshly ground
  pepper

1. In a large nonaluminum saucepan, bring broth, wine, and tarragon to a boil; reduce heat to a simmer. Add chicken breasts and poach them 15 to 20 minutes, until chicken is cooked through but still moist and tender. With a slotted spoon, transfer chicken to serving platter; keep warm. Reserve poaching liquid.

2. Stir dissolved cornstarch into poaching liquid. Bring to a boil, stirring constantly with a wire whisk. Continue cooking and stirring until the sauce thickens. Season with salt and pepper to taste. Pour over chicken breasts and serve.

162 BREAST OF CHICKEN WITH ASPARAGUS AND CARROTS EN PAPILLOTE
Prep: 15 minutes   Cook: 20 minutes   Serves: 4

En papillote literally means "in paper," referring to the charming parchment packets in which the French traditionally cooked. This modern version uses aluminum foil, more readily available and sturdier.

4 skinless, boneless chicken
  breast halves, cut
  crosswise into ¼-inch
  strips
Salt and freshly ground
  pepper
½ pound fresh asparagus, cut
  into 1-inch lengths

1 medium carrot, cut into
  julienne strips
1 small onion, sliced
2 tablespoons reduced-calorie
  margarine, melted
2 teaspoons lemon juice
½ teaspoon tarragon
¼ teaspoon salt
  Dash of cayenne pepper

1. Preheat oven to 450°. Tear off four lengths of heavy-duty aluminum foil large enough to permit adequate wrapping and to allow for heat circulation and expansion. Place sliced chicken in center of lower half of each length of foil; season with salt and pepper. Top with asparagus, carrot, and onion.

2. In a small bowl, combine margarine, lemon juice, tarragon, salt, and cayenne. Pour equally over each chicken-vegetable serving. Fold upper half of foil over ingredients making a series of locked folds; repeat folds for ends, pressing tight to seal.

3. Place foil packets in a single layer on a large baking sheet. Cook 18 to 20 minutes, until chicken tests done. To serve, cut an X in top of foil packet; fold back foil or remove to plate.

163 BAKED TOMATOES STUFFED WITH CHICKEN AND SPINACH
Prep: 15 minutes   Cook: 30 minutes   Serves: 4

¼ cup chopped onion	2 cups chopped cooked
1 cup skim milk	chicken
¼ cup flour	1 package (10 ounces) frozen
2 teaspoons instant chicken	chopped spinach, thawed
bouillon granules	and drained
4 slices diet (low-fat) Swiss	4 large tomatoes, tops cut off
cheese, cut into pieces	and insides scooped out

1. Preheat oven to 350°. In a medium-size saucepan, cook onion in ¼ cup water over medium heat until tender. In a small bowl, combine milk, flour, and bouillon; stir until smooth. Add to onion. Cook and stir until mixture thickens. Add cheese and remove from heat. Stir until cheese melts; set aside.

2. In a medium-size bowl, combine chicken, spinach, and 1 cup sauce; mix well and stuff tomatoes.

3. Place in an 8 x 8 x 2-inch baking dish; pour ½ cup water around tomatoes. Cover and bake 30 minutes, until hot. Serve with remaining sauce.

164 CHICKEN FLORENTINE WITH FRESH MUSHROOMS
Prep: 15 minutes   Cook: 30 minutes   Serves: 4

The combination of flavors in this dish is very good, and it makes an impressive presentation.

4 skinless, boneless chicken	¼ teaspoon ground nutmeg
breast halves	¼ teaspoon salt
1 small onion, quartered	Freshly ground pepper
1 tablespoon reduced-calorie	4 teaspoons grated Parmesan
margarine	cheese
2 cups sliced fresh mushrooms	
1 package (10 ounces) frozen	
chopped spinach, cooked	
and drained, or 2 cups	
chopped cooked fresh	
spinach	

1. In a medium-size saucepan, combine chicken breasts and onion with water to cover. Cover and poach chicken over medium-low heat until just white throughout, about 20 minutes.

2. Meanwhile, melt margarine in a large frying pan. Add mushrooms and cook until tender, about 5 minutes.

3. Preheat broiler. Place spinach in an 8-inch square baking dish. Sprinkle with nutmeg, salt, and pepper to taste. Arrange chicken in a single layer over spinach. Top with mushrooms. Sprinkle with cheese. Broil for 1 to 2 minutes, until cheese is melted.

165   BAKED LEMON CHICKEN

Prep: 15 minutes   Marinate: 2 hours   Cook: 45 minutes   Serves: 4

Remove skin from chicken to further reduce calories.

4 **chicken breasts halves with bone**
1 **small onion, chopped**
2 **tablespoons chopped fresh dill**

1 **teaspoon grated lemon rind**
1/4 **teaspoon ground nutmeg**
3 **tablespoons fresh lemon juice**

1. Place chicken breasts, skin side up, in an 8-inch square baking dish. Sprinkle with onion, dill, lemon rind, and nutmeg.

2. Combine lemon juice with 2/3 cup cold water. Pour over chicken. Cover and marinate at least 2 hours, or overnight in refrigerator.

3. Preheat oven to 375°. Bake chicken uncovered 45 minutes, basting frequently with pan juices.

166   LIGHT BROILED CHICKEN

Prep: 10 minutes   Cook: 30 to 40 minutes   Serves: 4

Use this procedure for all grilled or broiled chicken. Vary the flavor with different low-calorie sauces. Try brushing with fresh lemon or lime juice, sprinkle with freshly ground pepper, or brush with mashed garlic and chili paste.

1/4 **cup low-calorie spicy Italian salad dressing**

1 **chicken (3 pounds), skinned and cut up**

Brush dressing all over chicken. Broil about 6 inches from heat 25 to 30 minutes, or grill slowly over direct heat for 40 minutes, basting occasionally with dressing.

167   BROCCOLI-TOMATO CHICKEN

Prep: 20 minutes   Cook: 10 minutes   Serves: 4

4 **skinless, boneless chicken breast halves, cut crosswise into 1/2-inch strips**
  Salt and freshly ground pepper
2 **tablespoons reduced-calorie margarine**

1/4 **cup chopped onion**
2 **cups fresh broccoli florets**
1 **teaspoon lemon juice**
1/2 **teaspoon dried thyme**
3 **medium tomatoes, cut into wedges**

1. Season chicken with salt and pepper. In a medium-size frying pan, melt margarine over medium heat. Add chicken and onion and cook until chicken is opaque, about 8 minutes.

2. Add broccoli, lemon juice, thyme, and salt and pepper to taste. Cover and simmer for 6 minutes. Add tomatoes and simmer, covered, 3 to 4 minutes, until hot.

168 VINEGAR CHICKEN
Prep: 20 minutes   Cook: 20 minutes   Serves: 4

2 tablespoons reduced-calorie margarine
1 chicken (3 pounds), cut up
4 garlic cloves, unpeeled
¼ teaspoon salt
¼ teaspoon freshly ground pepper

½ cup tarragon wine vinegar
2 medium tomatoes, peeled, seeded, and chopped
2 tablespoons finely chopped fresh parsley

1. In a large nonaluminum frying pan, melt margarine over medium heat. Add chicken and garlic. Cook, turning, until chicken is lightly browned, about 5 minutes a side.

2. Season chicken with salt and pepper. Add vinegar and bring to a boil. Add tomatoes and parsley. Cover, reduce heat, and simmer 20 minutes, until chicken is tender. Remove chicken to a serving platter. Cover loosely with foil to keep warm.

3. Remove garlic cloves; peel under cold water, mash, and return to sauce. Pour sauce over chicken and serve hot.

169 COLD LEMON CHICKEN
Prep: 10 minutes   Cook: 15 minutes   Serves: 4

A perfect light dish for a chic little luncheon or cold buffet.

2 tablespoons reduced-calorie margarine
4 skinless, boneless chicken breast halves
½ cup dry white wine
¼ cup lemon juice
¼ teaspoon salt

2 tablespoons reduced-calorie mayonnaise
1 tablespoon minced fresh dill, or 1 teaspoon dried dill weed
Lettuce leaves, sprigs of dill, and lemon slices, for garnish

1. Preheat oven to 350°. In a large frying pan, melt margarine over medium heat. Add chicken breasts and cook, turning once, until light brown, about 4 minutes a side. Transfer chicken to an 8-inch square baking dish.

2. Add wine to pan. Bring to a boil, scraping bottom of pan with a wooden spoon. Stir in 2 tablespoons of the lemon juice and the salt; pour mixture over chicken.

3. Cover baking dish with foil and bake for 15 minutes, basting occasionally. Let chicken cool to room temperature. Combine mayonnaise with remaining 2 tablespoons lemon juice and spread evenly over the chicken breasts. Serve on a bed of lettuce; garnish with dill and lemon slices.

170 ORIENTAL CHICKEN
Prep: 15 minutes   Cook: 10 minutes   Serves: 6

2 tablespoons dry sherry
2 tablespoons soy sauce
1 tablespoon cider vinegar
½ teaspoon ground ginger
1 teaspoon cornstarch
2 tablespoons vegetable oil
1 pound skinless, boneless chicken breasts, cut into 1-inch pieces

1 red bell pepper, cut into 1-inch cubes
3 scallions, cut into 1-inch lengths
1 cup sliced mushrooms
1 can (8 ounces) sliced water chestnuts, drained

1. In a small bowl, combine sherry, soy sauce, vinegar, ginger, and cornstarch; stir to blend well.

2. In a wok or large frying pan, heat oil over medium-high heat. Add chicken and stir-fry until white. Add red pepper, scallions, mushrooms, and water chestnuts; stir-fry 2 minutes.

3. Stir sauce and add to wok. Stir over heat until sauce thickens.

171 EMPRESS CHICKEN
Prep: 20 minutes   Marinate: 15 minutes   Cook: 25 minutes   Serves: 4

A savory Chinese poached chicken. Sesame oil, five-spice powder, and star anise are sold in oriental markets and by mail order.

¼ cup soy sauce
1 tablespoon dry sherry
1 garlic clove, crushed
1 teaspoon grated fresh ginger
1 teaspoon Oriental sesame oil
2 star anise pods

¼ teaspoon Chinese five-spice powder
2 pounds skinless, boneless chicken breast halves
1 tablespoon cornstarch dissolved in 2 tablespoons water

1. Combine soy sauce, sherry, garlic, ginger, sesame oil, star anise, and five-spice powder in a large bowl. Add chicken and marinate 15 minutes.

2. In a medium-size saucepan, bring 2 cups of water to a boil. Add chicken breasts with marinade. Reduce heat to low and poach chicken, turning occasionally, 15 minutes, just until opaque throughout. Remove chicken and set aside.

3. Boil poaching liquid until reduced by half. Add dissolved cornstarch and cook, stirring, until smooth and thick. Slice chicken thin. Pour sauce over slices. Serve warm or at room temperature.

172 CURRIED CHICKEN SALAD IN LETTUCE PACKAGES
Prep: 15 minutes   Cook: 1 minute   Serves: 4

8 large Boston lettuce leaves
2 cups chopped cooked chicken
½ cup chopped celery
8 pitted black olives, chopped
2 tablespoons chopped scallions
¼ cup reduced-calorie mayonnaise
½ teaspoon curry powder
¼ teaspoon salt
⅛ teaspoon freshly ground pepper
10 cherry tomatoes, cut in half

1. Bring a medium-size saucepan of water to a boil. Drop in lettuce leaves until wilted; drain immediately in a colander under cold running water. Pat dry with paper towels.

2. In a medium-size bowl, combine chicken, celery, olives, scallions, mayonnaise, curry, salt, and pepper. Mix well. Divide chicken mixture into 8 equal portions; place one portion on each lettuce leaf. Carefully fold edges of each leaf toward center to enclose filling. Secure each package with a wooden toothpick. Serve 2 packages to each person; garnish with tomato halves.

173 PEPPER CHICKEN CASSEROLE
Prep: 20 minutes   Cook: 45 minutes   Serves: 4

2 tablespoons vegetable oil
1¼ pounds skinless, boneless chicken breasts, cut into 1-inch cubes
2 medium-size red bell peppers, sliced
2 medium-size green bell peppers, sliced
2 cups sliced mushrooms
2 cups chopped onions
½ teaspoon dried oregano
½ teaspoon crushed hot red pepper
½ cup dry white wine
1 cup hot skim milk

1. Preheat oven to 350°. Heat oil in a 2-quart flameproof casserole. Add chicken, bell peppers, mushrooms, onions, oregano, and hot pepper. Cook over medium-low heat 5 to 8 minutes, until chicken is opaque and onion is tender.

2. Add wine and cook 5 minutes. Pour hot milk over chicken mixture, cover, and bake 30 minutes.

174   LEMON TARRAGON CHICKEN
Prep: 15 minutes   Cook: 20 minutes   Serves: 4

4 skinless, boneless chicken
   breast halves, pounded to
   ¼-inch thickness
  Salt and freshly ground
   pepper
2 cups sliced fresh mushrooms

2 tablespoons reduced-calorie
   margarine, softened
1 shallot, minced
½ teaspoon dried tarragon
½ teaspoon salt
4 teaspoons lemon juice

1. Preheat oven to 450°. Tear off four sheets of heavy-duty aluminum foil about 12 by 18 inches. Place a chicken breast on lower half of each foil sheet. Season with salt and pepper. Top with mushroom slices.

2. In a small bowl, combine margarine, shallot, tarragon, salt, and lemon juice; mix well and divide evenly over chicken and mushrooms.

3. Fold upper half of foil sheet over ingredients, make a series of locked folds to seal packets; press edges tight to seal, allowing space for heat circulation and expansion. Place foil packets on a large baking sheet. Place in oven and cook 20 minutes. To serve, cut an X in top of packet; fold foil back.

175   CHICKEN WITH GARLIC
Prep: 25 minutes   Cook: 1 hour   Serves: 4

This recipe has super flavor, especially if you are a garlic lover. The brown crusty flavor is desirable, so I don't suggest adding more liquid.

  Vegetable cooking spray
2 cups chopped celery
1 chicken (3 pounds), cut up
   and skinned
1 whole head of garlic,
   separated into cloves and
   peeled

2 teaspoons olive oil
¼ cup finely chopped fresh
   parsley
½ teaspoon dried tarragon
¼ teaspoon freshly ground
   pepper
1 cup dry white wine

1. Preheat oven to 375°. Spray a 5½-quart Dutch oven with vegetable cooking spray. Arrange celery on bottom of dish; top with chicken and garlic. Sprinkle with oil, parsley, tarragon, and pepper; pour wine over all.

2. Cover tightly with foil, then cover with lid and bake 1 hour, until chicken is tender.

176 LO-CAL BARBECUED CHICKEN
Prep: 15 minutes   Cook: 45 minutes   Serves: 4

This is a light alternative to sugar-filled barbecue sauces. Make sauce ahead and refrigerate.

1 tablespoon vegetable oil
1/4 cup chopped onion
1 tomato, seeded and finely chopped
1 garlic clove, minced
1 teaspoon ground chili powder
1 cup chicken broth

2 tablespoons Worcestershire sauce
Freshly ground pepper
1 tablespoon cornstarch dissolved in 1 tablespoon water
4 skinless, boneless chicken breast halves

1. Preheat broiler. In a medium-size saucepan, heat oil over medium heat. Add onion; cook until softened, about 3 minutes. Add tomato, garlic, and chili powder; cook 2 minutes, stirring frequently. Stir in broth, Worcestershire sauce, and pepper to taste. Bring to a boil, reduce heat, and simmer 10 minutes. Stir in cornstarch mixture. Cook, turning, until thickened, about 1 minute.

2. Place chicken breasts on rack in broiler pan. Broil 6 inches from heat for 20 minutes, turning 3 or 4 times. Brush with sauce. Broil, turning and basting frequently with sauce, until tender, 5 to 10 minutes longer. Serve with remaining sauce.

177 SUPREMES OF CHICKEN WITH MORELS
Prep: 20 minutes   Cook: 25 minutes   Serves: 4

This dish is redolent with the smoky flavor of morels. They are wild mushrooms found in forests in the northern Midwest, often available at food specialty stores. Serve with rice and a full-bodied white wine.

2 tablespoons reduced-calorie margarine
2 cups small fresh mushrooms
1 cup fresh morels (if unavailable, use 1/2 ounce dried, reconstituted), well rinsed and dried

1 1/2 cups canned chicken broth
4 skinless, boneless chicken breast halves, pounded to 1/4-inch thickness

1. Preheat oven to 350°. In a medium-size frying pan, melt margarine over medium heat. Add mushrooms and morels. Cook 6 to 7 minutes, until mushrooms are lightly browned. Add stock and simmer until only 1/2 cup liquid remains.

2. Arrange chicken breasts in an 8-inch square baking dish. Pour mushroom mixture over chicken and bake for 25 minutes, until chicken is opaque and firm to the touch. To serve, spoon pan juices and mushrooms evenly over chicken.

178   BROCCOLI-CHICKEN QUICHE
Prep: 25 minutes   Cook: 30 minutes   Serves: 6

This light "quiche" has no crust. To reduce calories even further, diet Swiss-style cheese can be substituted for the Swiss cheese.

1 cup chopped broccoli stems and florets	2 tablespoons chopped parsley
1 cup chopped cooked chicken	1½ cups evaporated skim milk
½ cup chopped onion	3 eggs
4 ounces Swiss cheese, shredded (about 1 cup)	½ teaspoon garlic powder
	⅛ teaspoon cayenne pepper
	⅛ teaspoon grated nutmeg

1. Preheat oven to 400°. Butter a 10-inch glass pie plate (or spray with vegetable cooking spray). Arrange broccoli, chicken, onion, cheese, and parsley in bottom of dish.

2. Combine remaining ingredients and beat smooth with electric mixer, blender, or food processor. Pour over broccoli mixture.

3. Bake uncovered 30 minutes, until knife inserted near center comes out clean. Cool 10 minutes. Cut into wedges and serve.

179   *BROILED COUNTRY-MUSTARD CHICKEN*
Prep: 10 minutes   Cook: 40 minutes   Serves: 4

2 tablespoons country-style Dijon mustard	1 garlic clove, crushed through a press
2 tablespoons reduced-calorie mayonnaise	¼ teaspoon freshly ground pepper
2 scallions, sliced	4 chicken breast halves
½ teaspoon dried basil	

1. Preheat broiler. In a small bowl, mix mustard, mayonnaise, scallions, basil, garlic, and pepper. Place chicken pieces, skin side up, on a broiling pan. Spread half the mustard mixture over chicken.

2. Broil about 6 inches from heat for 15 to 20 minutes a side, basting occasionally with remaining sauce.

Chapter 11

Chicken Little

Chicken's little cousin, the Cornish game hen, stars in this chapter. With all due respect to other members of the poultry family, it is surprising that the Cornish hen does not make a regular appearance on American tables at least once a month. Its slightly gamey taste makes it unique among domesticated birds, and its natural tenderness gives it an edge over its wild fowl brethren. It lends itself to both the skillet and the oven and, when quartered, even to the barbecue grill. What's more, with the Cornish hen's uniform size of 3/4 to 1 pound, each bird makes a perfect, and often elegant, individual serving.

180 APRICOT-GLAZED CORNISH HENS STUFFED WITH WILD RICE

Prep: 40 minutes   Cook: 1¼ hour   Serves: 6

These whole stuffed hens with their glistening apricot glaze make a fabulous presentation for a very special dinner party. If you really want to impress, arrange them all on a large platter, alternating the hens with bundles of asparagus spears topped with a single thin strip of roasted red pepper to simulate a ribbon.

1 **package (6 ounces) long grain and wild rice**	1 **jar (12 ounces) apricot preserves**
2 **teaspoons tarragon leaves**	4 **tablespoons butter**
Salt and freshly ground pepper	⅓ **cup orange-flavored liqueur, such as Grand Marnier**
6 **Cornish game hens**	**Parsley sprigs, for garnish**

1. Prepare rice according to package instructions. Add tarragon and season with salt and pepper to taste.

2. Preheat oven to 350°. Wash hens, inside and out, pat dry. Stuff hens loosely with cooked rice. Fold wings back and tie legs together. Season outside with salt and pepper. Place hens, breast side up, in a large shallow baking pan.

3. In a small saucepan, combine apricot preserves, butter, and liqueur. Heat, stirring, until well blended. Baste hens with apricot glaze. Bake for 1 hour and 15 minutes, basting frequently. Remove to a serving platter and garnish with parsley.

181 CRISPY DEVILED HENS

Prep: 15 minutes   Cook: 30 minutes   Serves: 4

This tasty dish is delicious cold. Without the sauce in Step 2, it makes a wonderful picnic dish.

2 **cups seasoned bread crumbs**	4 **Cornish game hens, halved lengthwise, backbones removed**
1 **tablespoon dry mustard**	
½ **teaspoon salt**	
¼ **teaspoon freshly ground pepper**	½ **cup dry white wine**
8 **tablespoons butter or margarine, melted**	1 **tablespoon Dijon mustard**

1. Preheat oven to 425°. In a shallow dish, combine bread crumbs, dry mustard, salt, and pepper. Dip hens in melted butter and roll in bread crumb mixture. Place hens in a greased 13 x 9 x 2-inch baking dish. Bake for 30 minutes, basting once with remaining butter.

2. While chicken is baking, prepare sauce. In a small saucepan, combine wine and Dijon mustard with ¼ cup water. Boil over high heat until reduced to ½ cup. Serve over hens.

182   COMPANY CORNBREAD-STUFFED HENS
Prep: 20 to 30 minutes   Cook: 1¼ hours   Serves: 4

The addition of bacon, pecans, and sherry elevates the good to the spectacular.

4 **Cornish game hens**
  Salt and freshly ground
    pepper
	1½ **cups packaged cornbread**
	    stuffing

4 **strips of bacon, chopped**	¾ **cup medium-dry sherry or** **water**
¼ **cup chopped onion**	8 **tablespoons butter or**
¼ **cup chopped celery**	**margarine, melted**
¼ **cup chopped pecans**	¼ **cup chopped fresh parsley**

1. Wash hens inside and out; pat dry. Season with salt and pepper.

2. In a large frying pan, cook bacon 3 to 4 minutes until crisp. Remove with a slotted spoon and drain on paper towels. Add onion and celery to pan and fry for 30 seconds.

3. Preheat oven to 350°. In a medium-size bowl, combine bacon, onion, celery, pecans, and cornbread stuffing. Add ¼ cup of the sherry and ¼ cup of the melted butter; mix well. Stuff hens loosely. Fold wings back and tie legs together. Place in a shallow baking pan. Baste with remaining melted butter.

4. Bake hens for 1 hour 15 minutes, basting every 15 minutes. When done, remove hens to a platter and keep warm. Skim fat from baking pan, add remaining ½ cup sherry and scrape bottom to mix in browned bits. Pour into a small saucepan, and boil over high heat until reduced by one-third. Add parsley and pour over hens.

183   FRUITED CORNISH GAME HENS
Prep: 35 minutes   Cook: 1¼ hours   Serves: 4

4 **tablespoons butter or** **margarine**	½ **teaspoon salt**
1 **small onion, chopped**	¼ **teaspoon cinnamon**
8 **ounces mixed dried fruit,**	4 **Cornish game hens**
chopped	**Salt and freshly ground**
½ **cup long-grain rice**	**pepper**

1. In a small saucepan, melt 1 tablespoon of the butter over medium heat. Add onion and cook until tender, 3 to 5 minutes. Add dried fruit, rice, salt, cinnamon, and 1⅓ cups water. Mix well, cover, and simmer 20 to 25 minutes, until rice is tender and liquid is absorbed.

2. Preheat oven to 350°. Sprinkle hens inside and out with salt and pepper. Spoon rice-fruit mixture into hen cavities. Arrange in a 13 x 9 x 2-inch baking pan. Melt remaining 3 tablespoons butter and drizzle over hens. Bake, basting occasionally with pan drippings, 1 hour and 15 minutes, until juices run clear.

Fruited Roast Chicken: Prepare the recipe as described above, but stuff a 5-pound roaster with all the fruited rice and cook for about 2½ hours.

184   GAME HENS IN WHITE WINE WITH HERBS
Prep: 20 minutes   Cook: 25 minutes   Serves: 2

Simple and elegant. Serve with California Sauvignon Blanc or an Italian Pinot Grigio.

2 **Cornish game hens, halved lengthwise, backbones removed**	⅛ **teaspoon freshly ground pepper**
¼ **teaspoon dried basil**	1 **tablespoon butter or margarine**
¼ **teaspoon dried oregano**	1 **tablespoon olive oil**
¼ **teaspoon salt**	2 **shallots, finely chopped**
	½ **cup dry white wine**

1. Preheat oven to 350°. Season hens with basil, oregano, salt, and pepper.

2. In a large frying pan, melt butter in oil over moderately high heat. Add hens and sauté, turning once, 4 minutes a side, until browned. Transfer to a small baking dish.

3. Add shallots to pan, reduce heat to low, and sauté until soft, 1 to 2 minutes. Add white wine and bring to a boil, scraping up browned bits from bottom of pan. Pour over hens.

4. Cover with foil and bake 20 minutes, basting occasionally with pan juices.

5. Raise heat to 425°, uncover, and bake 5 minutes, until hens are tender and skin is crisp.

185   HUNGARIAN CORNISH GAME HENS
Prep: 10 minutes   Cook: 45 minutes   Serves: 2

⅓ **cup flour**	1 **tablespoon vegetable oil**
½ **teaspoon salt**	1 **medium onion, chopped**
¼ **teaspoon freshly ground pepper**	¼ **pound mushrooms, sliced**
2 **Cornish game hens, quartered**	1 **tablespoon imported sweet paprika**
2 **tablespoons butter or margarine**	1 **tablespoon tomato paste**
	⅓ **cup white wine**
	½ **cup cream**

1. Combine flour, salt, and pepper in a large plastic bag. Place hen quarters in bag and shake to coat.

2. In a large frying pan, melt butter in oil over medium heat. Add hen quarters and cook, turning, until lightly browned on all sides, about 10 minutes. Remove and set aside.

3. Add onion, mushrooms, and paprika to pan drippings. Cook 2 minutes, until onion is soft. Stir in tomato paste and wine.

4. Reduce heat, return hens to pan, and simmer 30 minutes, until tender. Remove to a serving platter and cover with foil to keep warm.

5. Stir cream into sauce. Simmer until just heated through, about 2 minutes. Serve over hens.

186 CORNISH HEN AND VEGETABLES IN FOIL PACKETS
Prep: 20 minutes   Cook: 50 minutes   Serves: 4

The beauty of this dish is threefold. First of all, the individual packets can be prepared hours before dinner and refrigerated. Secondly, for those on a low-fat diet, this method of cooking is ideal: simply reduce the butter to 1 teaspoon a portion. And last but not least, the bright yellow squash, orange carrots, and red-skinned potatoes make a lovely presentation.

4 Cornish game hens, halved, backbones removed
  Salt and freshly ground pepper
8 small red potatoes, scrubbed and sliced
1 large yellow squash, sliced
4 carrots, sliced

1 large onion, sliced
¼ pound mushrooms, sliced
4 tablespoons butter or margarine, melted
1 tablespoon lemon juice
½ teaspoon coarsely cracked pepper

1. Preheat oven to 350°. Season hens with salt and freshly ground pepper. Place two hen halves, skin side down, on bottom half of a 12 x 18-inch sheet of heavy-duty aluminum foil. Layer one-quarter of potatoes, squash, carrots, onion, and mushrooms over the top of the hen halves. Repeat with remaining 3 hens and vegetables.

2. In a small bowl, combine butter, lemon juice, and pepper. Drizzle over vegetables, dividing equally among packets. Season lightly with salt and sprinkle 1 tablespoon water over each packet.

3. Bring top half of foil over food. Make a series of pleated folds all around to seal. Place on a baking sheet and bake for 50 to 60 minutes, until juices from hen run clear when thigh is pricked.

187 GRILLED GARLIC-LIME GAME HENS
Prep: 10 minutes   Marinate: 1 hour   Cook: 25 minutes   Serves: 4

4 Cornish game hens, halved, backbones removed
2 garlic cloves, finely chopped
2 tablespoons lime juice

1 tablespoon coarse (kosher) salt
½ to 1 teaspoon cayenne pepper

1. Place hens in a 13 x 9 x 2-inch baking dish. Rub garlic into skin; sprinkle with lime juice. Season with salt and cayenne pepper. Refrigerate for at least 1 hour.

2. Grill hens over charcoal, skin side down, for 10 to 12 minutes. Turn and grill 15 minutes, until hens are tender. Under broiler, broil for 10 to 15 minutes a side, until done.

Grilled Garlic-Lime Chicken: Follow the recipe above, but increase the cooking time to about 40 minutes.

188 CORNISH HENS STROGANOFF
Prep: 10 minutes   Cook: 30 minutes   Serves: 2

2 Cornish game hens, quartered	3 scallions, chopped
½ teaspoon salt	½ pound fresh mushrooms, sliced
¼ teaspoon freshly ground pepper	1 tablespoon imported sweet paprika
5 tablespoons flour	½ cup chicken broth
3 tablespoons butter or margarine	½ cup sour cream

1. Wash hen pieces, pat dry. Place salt, pepper, and 3 tablespoons of the flour in a plastic or paper bag. Put hen pieces in bag and shake to coat.

2. In a large frying pan, melt butter over moderate heat. Add hen pieces and cook, turning, until browned all over, about 10 minutes. Reduce heat, cover, and simmer 15 to 20 minutes, until tender. With tongs, remove to a serving platter and cover loosely with foil to keep warm.

3. Add scallions and mushrooms to frying pan. Increase heat to moderately high and sauté until tender. Remove from pan with a slotted spoon and set aside.

4. Reduce heat to moderate. Add remaining 2 tablespoons flour and the paprika to pan drippings. Cook, stirring, for 1 minute. Slowly stir in chicken broth, blending until smooth. Bring to a boil and cook, stirring, until thickened, about 2 minutes. Reduce heat and stir in sour cream until blended: do not boil. Pour over hens.

189 SAUTÉED CORNISH GAME HENS WITH POTATOES, CARROTS, AND ONIONS
Prep: 15 minutes   Cook: 35 minutes   Serves: 2

This is one of my favorite after-work suppers, even though it's a fine enough dish to offer to company. If one person prepares the vegetables while the other browns the birds, you can have a delectable meal in a skillet in less than half an hour.

2 Cornish game hens, halved, backbone removed	4 medium-size red potatoes, quartered
Salt and freshly ground pepper	4 medium-size white onions, halved
3 tablespoons vegetable oil	2 carrots, sliced
1 garlic clove, finely chopped	½ cup chicken stock
	¼ teaspoon dried thyme

1. Season hens with salt and pepper. Heat oil in a large frying pan. Brown hen halves, turning once, about 8 minutes.

2. Pour off all but 1 tablespoon drippings from skillet. Add garlic and cook 1 minute. Arrange potatoes, onions, and carrots around hens. Add stock and thyme. Cover and cook over medium heat for 25 minutes, until hens and vegetables are tender.

190 GAME HENS WITH FETA CHEESE AND OLIVES, GREEK-STYLE

Prep: 10 minutes   Cook: 30 minutes   Serves: 4

3 tablespoons olive oil
4 Cornish game hens, quartered
2 garlic cloves, crushed
¾ teaspoon dried oregano
Salt and freshly ground pepper
1 lemon, thinly sliced
¼ cup fresh lemon juice

1 can (28 ounces) Italian peeled tomatoes, drained and chopped
½ pound feta cheese, cut into ½-inch cubes
16 black olives, preferably Kalamata, halved and pitted

1. In a large frying pan, heat oil over medium heat. Add hen quarters and cook, turning, until browned all over, about 10 minutes.

2. Add garlic, oregano, and salt and pepper to taste. Cook 2 minutes. Add lemon slices, lemon juice, and tomatoes. Cover and simmer 15 minutes, until hens are tender. Stir in cheese and olives. Simmer 3 minutes and serve.

191 CORNISH HENS FLORENTINE

Prep: 30 minutes   Cook: 1¼ hours   Serves: 4

In culinary terms, Florentine means spinach. In this elegant presentation, whole hens are stuffed with a savory spinach, mushroom, and ricotta cheese filling. It's a fabulous dinner party dish that needs only a little wild rice or buttered fine egg noodles as accompaniment.

4 Cornish game hens
Salt and freshly ground pepper
1 package (10 ounces) frozen chopped spinach, thawed
5 tablespoons butter or margarine

⅓ cup chopped onion
1 garlic clove, finely chopped
1 cup coarsely chopped fresh mushrooms
1 cup ricotta cheese
¼ cup sour cream
⅛ teaspoon nutmeg

1. Wash hens inside and out, pat dry. Season with salt and pepper. Squeeze spinach to remove as much moisture as possible.

2. Melt 2 tablespoons of the butter in a frying pan. Add onion and garlic; sauté until tender, about 2 minutes. Add mushrooms; cook until liquid evaporates. Add spinach and cook for 1 minute. Remove from heat and let cool slightly. Add ricotta cheese, sour cream, ¼ teaspoon salt, ⅛ teaspoon pepper, and nutmeg; mix well.

3. Preheat oven to 350°. Stuff hens loosely with spinach mixture. Fold wings back and tie legs together. Place hens, breast side up, in a large shallow baking pan. Melt remaining 3 tablespoons butter and baste hens.

4. Bake, basting frequently, for 1 hour 15 minutes.

192 ROAST GAME HEN WITH PARSLEYED RED POTATOES AND CARROTS

Prep: 10 minutes   Cook: 1 hour 10 minutes   Serves: 4

4 Cornish game hens
  Salt and freshly ground
    pepper
16 small red potatoes
4 carrots, peeled and cut into
    1/2-inch pieces

4 tablespoons butter or
    margarine, melted
2 tablespoons chopped fresh
    parsley
2 tablespoons lemon juice

1. Preheat oven to 350°. Season hens generously with salt and pepper inside cavity and rub into skin. Place hens in a shallow roasting pan; surround with potatoes and carrots.

2. Combine butter, parsley, and lemon juice in a small bowl. Drizzle over all.

3. Bake, basting with pan juices every 20 minutes, for 1 hour and 10 minutes, until hens are tender and potatoes and carrots test done.

193 CORNISH HENS WITH NECTARINES

Prep: 15 minutes   Cook: 20 minutes   Serves: 2

2 Cornish game hens, split in
    half
1/4 teaspoon cinnamon
1/8 teaspoon nutmeg
  Salt and freshly ground
    pepper

3 tablespoons butter or
    margarine
1/2 cup chicken broth
1/2 cup dry red wine
2 nectarines, chopped

1. Sprinkle hen pieces evenly with cinnamon, nutmeg, salt, and pepper.

2. In a large frying pan, melt butter over medium heat. Add hen halves and cook, turning, until browned on both sides, about 10 minutes. Add broth, wine, and nectarines. Cover and simmer over low heat for 15 minutes, until hens are tender. Remove hens to a serving platter.

3. Increase heat and boil about 5 minutes, until sauce is reduced by half. Pour over hens and serve.

Chapter 12

Roasted

If ever there were a perfect meat, to my taste it's roast chicken. With crisp, golden brown skin over moist, succulent meat, the bonus of a savory stuffing and warm gravy to sop up with a crust of bread if desired, it makes for one of the best meals I know.

Roast chicken can be simple, with perhaps some carrots, potatoes, and onions—one of its most beguiling treatments, in fact—or dressed to kill, with apples and sausage. It can be basted with tarragon butter, roasted almost fat-free in a clay cooker, glazed with apricots, stuffed under the skin, dosed with rum.

For a large roaster, the capon (a castrated rooster) is preferred by some people for its flavor, meatiness, and tenderness. Capons can be substituted for large roasters in any of these recipes. They hold about the same amount of stuffing; cooking time will be the same, or slightly longer, depending on the weight of the capon.

The recipes that follow are for standard 3- to 4-pound whole chickens and for 5- to 7-pound roasters. Smaller chickens take roughly 25 minutes a pound in a 350-degree oven; larger birds roast in 15 to 20 minutes a pound. When the chicken is cooked through, the juices will run clear (as opposed to red or pink) when the thickest part of the thigh is pierced. Add an extra 15 to 20 minutes to the cooking time if the bird is stuffed.

194   SIMPLE CORNBREAD-STUFFED ROASTER

Prep: 15 minutes   Cook: 2½ hours   Serves: 6 to 8

8 **tablespoons (1 stick) butter**	½ **cup chicken broth**
1 **medium onion, chopped**	1 **egg, beaten**
½ **green bell pepper, chopped**	1 **roasting chicken, 5 to 7**
1 **package (8 ounces)**	**pounds**
cornbread stuffing	**Salt and freshly ground**
½ **teaspoon dried thyme**	**pepper**
2 **tablespoons chopped parsley**	

1. Preheat oven to 350°. In a large frying pan, melt 4 tablespoons of the butter over medium heat. Add onion and bell pepper. Cook until onion is soft, about 3 minutes. Stir in cornbread stuffing, thyme, and parsley. Add broth and beaten egg. Mix well.

2. Season roaster inside and out with salt and pepper. Fill loosely with cornbread stuffing. Tie legs together. Place in a large roasting pan. Melt remaining 4 tablespoons butter and brush over chicken.

3. Bake for 2 to 2½ hours, until juices run clear, basting every 30 minutes with pan juices. Place remaining stuffing in a greased baking dish and bake during last 30 minutes.

195   BACON ROAST CHICKEN WITH BROWN GRAVY

Prep: 20 minutes   Cook: 1½ hours   Serves: 4

The bacon here is used as a "baster." But if you prefer, it can be chopped up after use and added to the gravy.

1 **whole chicken, about**	1 **teaspoon dried thyme**
3 pounds	1 **carrot, cut in half**
1 **tablespoon butter or**	3 **slices of bacon**
margarine, softened	**Paprika**
Salt and freshly ground	1 **cup beef broth**
pepper	2 **tablespoons flour**

1. Preheat oven to 450°. Rub cavity of chicken with butter; season with salt and pepper and half the thyme. Place carrot inside and tie legs and wings to the body. Place in a shallow roasting pan. Lay bacon strips over the breast. Sprinkle with salt and paprika.

2. Roast 15 minutes. Reduce oven temperature to 350° and baste chicken with beef broth. Roast for 1 hour and 15 minutes, until tender, basting every 15 minutes.

3. Remove chicken to a warm platter and remove ties and bacon. Skim off as much fat as possible from drippings in pan. Heat drippings over medium heat. Dissolve flour in ¼ cup cold water and stir into drippings. Bring to a boil, scraping up brown bits from bottom of pan. Pour in any remaining broth and cook until thickened. If too thick, thin with water. Season to taste with salt and pepper.

196   ROAST CHICKEN WITH SAUSAGE-APPLE STUFFING

Prep: 15 minutes   Cook: 2½ hours   Serves: 8

A holiday favorite. Serve with glazed Brussels sprouts and chestnuts and candied sweet potatoes.

½ cup (1 stick) plus 2 tablespoons butter or margarine	1 cup chopped scallions
½ teaspoon dried thyme	1 pound seasoned bulk pork sausage
½ teaspoon crushed sage	1 egg, beaten
½ teaspoon dried rosemary, crumbled	2 cups cubed stale bread
½ teaspoon salt	2 tart apples, peeled, cored, and cut in ½-inch cubes
½ teaspoon freshly ground pepper	1 roasting chicken, about 6 pounds

1. Melt 1 stick butter in a small saucepan. Add thyme, sage, rosemary, salt, and pepper; set herb butter aside.

2. Preheat oven to 350°. In a large frying pan, melt remaining 2 tablespoons butter over medium heat. Add scallions and cook until wilted, 1 to 2 minutes. Scrape butter and scallions into a large bowl, set aside. Add sausage to pan and cook, stirring to crumble, until brown, about 10 minutes. Remove sausage with a slotted spoon and add to scallions.

3. Add egg, bread cubes, and apples; mix well. Loosely stuff chicken cavity; tie legs together. Place remaining stuffing in a small buttered baking dish.

4. Place chicken, breast side up, in a large roasting pan. Brush with herb butter and roast 2 to 2½ hours, until tender, basting every 30 minutes. Bake extra stuffing during last 30 minutes of roasting.

197   ROSEMARY ROAST CHICKEN WITH VEGETABLES

Prep: 20 minutes   Cook: 1½ hours   Serves: 4

1 whole chicken, about 3 pounds	4 medium potatoes, peeled and cut into 2-inch cubes
Salt and freshly ground pepper	4 small onions, peeled and quartered
1 teaspoon rosemary, crushed	4 carrots, peeled and cut into 1-inch pieces
2 tablespoons butter or margarine, softened	1 cup dry white wine

1. Preheat oven to 375°. Season chicken inside and out with salt and pepper. Place ½ teaspoon rosemary in cavity. Tie legs together and rub butter over skin. Place in a large gratin dish or roasting pan.

2. Roast chicken for 15 minutes. Arrange potatoes, carrots, and onions around chicken. Sprinkle remaining rosemary over chicken and vegetables. Pour wine over all and bake 1 hour and 15 minutes with pan drippings. (Add water as needed if wine evaporates.)

198 ROAST CHICKEN WITH RICE AND PINE NUT STUFFING

Prep: 40 minutes   Cook: 1½ hours   Serves: 4

1 whole chicken, about 3 pounds, giblets reserved	1 medium onion, chopped
1½ teaspoons salt	¼ cup pine nuts
½ teaspoons freshly ground pepper	1 cup converted rice
5 tablespoons butter	¼ cup raisins
	2 tablespoons fresh chopped parsley

1. Rinse chicken and pat dry. Season inside and out with ½ teaspoon salt and ¼ teaspoon pepper. Coarsely chop giblets.

2. In a large saucepan, melt 3 tablespoons of the butter over medium heat. Add onion and cook until soft, 3 to 5 minutes. Add giblets and pine nuts. Cook, stirring, 3 minutes, until giblets are no longer pink. Stir in rice, raisins, parsley, remaining salt and pepper, and 2¼ cups water. Bring to a boil, reduce heat to low, cover and simmer for 25 minutes, until rice has absorbed liquid.

2. Preheat oven to 375°. Stuff cavity loosely with rice mixture; spoon remainder into a buttered baking dish. Tie chicken legs together with string. Place in a small roasting pan. Melt remaining 2 tablespoons butter and brush over chicken. Bake for 1½ hours, basting with pan juices every 20 minutes, until juices run clear when thigh is pierced. Heat remaining rice stuffing in oven during last half-hour of roasting time.

199 CLAY POT ROAST CHICKEN

Prep: 20 minutes   Cook: 1¼ hours   Serves: 4

A clay pot is specialized equipment, but well worth the modest investment. It produces a rich, moist, flavorful chicken with little or no fat. Clay pots should be soaked in water before using.

1 whole chicken, about 3 pounds	½ teaspoon freshly ground pepper
12 pearl onions, peeled	½ teaspoon rosemary, crumbled
2 carrots, cut into 4-inch sticks	1 tablespoon chopped fresh parsley
2 tablespoons butter or margarine, melted	
1 garlic clove, chopped	

1. Soak top and bottom of a 2-quart clay pot in water about 15 minutes. Drain.

2. Rinse and dry chicken. Remove excess fat. Place chicken inside cooker. Place onions and carrots around chicken.

3. In a small bowl, combine butter, garlic, pepper, rosemary, and parsley. Drizzle over chicken and vegetables.

4. Cover and place cooker in middle of cold oven. Turn temperature to 450° and bake for 1 hour. Remove lid and roast uncovered 5 to 10 minutes to brown skin lightly.

200 CASSEROLE-ROASTED TARRAGON CHICKEN

Prep: 25 minutes   Cook: 1 hour   Serves: 4

This method of cooking produces an unusually tender, juicy chicken, aromatic with the grassy fragrance of tarragon, with its hint of licorice.

1 whole chicken, about
   3 pounds
1 teaspoon salt
½ teaspoon freshly ground
   pepper
1½ teaspoons dried tarragon
2 tablespoons butter
1 tablespoon vegetable oil

24 pearl onions, peeled, or 8
   small white onions,
   peeled and quartered
2 carrots, peeled and sliced
1 can (10¾ ounces) beef
   bouillon
1 tablespoon cornstarch,
   dissolved in 2 tablespoons
   of water

1. Sprinkle chicken inside and out with half the salt and pepper. Season inside with 1 teaspoon of the tarragon.

2. Preheat oven to 325°. In a large heatproof covered casserole, heat butter and oil over medium heat. Add chicken and brown on all sides, about 15 minutes. Remove chicken and set aside.

3. Remove all but 2 tablespoons of fat from casserole. Add onions and carrots. Cook, stirring occasionally, about 5 minutes, until onions are lightly browned.

4. Return chicken to casserole. Add remaining ½ teaspoon tarragon and remaining salt and pepper. Pour bouillon over all. Cover and bake 1 hour, until juices run clear when thigh is pierced. Remove to a serving platter and cover loosely with foil to keep warm.

5. Bring pan juices to a boil over medium-high heat. Stir in dissolved cornstarch. Cook, stirring, until thickened, about 2 minutes. Carve chicken and spoon a little sauce over meat. Pass remaining sauce separately.

201 HONEY-MINT ROAST CHICKEN

Prep: 10 minutes   Cook: 1⅓ hours   Serves: 6

1 roasting chicken, about
   5 pounds
   Salt and freshly ground
   pepper
½ teaspoon paprika
¼ cup honey

2 tablespoons lemon juice
2 tablespoons butter or
   margarine
2 teaspoons mint jelly
1 teaspoon grated lemon peel

1. Preheat oven to 350°. Place chicken in a large roasting pan, breast side up. Sprinkle cavity and skin with salt, pepper, and paprika. Roast 1 hour.

2. In a small saucepan, mix honey, lemon juice, butter, mint jelly, and lemon peel. Heat, stirring, until butter and jelly are melted.

3. Brush chicken with honey-mint glaze. Roast 20 minutes longer, until chicken is tender.

202 BANANA STUFFED RUM RUNNER

Prep: 30 minutes   Cook: 2 hours   Serves: 6

1 roasting chicken, about
   5 pounds
   Salt and freshly ground
   pepper
7 tablespoons butter or
   margarine
2 garlic cloves, finely chopped
1 cup seasoned bread crumbs
¼ cup fresh lime juice

1 tablespoon grated lime peel
   (green part only)
¼ cup rum
1 teaspoon brown sugar
¼ teaspoon ground nutmeg
¼ teaspoon cayenne pepper
4 firm ripe bananas, peeled
   and chopped

1. Preheat oven to 350°. Wash chicken and pat dry. Sprinkle inside and out with salt and pepper.

2. In a large frying pan, melt 3 tablespoons of the butter over medium heat. Add garlic and cook 1 minute. Add bread crumbs; cook, stirring, until crisp and brown.

3. Remove pan from heat. Stir in lime juice, lime peel, 1 tablespoon of the rum, brown sugar, nutmeg, and cayenne pepper; mix well. Add banana and toss to combine. Stuff into cavity; truss chicken.

4. Place chicken in a large roasting pan. Melt remaining 4 tablespoons butter and brush over chicken. Roast for 2 hours, until meat thermometer registers 185°. Baste occasionally with pan juices.

5. In a small saucepan, warm remaining rum. Ignite and drizzle over chicken before serving.

203 APPLE-PECAN-STUFFED CHICKEN WITH RAISINS

Prep: 20 minutes   Cook: 1½ hours   Serves: 4

1 whole chicken, about
   3 pounds
2 tablespoons vegetable oil
   Salt and freshly ground
   pepper
1½ cups seasoned stuffing mix
2 medium-size tart apples,
   peeled and grated

½ cup chopped pecans
¼ cup raisins
¼ cup finely chopped celery
2 tablespoons butter or
   margarine, melted
2 teaspoons lemon juice
½ teaspoon grated lemon peel

1. Preheat oven to 350°. Place chicken, breast side up, in a 12 x 8 x 2-inch baking dish. Rub with oil. Season inside and out with salt and pepper.

2. In a medium-size bowl, combine stuffing mix, apples, pecans, raisins, celery, melted butter, lemon juice, lemon peel, and ¼ cup water; mix well. Loosely stuff chicken cavity; tie legs together. Roast 1½ hours, until chicken is tender.

204 CASSEROLE-ROASTED CHICKEN WITH TOMATOES, PROSCIUTTO, AND ZUCCHINI

Prep: 25 minutes   Cook: 2 to 2¼ hours   Serves: 6

1 roasting chicken, 5 to 7 pounds	1 green bell pepper, cut into strips
Salt and freshly ground pepper	1 can (16 ounces) crushed tomatoes
4 tablespoons butter	¼ pound prosciutto, chopped
1 tablespoon vegetable oil	½ cup dry Marsala
2 medium onions, chopped	1 teaspoon dried basil
1 garlic clove, crushed	2 medium zucchini, sliced

1. Preheat oven to 350°. Season chicken inside and out with salt and pepper. In a large covered roasting pan, heat butter and oil over medium-high heat. Add chicken and brown all over, about 15 minutes. Remove chicken and set aside.

2. Pour off all but 3 tablespoons fat. Add onions and garlic. Cook over medium heat until onions are soft, about 3 minutes. Add bell pepper; cook 3 minutes. Add tomatoes, prosciutto, Marsala, and basil. Bring to a boil; return chicken to pan.

3. Cover tightly and bake 1¾ hours. Add zucchini and bake 15 to 30 minutes longer, until juices run clear when thigh is pierced.

205 ROAST CHICKEN WITH CASBAH STUFFING

Prep: 15 minutes   Cook: 2½ to 3 hours   Serves: 6

Couscous, used instead of bread or rice here, is available in specialty food stores or gourmet sections in grocery stores. This stuffing recipe can also be used for 12 chicken thighs; loosen skin from meat and stuff under the skin. Bake 1 hour and 15 minutes.

2 cups chicken broth	½ cup golden raisins
5 tablespoons butter or margarine	½ cup chopped carrots
2 teaspoons cinnamon	1 medium onion, finely chopped
1 teaspoon ground cardamom	⅓ cup lemon juice
½ teaspoon turmeric	1 roasting chicken, about 6 pounds
½ teaspoon cumin	Salt and freshly ground pepper
1 cup couscous	
¾ cup chopped dates	

1. Preheat oven to 350°. In a large saucepan over medium-high heat, combine chicken broth and 2 tablespoons of the butter. Heat to boiling; reduce heat to medium. Stir in cinnamon, cardamom, turmeric, cumin, and couscous. Cook 1 minute; remove from heat. Let stand 10 minutes to cool.

2. To couscous add dates, raisins, carrots, onion, and lemon juice. Mix well.

3. Place roaster, breast side up, in a large roasting pan. Fill loosely with stuffing mixture. Tie legs. Sprinkle skin with salt and pepper. Melt remaining 3 tablespoons butter and brush over chicken. Roasts 2½ to 3 hours, basting occasionally.

206 STUFFED SESAME CHICKEN
Prep: 25 minutes   Cook: 1½ hours   Serves: 8

A mahogany honey-soy glaze and toasted sesame seeds make this a handsome presentation.

2 tablespoons vegetable oil
1 large onion, chopped
¾ pound ground veal
2 cups stuffing croutons or cubed stale bread
½ cup heavy cream
1 can (3 ounces) water chestnuts, drained and chopped

2 eggs, beaten
¼ cup soy sauce
2 teaspoons grated fresh ginger
2 whole chickens, 3 pounds each
4 tablespoons butter, melted
¼ cup honey
¼ cup sesame seeds

1. Preheat oven to 350°. In a medium-size frying pan, he.. .eget...e oil over medium heat. Add onion and cook until soft, about 3 minutes. Add veal; cook until meat is lightly browned, 5 to 7 minutes.

2. In a large bowl, combine stuffing croutons and cream. Let stand 1 minute. Add water chestnuts, eggs, 2 tablespoons of the soy sauce, and ginger. Mix well. Blend in veal-onion mixture.

3. Spoon stuffing into chicken cavities, filling loosely; reserve any excess. Tie chicken legs with string; place in a large roasting pan.

4. Combine butter, honey, and remaining 2 tablespoons soy sauce; brush over chickens. Bake, basting every 30 minutes, 1½ hours, until juices run clear. Place the excess stuffing in a small baking dish and bake 30 minutes before chickens are done.

5. Sprinkle chickens with sesame seeds. Bake 10 minutes longer, until seeds are lightly browned.

207 ROAST CHICKEN WITH LEMON
Prep: 5 minutes   Cook: 1¼ hours   Serves: 4

1 whole chicken, about 3 pounds
Salt and freshly ground pepper

1 garlic clove, split in half
1 lemon, quartered
1 small onion, quartered

1. Preheat oven to 350°. Rinse chicken inside and out; pat dry. Season inside and out with salt and pepper. Rub garlic over the skin, then place inside cavity. Stuff lemon and onion inside cavity. Tie legs together. Place chicken breast side up in a roasting pan.

2. Bake 1 hour and 15 minutes, until juices run clear.

208 ROAST ORANGE CHICKEN IN CLAY POT
Prep: 20 minutes   Cook: 1¼ hours   Serves: 4

⅓ cup brown sugar
1 teaspoon grated orange peel
1 cup orange juice
  Dash of hot pepper sauce
1 whole chicken, about
   3 pounds

1 tablespoon butter or
   margarine, softened
2 orange slices, halved
1 tablespoon cornstarch
   dissolved in 2 tablespoons
   water

1. Soak top and bottom of a 2-quart clay pot in water about 15 minutes. Drain.

2. In a small bowl combine brown sugar, orange peel, orange juice, and hot sauce.

3. Rinse and dry the chicken; remove excess fat around the cavity. Rub with butter and place inside pot. Pour sauce over all. Secure orange slices on top of chicken with wooden toothpicks.

4. Cover and place cooker in the middle of a cold oven. Turn the oven on to 475° and bake 1 hour. Remove the lid and bake uncovered for 10 minutes to brown the skin lightly.

5. Remove chicken to a heated platter. Place sauce in a small saucepan and heat over medium-high heat. Add dissolved cornstarch to liquid and cook, stirring constantly, until sauce thickens and bubbles. Serve with chicken.

209 ROAST CHICKEN WITH FENNEL STUFFING
Prep: 30 minutes   Cook: 1½ hours   Serves: 4

Fennel is a winter vegetable that resembles overgrown celery. It has a delicate anise flavor. The tough fibrous stalks are discarded and only the large bulb is used. Sometimes the feathery green leaves are added for color. The stuffing here becomes a light vegetable purée.

2 tablespoons olive oil
3 tablespoons butter
1 shallot, finely chopped
1 garlic clove, crushed
   through a press
1 large fennel bulb, chopped;
   reserve 3 tablespoons
   chopped green leaves

2 tablespoons Pernod
¼ teaspoon salt
¼ teaspoon freshly ground
   pepper
1 whole chicken, about
   3 pounds

1. In a large frying pan, heat oil and 1 tablespoon of the butter over medium heat. Add shallot; cook until softened, about 2 minutes. Add garlic, fennel, and fennel leaves. Cover and cook over low heat 20 minutes, until fennel is tender but not brown. Add Pernod, salt, and pepper; mix well.

2. Preheat oven to 375°. Stuff chicken loosely with fennel mixture. Tie legs together and place in a small roasting pan, breast side up. Melt remaining butter and brush over chicken. Bake 1½ hours, basting frequently with pan juices, until juices run clear when thigh is pierced.

210 EASY LEMON-MUSHROOM-STUFFED CHICKEN

Prep: 20 minutes   Cook: 2½ hours   Serves: 6

7 tablespoons butter or margarine
1 medium onion, finely chopped
¼ pound mushrooms, sliced
3½ cups seasoned croutons
1 egg, beaten
2 tablespoons chopped parsley
2 teaspoons grated lemon peel
1 garlic clove, crushed through a press
1 tablespoon fresh lemon juice
1 roasting chicken, about 6 pounds
Salt and freshly ground pepper

1. Preheat oven to 350°. In a large frying pan, melt 4 tablespoons of the butter over medium heat. Add onion and mushrooms and cook until onion is tender and mushrooms are lightly browned, about 5 minutes. Remove from heat. Add croutons, egg, parsley, lemon peel, and ¾ cup water; toss to mix well.

2. In a small saucepan, melt remaining 3 tablespoons butter. Add garlic and lemon juice; set aside.

3. Place chicken in a large roasting pan. Fill loosely with stuffing. Tie legs together. Season skin with salt and pepper. Brush with garlic butter.

4. Roast 2½ hours, basting occasionally, until chicken is tender.

211 MARTHA STEWART'S HERB-ROASTED CHICKEN WITH BAKED SHALLOTS

Prep: 10 minutes   Cook: 1¼ hours   Serves: 4

1 roasting chicken, 5 to 6 pounds
Coarse (kosher) salt and freshly ground pepper to taste
Juice of 1 lemon
10 sprigs fresh thyme
6 sprigs fresh rosemary
6 sprigs fresh sage
16 shallots, peeled and left whole
6 garlic cloves, unpeeled
½ cup dry white wine

1. Preheat oven to 400°.

2. Rub inside of chicken with salt and pepper and lemon juice. Fill cavity with half the fresh herbs. Truss bird firmly with kitchen string.

3. Put chicken, breast side up, in a shallow heavy roasting pan. Put pan in middle of oven and roast for 15 minutes.

4. After 15 minutes, put shallots and garlic around chicken. Add most of remaining herbs to pan, leaving a few for decoration. Pour white wine over shallots and garlic and return pan to oven. Roast for another 45 minutes, until thigh juices run clear.

5. Arrange bird on a heated serving platter and distribute shallots and garlic around it. Decorate with remaining herbs and serve.

212 SLEEPING ITALIAN ROASTER
Prep: 20 minutes   Cook: 1½ hours   Serves: 8

By removing the backbone and butterflying the bird, this roaster cooks faster and is easier to carve.

1 **roasting chicken, about 6 pounds, backbone removed**
5 **tablespoons butter or margerine**
1 **large onion, chopped**
2 **cups grated zucchini**
1 **cup ricotta cheese**
1 **egg, beaten**

2 **cups stale bread cubes**
½ **teaspoon dried marjoram**
1 **teaspoon salt**
¼ **teaspoon freshly ground pepper**
1 **garlic clove, crushed through a press**
1 **teaspoon dried basil**
½ **teaspoon dried oregano**

1. Preheat oven to 350°. Flatten chicken and place in a large roasting pan, skin side up. Starting at the breast, gently pull skin away from meat without tearing, slowly working your hand between skin and meat along thighs and legs.

2. In a large frying pan, melt 3 tablespoons of the butter over medium heat. Add onion and cook until tender, about 3 minutes. Add zucchini and cook until wilted, about 3 minutes longer; remove from heat. Add ricotta cheese, egg, bread cubes, marjoram, salt, and pepper; mix well.

3. Spoon stuffing under the skin working over breast, thigh, and leg areas, smoothing it evenly under skin.

4. In a small saucepan, melt remaining 2 tablespoons butter. Add garlic, basil, and oregano. Brush chicken with seasoned butter. Roast 1½ hours until tender and juices run clear, basting every 20 or 30 minutes.

213 HERBED-ROASTED CHICKEN IN A BAG
Prep: 10 minutes   Cook: 50 minutes   Serves: 4

1 **tablespoon flour**
2 **small onions, quartered**
2 **celery ribs, coarsely chopped**
1 **whole chicken, about 3 pounds**
Salt and freshly ground pepper

2 **tablespoons butter, melted**
1 **teaspoon dried thyme**
½ **teaspoon rosemary, crumbled**
½ **teaspoon crushed sage**

1. Preheat oven to 325°. Shake flour in a 10 x 16-inch oven cooking bag. Place in a 13 x 9 x 2-inch baking dish. Scatter onions and celery in bottom of bag.

2. Season chicken cavity with salt and pepper. Place in bag on top of vegetables.

3. Combine butter, thyme, rosemary, and sage in a small bowl. Brush chicken with herbed butter.

4. Close bag with nylon tie. Make six ½-inch slits in top for steam to escape. Bake 50 minutes, until juices run clear.

Chapter 13

Chicken in the Oven

The biggest difference between these chicken recipes and those in the preceding "Roasted" chapter is that here the chickens are cut up, or single parts are used. Consequently, cooking times are only 45 minutes to an hour at most. These recipes employ all sorts of sauces and seasonings, which seep in slowly as the chicken bakes, because so much surface area of the meat is exposed.

214 FORTY CLOVES OF GARLIC
Prep: 10 minutes   Cook: 1½ hours   Serves: 4

You may be surprised at how mild all this garlic becomes. With long, slow cooking, the cloves perfume the chicken and can be eaten separately as a vegetable or spread on bread.

2 tablespoons butter	½ teaspoon dried thyme
1 tablespoon olive oil	1 teaspoon salt
1 chicken (3 pounds), cut up	¼ teaspoon freshly ground
40 garlic cloves, unpeeled	pepper
2 tablespoons lemon juice	

1. Preheat oven to 350°. In a large Dutch oven, melt butter in oil. Add chicken and cook, turning, until golden, 5 to 10 minutes.

2. Tilt pan and spoon off all but 2 tablespoons fat. Add garlic and stir to coat. Sprinkle with lemon juice, thyme, salt, pepper, and ¼ cup water.

3. Cover tightly and bake 1½ hours.

215 ZUCCHINI-STUFFED CHICKEN WITH POTATOES
Prep: 25 minutes   Cook: 1¼ hours   Serves: 4

¾ pound zucchini, shredded	½ cup ricotta cheese
1 teaspoon salt	2 tablespoons grated
4 medium potatoes, thinly	Parmesan cheese
sliced	1 egg, beaten
Freshly ground pepper	3 pounds chicken thighs
6 tablespoons butter or	(8 pieces)
margarine	1 tablespoon minced parsley
½ cup chopped onion	½ teaspoon dried tarragon
1 garlic clove, finely chopped	½ teaspoon dried basil
1 cup seasoned croutons	

1. Spread shredded zucchini on paper towels. Sprinkle with salt. Let zucchini sweat for 15 minutes; blot with additional towels to remove excess water.

2. Line a lightly greased 13 x 9 x 2-inch baking dish with two layers of sliced potatoes. Season with salt and pepper to taste.

3. In a medium-size frying pan, melt 2 tablespoons of the butter over medium heat. Add onion and sauté about 3 minutes, until tender. Add garlic and cook 1 minute. Add zucchini; cook another 3 minutes. Remove from heat. Add croutons, ricotta cheese, Parmesan cheese, and egg; mix well.

4. Preheat oven to 450°. Prepare chicken thighs by pulling the skin away from the meat without removing it. Stuff zucchini mixture between skin and meat. Place skin side up on top of potatoes.

5. In a small saucepan, melt remaining 4 tablespoons butter, add parsley, tarragon, and basil. Brush chicken thighs with herb butter. Bake uncovered for 15 minutes; baste. Reduce heat to 375°. Bake 45 minutes longer, until chicken is tender, basting every 15 minutes.

216 LIME-HONEY-GLAZED CHICKEN
Prep: 10 minutes   Marinate: 3 hours   Cook: 50 minutes   Serves: 4

2 teaspoons cinnamon	1 garlic clove, finely chopped
1 chicken (3 pounds), cut up	½ teaspoon salt
½ cup honey	¼ teaspoon freshly ground
½ cup dry sherry	pepper
2 tablespoons fresh lime juice	

1. Sprinkle cinnamon over chicken and arrange in a 12 x 8 x 2-inch baking dish.

2. In a small bowl, combine remaining ingredients. Pour over chicken pieces. Cover and marinate in refrigerator at least 3 hours, turning pieces occasionally.

3. Preheat oven to 350°. Bake 50 minutes, basting frequently with pan juices.

217 FRANK'S OTHER FAVORITE
Prep: 10 minutes   Cook: 50 minutes   Serves: 4

Along with "Chicken à la Nancy" (p. 80) this recipe for "Sweet 'N Smoky Chicken" is Frank Perdue's personal favorite.

1 large onion, sliced	¼ cup ketchup
1 chicken (3 pounds), cut up	¼ cup maple syrup
½ teaspoon hickory-smoked	2 tablespoons cider vinegar
salt	1 tablespoon Dijon mustard
⅛ teaspoon freshly ground	
pepper	

1. Preheat oven to 350°. Place onion slices in a 13 x 9 x 2-inch baking dish. Arrange chicken in a single layer, skin side up, on top of onion. Sprinkle with hickory salt and pepper.

2. In a small bowl, combine ketchup, maple syrup, vinegar, and mustard, mixing well. Pour over chicken. Bake uncovered for 50 minutes, until chicken is tender.

218 QUICK-AND-EASY BOURBON BARBECUE
Prep: 10 minutes   Marinate: 2 hours   Cook: 1¼ hours   Serves: 4

For great barbecue, you don't necessarily need a grill. Here's an oven-baked version, tangy and finger-licking good.

1 chicken (3 pounds), cup up	2 tablespoons Worcestershire
1 bottle (14-ounces) hickory-	sauce
smoked barbecue sauce	2 tablespoons bourbon
	2 tablespoons Dijon mustard

1. Arrange chicken pieces in 13 x 9 x 2-inch baking dish.

2. In a bowl, combine barbecue sauce, Worcestershire, bourbon, and mustard. Pour over chicken. Cover and marinate at least 2 hours, or refrigerate overnight, turning once.

3. Preheat oven to 350°. Bake uncovered, basting every 15 minutes, for 1 hour and 15 minutes, until chicken is tender.

219 COLA OVEN BARBECUE
Prep: 10 minutes   Cook: 2¼ hours   Serves: 4

2 tablespoons butter
1 medium onion, finely
   chopped
2 garlic cloves, finely chopped
1 bay leaf, crumbled
2 cups ketchup
6 ounces cola

1 tablespoon Worcestershire
   sauce
1 teaspoon dry mustard
2 teaspoons cider vinegar
   Salt and freshly ground
   pepper
1 chicken (3 pounds), cut up

1. In a large nonaluminum saucepan, melt butter over low heat. Add onion and garlic and cook until onion is soft, about 5 minutes. Add bay leaf, cola, ketchup, Worcestershire, mustard, vinegar, and salt and pepper to taste. Simmer sauce 1 hour, stirring occasionally.

2. Preheat oven to 350°. Pour ½ cup sauce in bottom of a 13 x 9 x 2-inch baking dish. Arrange chicken pieces skin side up in dish. Spoon ½ cup more sauce over chicken. Bake for 30 minutes. Turn chicken, baste, and bake another 30 minutes.

3. Turn oven to broil. Spoon ½ remaining sauce over chicken. Broil until crisp, about 4 minutes. Turn chicken over and spoon on remaining sauce; broil until crisp.

220 BAKED LEMON CHICKEN WITH RAISINS AND COGNAC
Prep: 1 hour   Cook: 1 hour   Serves: 6

¾ cup golden raisins
¼ cup Cognac
3 tablespoons butter or
   margarine
1 tablespoon vegetable oil
4 pounds chicken parts

4 medium onions, sliced
   Rind of 1 lemon, minced
   (yellow part only)
3 tablespoons fresh lemon
   juice

1. In a small bowl, combine raisins, Cognac, and ½ cup water; soak for 45 minutes.

2. In a large frying pan, heat butter and vegetable oil over medium heat. Sauté chicken in batches until brown, about 5 minutes a side. Transfer to a 14 x 12 x 2½-inch roasting pan.

3. Preheat oven to 350°. Add onions to drippings in frying pan and cook until tender, about 5 minutes. Add raisin-Cognac mixture, lemon rind, and lemon juice. Mix and pour over chicken. Bake for 50 minutes, until chicken is tender.

221 ITALIAN-STYLE OVEN DINNER
Prep: 15 minutes   Cook: 1¼ hours   Serves: 6 to 8

4 baking potatoes, cut into wedges
½ teaspoon salt
2 garlic cloves, minced
1 red bell pepper, sliced
1 green bell pepper, sliced
1 can (28 ounces) Italian peeled tomatoes, drained and cut up

1 pound Italian hot or sweet sausage cut into 2-inch segments
1 chicken (3 pounds), cut up
1 tablespoon olive oil
½ teaspoon coarsely cracked black pepper

1. Preheat oven to 350°. Arrange potatoes in a large roasting pan. Sprinkle with ¼ teaspoon of the salt and the garlic. Layer peppers, tomatoes, and sausage over potatoes. Arrange chicken on top.

2. Brush chicken with olive oil. Sprinkle with remaining salt and pepper. Bake uncovered 1 hour and 15 minutes, until tender.

222 ORIENTAL HOT AND SPICY CHICKEN
Prep: 10 minutes   Cook: 1 hour   Serves: 4

3 pounds chicken thighs, skinned
3 tablespoons butter or margarine
2 tablespoons Oriental sesame oil

1 tablespoon sesame seeds
1 tablespoon cider vinegar
2 teaspoons soy sauce
1 teaspoon hot pepper sauce
1 teaspoon dry mustard
1 garlic clove, crushed

1. Preheat oven to 350°. Place chicken thighs in a 13 x 9 x 2-inch baking dish.

2. In a small saucepan, mix butter, sesame oil, sesame seeds, vinegar, soy sauce, hot sauce, mustard, and garlic. Cook over medium heat until butter melts and garlic is fragrant.

3. Brush half of butter mixture over chicken, coating completely. Bake uncovered for 30 minutes. Turn chicken and brush with remaining butter. Bake 20 minutes more, until tender.

223 ZESTY CHICKEN LEGS
Prep: 10 minutes   Cook: 1 hour   Serves: 4

2 tablespoons vegetable oil
3 pounds chicken legs
1 cup chopped celery
1 cup chopped onion
1 cup tomato juice

3 tablespoons cider vinegar
½ teaspoon salt
¼ teaspoon freshly ground pepper
¼ teaspoon hot pepper sauce

1. Preheat oven to 350°. In a large frying pan, heat oil over medium heat. Add chicken and cook, turning, until brown, about 10 minutes. Transfer to a 13 x 9 x 2-inch baking dish.

2. Add celery and onion to the pan drippings and sauté until tender but not brown, 3 to 5 minutes. Stir in tomato juice, vinegar, salt, pepper, and hot sauce. Heat to boiling; pour over chicken.

3. Bake chicken uncovered, basting occasionally, 45 minutes, until tender. Skim excess fat from sauce and pour over chicken.

224 HONEY-MUSTARD BAKED CHICKEN
Prep: 10 minutes   Cook: 1 hour   Serves: 4

Mustard and honey make a delicious glaze for chicken, lightly spiced, slightly sweet.

1 chicken (3 pounds), cut up
½ cup (1 stick) butter or
    margarine, melted
½ cup honey

¼ cup Dijon mustard
½ teaspoon salt
¼ teaspoon freshly ground
    pepper

1. Preheat oven to 350°. Place chicken pieces in a 13 x 9 x 2-inch baking dish.

2. Combine butter, honey, mustard, salt, and pepper. Spread over chicken. Bake 1 hour, basting with pan juices every 15 minutes, until chicken is tender and golden brown.

225 BAKED PARMESAN CHICKEN
Prep: 10 minutes   Cook: 55 minutes   Serves: 4

1 chicken (3 pounds), cut up
    Salt and freshly ground
    pepper
3 tablespoons butter or
    margarine

½ cup grated Parmesan cheese
2 tablespoons flour
1 cup milk
½ cup shredded Swiss cheese
¼ cup bread crumbs

1. Preheat oven to 350°. Season chicken with salt and pepper. In a large frying pan, melt butter over medium heat. Add chicken and cook, turning, until browned, about 10 minutes.

2. Sprinkle ¼ cup of the Parmesan cheese over bottom of a 13 x 9 x 2-inch baking dish. Arrange chicken in dish.

3. In same frying pan, whisk flour into pan drippings. Cook, stirring, for 1 minute. Gradually add milk and cook, stirring constantly, until smooth and thick. Remove from heat and stir in Swiss cheese. Pour sauce over chicken.

4. Top chicken with remaining ¼ cup Parmesan cheese. Sprinkle with bread crumbs. Bake for 45 minutes, until chicken is tender.

226   BONED STUFFED CHICKEN THIGHS
Prep: 15 minutes   Cook: 1 hour   Serves: 4

To cut costs, bone thighs at home: place on a cutting board with skin side down. With a sharp knife, cut along thin side, joint to joint. Cut meat from one joint and scrape meat from bone. Cut meat from other joint.

3 slices bacon	2 tablespoons dry sherry
½ cup finely chopped celery	1 teaspoon garlic salt
½ cup finely chopped onion	8 chicken thighs, boned
½ cup seasoned bread crumbs	

1. In a small frying pan, cook bacon over medium heat 5 minutes, until crisp. Remove and drain on paper towels. Crumble and set aside.

2. Preheat oven to 350°. Remove all but 2 tablespoons bacon drippings from frying pan, reserving the excess. Add celery and onion to pan drippings; cook until tender, 3 to 5 minutes. Remove from heat; stir in crumbled bacon, bread crumbs, sherry, and garlic salt.

3. Place 2 tablespoons of stuffing into each chicken thigh and secure with a wooden toothpick. Arrange in a 12 x 8 x 2-inch baking dish. Brush with reserved bacon drippings. Bake 1 hour, until chicken is tender. Remove picks before serving.

227   BAKED CHICKEN WITH CITRUS SAUCE
Prep: 25 minutes   Cook: 1 hour   Serves: 4

This is a great entrée for a party.

1 cup bread crumbs	1 chicken (3 pounds), cut up
¼ cup grated Parmesan cheese	1 tablespoon cornstarch
¼ cup sesame seeds	¼ teaspoon ground ginger
2 tablespoons chopped fresh parsley	Shredded rind and juice of 1 orange
½ teaspoon salt	1 jar (10 ounces) currant jelly
¼ teaspoon freshly ground pepper	2 tablespoons Dijon mustard
¼ teaspoon paprika	3 drops hot pepper sauce
4 tablespoons butter or margarine, melted	Shredded rind of 1 lemon

1. Preheat oven to 350°. In a shallow dish, combine bread crumbs, Parmesan cheese, sesame seeds, parsley, salt, pepper, and paprika. Place melted butter in a second shallow dish.

2. Dip chicken pieces in melted butter; then dredge in crumb mixture, turning to coat. Arrange chicken in a 13 x 9 x 2-inch baking dish. Bake for 50 minutes, until golden brown and tender.

3. In a small saucepan, combine cornstarch and ginger. Stir in orange juice, currant jelly, mustard, and hot pepper sauce. Cook over medium heat, stirring until smooth; add shredded orange and lemon rind. Serve separately with chicken.

228   CHICKEN ROMANO
Prep: 20 minutes   Cook: 30 minutes   Serves: 4

1 pound fresh spinach, rinsed, steamed, and chopped	¼ teaspoon nutmeg
3 tablespoons butter or margarine	½ cup shredded Swiss cheese
3 tablespoons flour	2 cups chopped, cooked chicken
1¾ cups milk	½ pound mushrooms, halved
1 teaspoon salt	¼ cup seasoned bread crumbs
¼ teaspoon pepper	¼ cup grated Parmesan cheese

1. Preheat oven to 350°. Place spinach in a large saucepan with 2 tablespoons water. Cover and steam until tender, about 3 minutes. Drain well; press between paper towels to squeeze out excess water. Transfer to a 12 x 8 x 2-inch baking dish.

2. In a large saucepan, melt butter over medium heat. Stir in flour and cook, stirring, for 1 minute without browning. Gradually whisk in milk. Add salt, pepper, and nutmeg. Cook, stirring constantly, until mixture thickens and comes to a boil. Reduce heat to low, add Swiss cheese, and cook until melted.

3. Remove sauce from heat. Add chicken and mushrooms. Pour over spinach.

4. Combine bread crumbs and Parmesan cheese; sprinkle over chicken. Bake for 20 minutes, until bubbly and lightly browned on top.

229   OVEN CHICKEN CROQUETTES
Prep: 20 minutes   Chill: 2 hours   Cook: 40 minutes   Serves: 4

Old-fashioned creamy chicken croquettes made without frying. Serve with fresh cranberry relish.

5 tablespoons butter	1¼ cups bread crumbs
3 tablespoons flour	3 tablespoons chopped fresh parsley
½ cup milk	¼ teaspoon salt
½ cup chicken broth	2 eggs, beaten
2 cups finely chopped cooked chicken	¼ cup grated Parmesan cheese

1. In a medium-size saucepan, melt 3 tablespoons of the butter over medium heat. Add flour and cook, stirring, for 1 to 2 minutes without browning. Gradually whisk in milk and broth and cook, stirring constantly, until smooth and thickened. Remove from heat; let cool for 5 minutes.

2. In a large bowl, combine chicken, 1 cup of the bread crumbs, parsley, salt, and eggs. Mix well. Pour in sauce, blend, and cover. Chill 2 hours, until set.

3. Preheat oven to 350°. Combine Parmesan cheese and remaining ¼ cup bread crumbs in a shallow dish. Shape chicken mixture into 2½- to 3-inch balls, then roll into ovals (makes about 8). Roll croquettes in bread crumb mixture.

4. Arrange croquettes in a greased 12 x 8 x 2-inch baking dish. Melt remaining 2 tablespoons butter and drizzle over croquettes. Bake 30 minutes, until golden brown.

230 CHICKEN THIGHS STUFFED WITH BROCCOLI AND CARROTS
Prep: 10 minutes   Cook: 50 minutes   Serves: 4

2 tablespoons butter or
    margarine
1 cup grated carrots
1 cup finely chopped broccoli
1 onion, chopped

2 pounds deboned chicken
    thighs (8 pieces)
1 cup seasoned bread crumbs
¼ cup grated Parmesan cheese
4 tablespoons butter, melted

1. In a medium-size frying pan, melt butter over medium-high heat. Add carrots, broccoli, and onion and cook, tossing often, 5 minutes, until broccoli is crisp-tender.

2. Preheat oven to 350°. Place 2 to 3 tablespoons vegetable mixture in center of each chicken thigh. Fold up chicken and secure with wooden toothpicks.

3. Combine bread crumbs and Parmesan cheese in a shallow dish. Place melted butter in separate shallow dish. Dip chicken first in butter, then roll in bread crumbs. Place in a 12 x 8 x 2-inch baking dish. Bake 45 minutes, until chicken is tender.

231 CHICKEN WITH WINE HERB SAUCE
Prep: 10 minutes   Cook: 50 minutes   Serves: 4

2 tablespoons butter or
    margarine
2 tablespoons chopped onion
2 tablespoons chopped parsley
½ teaspoon dried oregano
½ teaspoon poultry seasoning

¼ teaspoon dried tarragon
¼ teaspoon dried marjoram
½ cup dry white wine
1 chicken (3 pounds), cut up
¼ cup grated Parmesan cheese
1 teaspoon paprika

1. Preheat oven to 350°. In a small saucepan, melt butter over medium heat. Add onion and cook until tender, about 3 minutes. Stir in parsley, oregano, poultry seasoning, tarragon, marjoram, and wine. Boil 5 minutes, until sauce is reduced by one-third.

2. Arrange chicken in a 13 x 9 x 2-inch baking dish. Brush herb sauce over chicken. Sprinkle with Parmesan cheese and paprika. Bake 45 minutes, until tender.

232 BAKED CHICKEN CACCIATORA
Prep: 20 minutes   Cook: 55 minutes   Serves: 4

½ cup flour
1 chicken (3 pounds), cut up
¼ cup vegetable oil
1 can (8 ounces) tomato sauce
½ cup dry red wine
½ teaspoon dried oregano
½ teaspoon salt

¼ teaspoon freshly ground
    pepper
4 garlic cloves, minced
2 green bell peppers, cored,
    seeded, and sliced
½ pound mushrooms, sliced
¼ cup grated Parmesan cheese

1. Place flour in a paper bag; shake chicken pieces in flour to coat. In a large frying pan, heat oil. Add chicken and cook, turning, until browned, about 10 minutes. Remove to a 13 x 9 x 2-inch baking dish.

2. While chicken is browning, mix tomato sauce, wine, oregano, salt, and pepper in a small bowl.

3. Add garlic to pan drippings and sauté 1 minute. Add bell peppers and mushrooms; cook 5 minutes. Stir in tomato sauce mixture. Pour over chicken.

5. Cover with foil and bake at 350° for 45 minutes, until chicken is tender. Sprinkle with Parmesan cheese.

---

233   VIA VENETO CHICKEN
Prep: 20 minutes   Cook: 1½ hours   Serves: 8

6 tablespoons butter or margarine	2 chickens (3 pounds each), quartered
1¼ cups flour	2 tablespoons vegetable oil
2 cups milk	3 large onions, sliced
½ teaspoon white pepper	¼ pound boiled ham, cut into thick strips
½ cup grated white Cheddar cheese	1 can (28 ounces) Italian peeled tomatoes, drained and finely chopped
¼ teaspoon freshly ground black pepper	1 teaspoon dried basil

1. Preheat oven to 350°. In a medium-size saucepan, melt 4 tablespoons of the butter over medium heat. Whisk in ¼ cup of the flour and cook, stirring, 2 minutes without browning. Gradually whisk in milk. Bring to a boil and cook, stirring, until thickened; season with white pepper. Remove from heat and stir in Cheddar cheese.

2. Place remaining 1 cup flour and black pepper in a plastic or paper bag. Add chicken quarters and shake to coat. In a large frying pan, melt remaining 2 tablespoons butter in oil over medium heat. Brown chicken in pan in batches, about 4 minutes on each side; remove to a large roasting pan.

3. Add onions to frying pan and cook 3 minutes, until softened. Add ham, tomatoes, cheese sauce, and basil. Cook 5 minutes. Pour sauce over chicken and cover. Bake 1 hour.

4. Arrange chicken on a large heated platter. Coat lightly with sauce. Pass remaining sauce separately.

234   GARLICKY BAKED CHICKEN
Prep: 20 minutes   Cook: 55 minutes   Serves: 4

This is a variation of the traditional forty-clove chicken. After long cooking, the garlic becomes mild and buttery, a treat to spread on bread.

1 whole chicken, (3 pounds), cut up
2 large heads of garlic, separated into cloves
3 celery ribs, cut into 1-inch pieces
¾ cup dry white wine
¼ cup olive oil
3 tablespoons fresh lemon juice

2 tablespoons chopped parsley
2 tablespoons chopped fresh basil, or ¾ teaspoon dried
¼ teaspoon salt
¼ teaspoon freshly ground pepper
¼ teaspoon crushed hot pepper
½ teaspoon grated lemon rind

1. Preheat oven to 375°. Arrange chicken in a 13 x 9 x 2-inch baking dish, skin side up. Sprinkle garlic cloves and celery over chicken.

2. Combine wine, oil, lemon juice, parsley, basil, salt, pepper, and hot pepper. Pour over chicken. Sprinkle lemon rind on top.

3. Bake, covered, for 40 minutes. Uncover and bake 15 minutes, until chicken is tender.

235   CHICKEN GUIANAS
Prep: 30 minutes   Cook: 50 minutes   Serves: 4

The flavor of this is typical of many South American dishes, but canned tomato soup provides an easy shortcut.

2 tablespoons vegetable oil
1 chicken (3 pounds), cut up
1 medium-size onion, chopped
½ cup chopped celery
1 can (10 ¾ ounces) condensed tomato soup

¾ teaspoon nutmeg
3 cups shredded potatoes
1 cup shredded carrots
⅓ cup orange juice
½ teaspoon salt
⅛ teaspoon freshly ground pepper

1. Preheat oven to 375°. In a large frying pan, heat oil over medium heat. Add chicken and cook until brown, about 5 minutes a side. Remove chicken and set aside.

2. Add onion and celery to pan. Cook until onion is tender, about 3 minutes. Stir in soup and nutmeg. Bring to a boil; remove and reserve ½ cup of soup mixture.

3. To remaining soup mixture in pan, add potatoes, carrots, orange juice, salt, and pepper. Stir well and turn into a greased 13 x 9 x 2-inch baking dish. Top with chicken. Pour ½ cup reserved soup mixture over chicken. Bake 50 minutes, until chicken is tender.

236 CABBAGE AND CHICKEN
Prep: 30 minutes   Cook: 1 hour   Serves: 4

½ cup flour
1½ teaspoons seasoned salt
1 teaspoon celery seed
3 pounds chicken legs
½ cup vegetable oil
1 medium onion, chopped
1 can (14 ounces) Italian peeled tomatoes
1 can (8 ounces) tomato sauce

2 apples, peeled, cored, and chopped
2 teaspoons caraway seed
1 teaspoon salt
1 teaspoon sugar
4 cups shredded cabbage
1 cup shredded mozzarella cheese

1. In a paper or plastic bag, mix flour, seasoned salt, and celery seed. Add chicken legs, a few pieces at a time, and shake to coat.

2. In a large frying pan, heat oil over medium heat. Add chicken and cook, turning, until browned, about 10 minutes. Transfer to a 13 x 9 x 2-inch baking dish.

3. Preheat oven to 350°. In the same pan, cook onion about 3 minutes, until tender. Add tomatoes, tomato sauce, apples, caraway seed, salt, and sugar. Bring to a boil. Add cabbage and mix well. Spoon mixture over chicken.

4. Cover with foil and bake 1 hour, until chicken is tender. Remove foil; sprinkle mozzarella cheese over chicken. Return to oven for about 5 minutes, until cheese melts.

237 BAKED CHICKEN WITH POTATOES LYONNAISE
Prep: 15 minutes   Cook: 1 hour   Serves: 4

1 chicken (3 pounds), cut up
6 tablespoons butter or margarine, melted
2 garlic cloves, crushed through a press
¾ teaspoon dried thyme
2 tablespoons minced fresh parsley

4 medium baking potatoes, peeled and thinly sliced
Salt and freshly ground pepper
2 medium onions, thinly sliced

1. Preheat oven to 350°. Gently pull chicken skin away from flesh without removing; leave skin attached at several points. Combine melted butter, garlic, thyme, and parsley in a small bowl. Using a pastry brush, paint the butter mixture all over chicken and under the skin.

2. Arrange potato slices, overlapping slightly, in a lightly greased 13 x 9 x 2-inch baking dish. Season with salt and pepper. Arrange onion slices on top.

3. Place chicken pieces, skin side up, on top of potato-onion slices. Brush again with garlic butter. Bake for 1 hour, basting every 20 minutes with remaining garlic butter.

238 PEPPER CHICKEN PROVENÇALE
Prep: 20 minutes   Cook: 50 minutes   Serves: 4

1 cup seasoned bread crumbs
½ teaspoon salt
¼ teaspoon pepper
1 cup plain yogurt
3 pounds chicken thighs
  or legs

1 red pepper, cut into ¼-inch
  strips, seeds reserved
1 green pepper, cut into
  ¼-inch strips, seeds
  reserved

1. Preheat oven to 350°. In a shallow dish, combine bread crumbs, salt, and pepper. Spoon yogurt into a separate dish and stir until creamy.

2. Dip chicken pieces in yogurt, then dredge in seasoned bread crumbs.

3. Place chicken pieces, skin side up, in a 13 x 9 x 2-inch baking dish. Sprinkle with reserved pepper seeds. Bake uncovered 30 minutes.

4. Place pepper strips around chicken and continue to bake about 20 minutes, until chicken is tender.

Chapter 14

Chicken in the Skillet

It should come as no surprise that one of the simplest, most delicious ways to cook chicken is the classic French sauté. It's quick, it lends itself to almost infinite flavor variations, and all you need to wash is a single skillet. Basically, the technique involves browning a cut-up chicken quickly to seal in the juices. Then liquid and seasonings are added and the bird is braised for no more than 25 minutes, until it is just done, still moist and juicy.

To accomplish a proper sauté, you must have a good heavy skillet. Tin-lined copper is excellent, but expensive, and it needs polishing. Enameled cast-iron is versatile, but heavy. Cast-iron is all right for some recipes, but cannot be used with wine, tomatoes, or spinach; it reacts unpleasantly with acid. Stainless steel doesn't react, but it can have hot spots. Your best choice besides copper is probably a copper-clad stainless steel skillet or a heavy aluminum pan with a nonstick lining. Choose one that is at least 10 inches in diameter (12 is better) and that comes with a cover. Or buy a separate cover that fits.

239 CHICKEN SAUTÉED WITH RASPBERRY VINEGAR

Prep: 5 minutes   Cook: 30 minutes   Serves: 4

2 tablespoons butter
1 tablespoon vegetable oil
1 chicken (3 pounds), cut up
½ cup raspberry vinegar

1 cup chicken broth
1 cup heavy cream
   Salt and freshly ground
   pepper

1. In a large frying pan, melt butter and oil over medium heat. Add chicken and brown all over, about 10 minutes. Remove chicken and set aside.

2. Pour out fat from pan. Add raspberry vinegar, bring to a boil, and cook until reduced to 2 tablespoons. Add chicken broth and return chicken to pan. Cover and simmer 15 to 20 minutes, until chicken is tender. Remove chicken to a serving platter.

3. Increase heat to medium, bring pan juices to a boil, and cook until reduced by half. Add cream and boil until sauce is thickened slightly, about 3 minutes. Season with salt and pepper to taste. Pour over chicken and serve.

240 SAFFRON CHICKEN WITH OLIVES

Prep: 10 minutes   Cook: 55 minutes   Serves: 4

1 chicken (3 pounds), cut up
   Salt
2 tablespoons vegetable oil
4 garlic cloves, halved
1 bay leaf
¼ teaspoon ground saffron
¼ teaspoon thyme

¼ teaspoon freshly ground
   pepper
4 tomatoes, peeled and
   quartered
20 pimiento-stuffed olives
1¼ cups dry white wine
1¼ cups chicken broth

1. Season chicken with salt. In a large frying pan, heat oil over medium heat. Add chicken and cook, turning, until browned, about 10 minutes.

2. Add garlic, bay leaf, saffron, thyme, and pepper. Mix well. Add remaining ingredients; reduce heat. Simmer, uncovered, 45 minutes, until chicken is tender.

3. Remove garlic halves and bay leaves. Serve with French bread for soaking up the sauce.

241 CHICKEN PILAF

Prep: 10 minutes   Cook: 45 minutes   Serves: 4

1 chicken (3 pounds), cut up
   Salt and freshly ground
   pepper
2 tablespoons vegetable oil
2 large onions, chopped

1 cup rice
2¾ cups boiling chicken broth
½ can (3 ounces) tomato paste
½ cinnamon stick

1. Season chicken with salt and pepper. In a large frying pan, heat oil over medium heat. Add chicken and brown all over, about 10 minutes. Remove with tongs and set aside.

2. Add onions to pan and cook until just beginning to brown, 3 to 5 minutes. Add rice and cook, stirring, until coated with oil and translucent, about 3 minutes. Stir in broth and tomato paste; add cinnamon stick and arrange chicken on top. Cover and cook over low heat until chicken is tender and rice has absorbed liquid, 20 to 25 minutes.

3. When ready to serve, mound rice on platter and arrange chicken on rice. Discard cinnamon stick. If desired, serve with yogurt.

---

242 CHICKEN TARRAGON
Prep: 10 minutes   Cook: 45 minutes   Serves: 4

Tarragon has a wonderful grassy aroma that reminds me of new-mown hay. Its delicate anise flavor combines beautifully with chicken.

1 chicken (3 pounds), cut up	2 tablespoons flour
Salt and freshly ground	½ cup white wine
pepper	2 tablespoons chopped fresh
3 tablespoons butter	tarragon, or 1½ teaspoons
1 small onion, finely chopped	dried
1 garlic clove, crushed	¾ cup heavy cream

1. Season chicken pieces with salt and pepper. In a large frying pan or flameproof casserole, heat butter over medium-low heat. Add chicken and cook for 5 minutes. Turn chicken, add onion and garlic, and cook for 5 to 7 minutes, until onion is softened but not browned.

3. Sprinkle flour over chicken and toss for 1 minute. Add wine, tarragon and 1 cup water. Cover and simmer for 20 minutes, until tender. Remove chicken to a serving platter. Cover with foil to keep warm.

4. Boil sauce in pan, stirring often, until reduced by half, about 5 minutes. Add cream and simmer for 3 minutes. Season with salt and pepper to taste. Pour sauce over chicken and serve.

---

243 ROSEMARY CHICKEN
Prep: 5 minutes   Cook: 40 minutes   Serves: 4

1 chicken (3 pounds), cut up	4 garlic cloves
Salt and freshly ground	½ teaspoon dried rosemary
pepper	¼ cup dry white wine
1 tablespoon vegetable oil	¼ cup chicken broth
1 tablespoon butter	

1. Season chicken with salt and pepper. In a large frying pan, heat oil and butter over medium heat. Add garlic cloves and cook 2 minutes, without browning. Add chicken and cook, turning, until lightly browned, about 10 minutes.

2. Sprinkle with rosemary; add wine and chicken broth. Cover and cook over low heat, turning once, 30 minutes, until tender.

3. To serve, remove chicken to a warm platter. Discard garlic cloves and pour any remaining pan juices over chicken.

244   CHICKEN WITH GREEN PEPPERCORNS
Prep: 10 minutes   Cook: 45 minutes   Serves: 4

Green peppercorns are the unripened berries that later become black pepper. They have an herbal peppery quality that works beautifully with chicken.

1 chicken (3 pounds), cut up
  Salt and freshly ground
    pepper
3 tablespoons vegetable oil
2 shallots, finely chopped
1 garlic clove, crushed
1 cup dry red wine
½ teaspoon dried thyme

1 can (14 ounces) Italian peeled
  tomatoes, drained and
  chopped
1 cup beef stock
2 tablespoons tomato paste
1 tablespoon green
  peppercorns

1. Sprinkle chicken pieces with salt and pepper. In a large frying pan, heat oil over medium heat. Add chicken. Cook, turning, until browned all over, about 10 minutes. Remove from pan and set aside. Discard all but 2 tablespoons oil.

2. Add shallots and garlic to pan. Sauté until softened, 1 to 2 minutes. Pour in wine and bring to a boil, scraping up browned bits from bottom of pan. Boil until liquid reduces to about ⅓ cup.

4. Add thyme, tomatoes, beef stock, and tomato paste and mix well. Return chicken to pan. Simmer, uncovered, about 30 minutes, or until tender. Remove chicken to a serving platter.

5. Increase heat and boil sauce until thick, about 2 minutes. Stir in green peppercorns and serve over chicken.

245   TARRAGON CHICKEN WITH MUSHROOMS
Prep: 10 minutes   Cook: 40 minutes   Serves: 4

2 tablespoons butter or
  margarine
½ pound mushrooms, sliced
1 chicken (3 pounds), cut up
½ teaspoon salt
¼ teaspoon freshly ground
  pepper

2 tablespoons olive oil
½ cup dry white wine
1 tablespoon chopped fresh
  tarragon, or 1 teaspoon
  dried

1. In a large frying pan, melt butter over medium heat. Add mushrooms and cook about 5 minutes, until lightly brown. Remove from pan and set aside.

2. Season chicken with salt and pepper. In same pan, heat olive oil. Add chicken and cook over medium heat until brown, about 5 minutes a side.

4. Drain off excess fat. Add wine and tarragon. Cover, reduce heat, and simmer 25 minutes. Add reserved mushrooms and cook 5 minutes more.

246   CUCUMBERED CHICKEN THIGHS
Prep: 30 minutes   Cook: 30 minutes   Serves: 4

If you've never eaten cooked cucumbers, you'll be pleasantly surprised at the way it brings out their flavor. This is a light, elegant dish. Accompany simply with rice and a crisp chilled white wine.

1 **pound cucumbers, peeled, seeded, and sliced**	1 **garlic clove, crushed**
Salt	1 **large onion, finely chopped**
4 **tablespoons butter**	2 **tablespoons chopped fresh chives**
2 **pounds chicken thighs, skin removed**	½ **cup heavy cream**
¾ **cup chicken broth**	**Freshly ground pepper**

1. Arrange cucumbers on paper towels. Sprinkle with salt and let stand 20 minutes. Pat dry with additional paper towels.

2. Meanwhile, in a large frying pan, melt 2 tablespoons of the butter over moderately low heat. Add chicken thighs and cook about 5 minutes a side without browning. Add broth; cover and simmer 10 minutes, until tender.

3. In a medium-size saucepan, melt remaining 2 tablespoons butter over medium heat. Add garlic and onion and cook until onion is soft, about 3 minutes.

4. Add cucumber and chives to saucepan. Cook 2 minutes, until cucumbers are crisp-tender. Add cream and cook until sauce reduces and thickens, about 5 minutes. Season with pepper. Serve over chicken thighs.

247   PILAF OF CHICKEN AND CRAB WITH CASHEWS
Prep: 10 minutes   Cook: 30 minutes   Serves: 4

2 **tablespoons vegetable oil**	1 **can chicken broth plus water to equal 2¼ cups**
2 **medium onions, chopped**	2 **cups chopped cooked chicken**
1 **garlic clove, crushed**	¼ **pound fresh lump crabmeat, or 1 can (6 ounces), drained**
2 **medium tomatoes, chopped**	½ **cup salted cashew pieces**
1 **teaspoon curry powder**	
1 **cup converted rice**	

1. In a large frying pan, heat oil over medium heat. Add onion and garlic and cook until onion is soft, about 3 minutes. Add tomatoes, curry powder, and rice. Mix well·and cook 2 minutes.

2. Stir in diluted broth; bring to a boil. Reduce heat to moderately low, cover, and cook 20 minutes, until liquid is absorbed and rice is tender.

3. Add chopped chicken and crabmeat. Cook 5 to 10 minutes, stirring occasionally, until heated through. Remove to a serving platter and top with cashews.

248 CHICKEN DIJONNAISE
Prep: 15 minutes   Cook: 30 minutes   Serves: 4

2 tablespoons butter or
    margarine
1 tablespoon vegetable oil
1 chicken (3 pounds), cut up
2 tablespoons flour

1 cup chicken broth
½ cup dry white wine
2 tablespoons Dijon mustard
½ cup heavy cream

1. In a large frying pan, melt butter in oil over medium heat. Add chicken and brown all over, about 10 minutes.

2. Stir flour into pan juices. Cook, stirring, for 1 minute without browning. Stir in chicken broth and white wine. Cover and simmer for 15 to 20 minutes, until chicken is tender. Remove chicken to a serving platter and cover with foil to keep warm.

3. Whisk mustard and cream into pan juices. Simmer for 3 minutes and serve over chicken.

249 MEDITERRANEAN CHICKEN WITH SUN-DRIED TOMATOES AND OLIVES
Prep: 5 minutes   Cook: 40 minutes   Serves: 4

2 tablespoons olive oil
1 chicken (3 pounds), cut up
2 garlic cloves, crushed
2 shallots, finely chopped
¾ cup dry white wine
1 lemon, thinly sliced

¼ pound sun-dried tomatoes,
    cut into thin strips
12 black Italian olives
¼ teaspoon freshly ground
    pepper

1. In a large frying pan, heat oil over medium heat. Add chicken and cook, turning, until browned, about 5 minutes a side.

2. Add garlic and shallots and cook 2 minutes. Pour wine over chicken, cover, reduce heat, and simmer 15 minutes.

3. Add lemon, sun-dried tomatoes, olives, and pepper. Cover and simmer 10 minutes, until chicken is tender.

250 SMOTHERED SWEET-AND-SOUR CHICKEN
Prep: 10 minutes   Cook: 30 minutes   Serves: 4

3 tablespoons vegetable oil
3 pounds chicken legs
1 large onion, chopped
3 tablespoons ketchup
2 tablespoons lemon juice
2 tablespoons soy sauce
2 tablespoons sugar

½ teaspoon freshly ground
    pepper
1 tablespoon cornstarch
    dissolved in ¼ cup cold
    water
Lemon slices

1. In a large frying pan, heat oil over medium heat. Add chicken and cook, turning, until golden brown, about 10 minutes.

2. Meanwhile, in a small bowl, combine onion, ketchup, lemon juice, soy sauce, sugar, pepper, and ½ cup water; blend well.

3. Pour sweet-and-sour mixture over chicken. Cover, reduce heat to low, and cook 20 minutes, until tender. Remove chicken to a serving platter.

4. Add cornstarch mixture to sauce. Raise heat, bring to a boil, and cook, stirring, until sauce thickens, about 2 minutes. Pour over chicken and garnish with lemon slices.

---

251 CHICKEN LEGS WITH YELLOW SQUASH
Prep: 5 minutes   Cook: 40 minutes   Serves: 4

3 **pounds chicken thighs and/ or drumsticks**	1 **large tomato, chopped**
Salt and freshly ground pepper	½ **teaspoon dried basil**
	¼ **teaspoon dried marjoram**
3 **tablespoons vegetable oil**	¼ **teaspoon paprika**
2 **medium yellow squash, sliced**	⅛ **to ¼ teaspoon cayenne pepper, to taste**
1 **large onion, sliced**	½ **cup dry white wine**

1. Season chicken with salt and pepper. In a large frying pan, heat oil over medium heat. Add chicken and cook, turning, until browned, about 10 minutes.

2. Add squash, onion, tomato, basil, marjoram, paprika, and cayenne; mix well. Pour wine over all. Cover, reduce heat, and simmer 30 minutes, adding water if liquid evaporates.

---

252 SAUTÉED CHICKEN WITH FRESH VEGETABLES
Prep: 5 minutes   Cook: 40 minutes   Serves: 4

1 **chicken (3 pounds), cut up**	16 **pearl onions, peeled**
Salt and freshly ground pepper	1 **bay leaf**
	1 **tablespoon chopped fresh dill**
3 **tablespoons vegetable oil**	
4 **medium potatoes, quartered**	1 **cup beef stock**
4 **carrots, thickly sliced**	1 **tablespoon chopped parsley**
1 **container (10 ounces) fresh Brussels sprouts**	

1. Season chicken with salt and pepper. In a large flameproof casserole, heat oil over medium heat; add chicken and cook, turning, until browned, about 10 minutes.

2. Add potatoes, carrots, Brussels sprouts, onions, bay leaf, dill, and beef stock. Cover and simmer 30 minutes, until chicken and vegetables are tender. Sprinkle with parsley.

253 CHICKEN THIGHS WITH ORANGE CREAM SAUCE

Prep: 5 minutes   Cook: 35 minutes   Serves: 4

Subtle, elegant, and simple. Serve with rice and buttered asparagus or glazed carrots and snow peas.

8 chicken thighs
  Salt and freshly ground pepper
3 tablespoons vegetable oil
2 tablespoons brandy
2 tablespoons chopped chives
¼ teaspoon dried thyme

¾ cup chicken broth
½ cup heavy cream
2 tablespoons fresh orange juice
1 teaspoon grated orange rind
¼ teaspoon nutmeg

1. Season chicken thighs with salt and pepper. In a large frying pan, heat oil over medium heat. Add chicken and cook, turning, until browned, about 10 minutes.

2. Remove all but 1 tablespoon pan drippings. Pour brandy over chicken and ignite. Shake pan until flames subside. Add chives, thyme, and broth. Reduce heat, cover, and simmer 20 minutes, until chicken is tender. Remove to a serving platter and cover loosely with foil to keep warm.

3. Stir cream, orange juice, orange rind, and nutmeg into pan juices. Bring to a boil and cook 2 minutes, until thickened slightly. Season with salt and pepper to taste. Pour sauce over chicken and serve.

254 CONFETTI PEPPER CHICKEN WITH TOMATO CREAM SAUCE

Prep: 5 minutes   Cook: 45 minutes   Serves: 4

1 chicken (3 pounds), cut up
  Salt and freshly ground pepper
3 tablespoons vegetable oil
½ green bell pepper, diced
½ red bell pepper, diced

1 medium onion, chopped
1 teaspoon dried basil
3 tablespoons flour
1½ cups milk
½ cup dry white wine
3 tablespoons tomato paste

1. Season chicken with salt and pepper. In a large frying pan, heat oil over medium heat. Add chicken and cook, turning, until brown all over, about 10 minutes. Remove with tongs and set aside.

2. Add green pepper, red pepper, onion, and basil to pan drippings. Cook until vegetables are soft, about 5 minutes. Sprinkle flour over vegetables, cook 1 to 2 minutes, stirring constantly. Gradually whisk in milk. Bring to a boil, stirring, until thickened. Add wine and tomato paste and blend well.

3. Return chicken to pan. Cover and simmer over low heat 30 minutes, until chicken is tender.

255 CHICKEN WITH BLACK OLIVES AND ANCHOVIES
Prep: 15 minutes   Cook: 50 minutes   Serves: 4

Highly seasoned with anchovies, olives, and herbs, this dish needs only buttered noodles and a salad. Use good imported Mediterranean or Kalamata olives for best taste.

1 chicken (3 pounds), cut up
Salt and freshly ground
    pepper
3 tablespoons olive oil
1 small onion, chopped
1 garlic clove, crushed
    through a press
½ cup dry white wine
	2 tablespoons white wine
	    vinegar
	½ cup chicken stock
	½ teaspoon dried oregano
	1 bay leaf
	½ cup pitted black olives,
	    halved
	4 anchovy fillets, rinsed,
	    dried, and chopped

1. Season chicken with salt and pepper. In a large frying pan, heat oil over medium heat. Add chicken and cook, turning, until brown all over, about 10 minutes. Remove to a platter.

2. Pour off all but 2 tablespoons of fat. Add onion and garlic and cook until onion is soft, about 5 minutes. Add wine and vinegar and bring to a boil, scraping up browned bits from bottom of pan with a wooden spoon. Cook until liquid is reduced to ¼ cup.

3. Add chicken stock, oregano, and bay leaf and cook 2 minutes. Return chicken to pan. Cover, reduce heat to low, and simmer 30 minutes, until tender.

4. Arrange chicken on a serving platter. Bring sauce to a boil and cook until thickened, about 3 minutes. Remove and discard bay leaf. Add olives and anchovies, cook 2 minutes, and pour over chicken.

256 CHICKEN WITH LEEKS AND PEPPERS
Prep: 15 minutes   Cook: 40 minutes   Serves: 4

1 teaspoon celery seed
1 teaspoon chili powder
1 teaspoon onion salt
1 chicken (3 pounds), cut up
3 tablespoons vegetable oil
	2 large green bell peppers, cut
	    into ¼-inch strips
	1 large red bell pepper, cut
	    into ¼-inch strips
	2 leeks (white part only), sliced

1. In a small bowl, combine celery seed, chili powder, and onion salt. Sprinkle spice mixture over chicken pieces, coating well.

2. In a Dutch oven, heat oil over medium heat. Add chicken and cook, turning, until brown, about 10 minutes.

3. Reduce heat to low, cover, and cook about 20 minutes, until chicken is tender. Remove to a serving platter and keep warm.

4. Pour off all but 2 tablespoons fat from pan. Return to medium heat. Add peppers and leeks. Cook about 5 minutes, stirring, until leeks are soft. Serve over chicken.

257 CHICKEN CACCIATORA
Prep: 10 minutes   Cook: 45 minutes   Serves: 4

3 tablespoons vegetable oil
1 chicken (3 pounds), cut up
1 medium onion, sliced
3 garlic cloves, minced
½ pound mushrooms, sliced
1 large bell pepper, cut into 1-inch pieces

1 can (16 ounces) tomatoes
1 can (8 ounces) tomato sauce
1 teaspoon dried oregano
1 teaspoon salt
½ teaspoon freshly ground pepper

1. In a large frying pan, heat vegetable oil over medium heat. Add chicken and brown on all sides, about 10 minutes. Remove and drain on paper towels.

2. Add onion, garlic, mushrooms, and bell pepper to pan and sauté until onion and pepper are softened, about 5 minutes. Add remaining ingredients. Stir well.

3. Return chicken to pan. Bring to a boil; reduce heat. Cover and simmer 30 minutes, until chicken is tender.

Chapter 15

Chicken in the Pot (Stews)

Stews go by many names. Sometimes they are called ragouts; when they are light, they are termed blanquettes. When they come from Louisiana and are thickened with okra or filé powder, they are called gumbos. Sometimes, the line dividing a stew from a soup is hard to define.

It really doesn't matter what you call it, as long as it tastes good. Whether you serve an egg- and cream-enriched Waterzooie of Chicken with its silken broth in a bowl or a rustic cinnamon-scented Chicken Kampama over rice or pasta on a plate, it's all hearty, flavorful food that's sure to please. Most stews need only a crisp green salad and some crusty bread to make up a lovely well-balanced meal.

Most of the preparation time in these recipes involves chopping and cutting up the vegetables. Once preparations are completed, the cooking takes care of itself. Unlike strong red meats, which need hours of cooking to produce a tender, flavorful stew, chicken cooks in under an hour.

258   RAGOUT OF CHICKEN WITH BACON AND VEGETABLES

Prep: 20 minutes   Cook: 40 minutes   Serves: 4

If too much liquid evaporates during cooking, add more wine, broth, or water.

2 tablespoons butter or margarine
¼ pound bacon, cut into 1-inch pieces
1 chicken (3 pounds), cut up
2 large onions, sliced
1 garlic clove, crushed
8 small red potatoes, halved

2 celery ribs, sliced diagonally
2 carrots, sliced diagonally
½ pound fresh mushrooms, sliced
2 tablespoons chopped fresh basil or tarragon
½ cup dry white wine
½ cup chicken broth

1. In a large Dutch oven, melt butter over medium-low heat. Add bacon and cook until lightly browned. Remove with a slotted spoon and set aside. Add chicken, and cook, turning, until chicken is browned, about 10 minutes. Remove and set aside.

2. Add onions and garlic to pan and cook, stirring, until onion is soft, about 3 minutes. Add potatoes, celery, carrots, mushrooms, basil, wine, and broth. Return chicken to Dutch oven. Reduce heat, cover, and simmer 40 minutes, until chicken is tender.

259   CHICKEN AND OKRA GUMBO

Prep: 1 hour   Cook: 50 minutes   Serves: 6

One Cajun classic is gumbo, a hodgepodge stew made with a combination of ingredients. It is traditionally thickened with okra and/or filé powder (ground sassafras leaves).

1 pound okra, sliced
5 tablespoons vegetable oil
2 large onions, chopped
3 celery ribs, chopped
1 chicken (3 pounds), cut up
¼ cup flour
Salt

Freshly ground pepper
1 teaspoon cayenne pepper
Chopped scallions and parsley
2 tablespoons filé powder (or ¼ pound additional okra)

1. In a large Dutch oven, sauté okra in 2 tablespoons of the oil over medium heat until golden brown, about 15 minutes. Add onions and celery; cook until wilted. Add 4 cups water; simmer 15 minutes.

2. In a large frying pan, heat remaining 3 tablespoons oil over medium-low heat. Add chicken and brown about 5 minutes a side. With tongs, transfer chicken to okra mixture. Stir flour into fat in pan. Cook, stirring, until a nut-brown roux is made, about 20 minutes. Remove from heat and whisk in about 1 cup liquid from okra. Stir into remaining liquid in Dutch oven.

3. Bring to a boil, stirring. Reduce heat and simmer until chicken is tender, about 50 minutes. Season with salt, black pepper, and cayenne to taste.

4. Add scallions, parsley, and filé just before serving. Serve over rice, with French bread.

260 BLANQUETTE OF CHICKEN
Prep: 30 minutes   Cook: 1 hour 10 minutes   Serves: 4

1 whole chicken, about 3 pounds	1 cup dry white wine
Salt and freshly ground pepper	1 cup chicken broth
4 slices of bacon, diced	½ pound mushrooms, quartered
1 tablespoon vegetable oil	1 teaspoon dried thyme
1 large onion, chopped	1 tablespoon chopped parsley
2 garlic cloves, chopped	2 tablespoons flour mashed with 2 tablespoons butter

1. Truss chicken and season with salt and pepper.

2. In a large flameproof casserole, brown bacon pieces over low heat. Remove bacon with a slotted spoon and drain on paper towels. Add oil to bacon drippings. Add chicken and cook over medium heat, turning, until browned well all over, about 20 minutes. Remove from pan.

3. Add onion and garlic to pan drippings and cook until tender, about 3 minutes. Stir in white wine, chicken broth, mushrooms, thyme, and parsley. Return chicken and bacon to casserole.

4. Cover and cook over low heat 1 hour, until chicken is tender. Remove chicken to a heated serving platter and cover lightly with foil to keep warm.

5. Bring cooking liquid in casserole to a boil. Gradually stir in flour-butter paste. Cook, stirring constantly, until sauce thickens, about 2 minutes. Pour over chicken.

261 CHICKEN PAPRIKA
Prep: 10 minutes   Cook: 45 minutes   Serves: 4

Sour cream and sweet paprika are the hallmarks of good Hungarian cooking. Serve with noodles or, for a real treat, homemade spaetzle.

1 chicken (3 pounds), cut up	2 large tomatoes, coarsely chopped
Salt and freshly ground pepper	2½ tablespoons imported sweet paprika
2 tablespoons vegetable oil	½ cup sour cream
2 medium onions, finely chopped	

1. Season chicken with salt and pepper. In a large frying pan, heat oil over medium heat. Brown chicken lightly on all sides, about 10 minutes. Remove chicken and set aside.

2. Add onion to pan. Cook, stirring, until tender and beginning to brown, 5 to 10 minutes. Add tomatoes and paprika. Return chicken to pan. Cover tightly and simmer 30 to 40 minutes, until tender.

3. Remove chicken to a serving platter. Stir sour cream into tomato mixture. Heat until warm; do not boil. Season with salt and pepper to taste. Pour over chicken.

262   COUNTRY CAPTAIN
Prep: 30 minutes   Cook: 50 minutes   Serves: 4

Some say the original version of this recipe was created by a Georgia hostess for a party honoring President Franklin D. Roosevelt. Other reports maintain the dish actually originated in India. Wherever it's from, it is delicious.

½ cup flour
1 chicken (3 pounds), cut up
3 tablespoons vegetable oil
1 cup chopped onion
½ cup chopped green bell pepper
½ cup chopped red bell pepper
1 garlic clove, finely chopped
2 teaspoons curry powder
½ teaspoon salt

¼ teaspoon freshly ground pepper
¼ teaspoon mace
1 can (16 ounces) whole tomatoes, cut up, with juices
1 tablespoon chopped parsley
½ cup raisins
¼ cup slivered almonds, toasted

1. Place flour in a shallow dish. Roll chicken pieces in flour to coat; shake off excess.

2. In a large Dutch oven, heat oil over medium heat. Add chicken and cook, turning, until brown, about 10 minutes. Remove chicken and set aside.

3. To the same pan, add onion, bell peppers, and garlic. Cook until onion and peppers are tender, about 5 minutes. Add curry powder, salt, pepper, and mace. Stir until well blended. Add tomatoes, parsley, and raisins.

4. Bring to a boil and return chicken to pan. Reduce heat and simmer, partly covered, 30 to 40 minutes, until chicken is tender. Serve over rice; garnish with almonds.

263   CHICKEN MARENGO
Prep: 25 minutes   Cook: 45 minutes   Serves: 4

This dish was said to be a favorite of Napoleon's. It's a wonderfully easy dish for entertaining, and it reheats beautifully. Serve with steamed white rice.

1 chicken (3 pounds), cut up
Salt and freshly ground pepper
3 tablespoons vegetable oil
2 medium onions, thinly sliced
2 garlic cloves, chopped
¼ pound mushrooms, sliced
1 tablespoon chopped parsley

½ teaspoon dried thyme
¼ teaspoon rosemary, crumbled
1 bay leaf
1 can (14 ounces) Italian peeled tomatoes, with their juices, coarsely cut up
¼ cup dry white wine

1. Season chicken with salt and pepper. In a large frying pan, heat oil over medium heat. Add chicken and brown lightly on both sides, about 8 minutes. Remove and set aside. Remove all but 3 tablespoons fat from pan. Add onions, garlic, and mushrooms and cook until tender, about 5 minutes.

Return chicken to pan. Sprinkle with parsley, thyme, rosemary, and bay leaf.

2. Add tomatoes and wine, partly cover and simmer 45 to 50 minutes, until chicken is tender. Remove bay leaf and serve.

264 BRUNSWICK STEW
Prep: 15 minutes   Cook: 1¾ hours   Serves: 8

- 1 chicken (3 pounds), cut up
- Freshly ground pepper
- 1 ham bone
- 1 bay leaf
- 1½ teaspoons salt
- 6 whole peppercorns
- 2 potatoes, peeled and chopped
- 1 can (16 ounces) Italian peeled tomatoes, drained and chopped

- 2 onions, chopped
- 1 package (10 ounces) frozen corn
- 1 package (10 ounces) frozen lima beans
- 1 package (10 ounces) frozen okra
- ½ teaspoon crushed hot pepper

1. In a Dutch oven, combine chicken pieces, freshly ground pepper, ham bone, bay leaf, salt, and peppercorns in 2 quarts of water. Bring to a boil, reduce heat and simmer 45 to 60 minutes, until meat begins to fall off the bones. Strain broth and reserve. Discard skin and bones. Cut meat into bite-size pieces.

2. Return broth to Dutch oven. Add remaining ingredients and chicken. Cover and cook over low heat 45 minutes, until flavors are well blended. Season with additional salt and pepper to taste. Remove bay leaf before serving.

265 CHICKEN WITH CARROTS AND MUSHROOMS
Prep: 10 minutes   Cook: 40 minutes   Serves: 4

- 3 tablespoons olive oil
- 1 chicken (3 pounds), cut up
- 1 medium onion, chopped
- 1 cup sliced carrots
- 1 can (28 ounces) crushed tomatoes

- ½ pound mushrooms, sliced
- ¾ teaspoon dried thyme
- 1 bay leaf
- Salt and freshly ground pepper

1. In a large frying pan or flameproof casserole, heat oil over medium heat. Add chicken and cook, turning, until brown all over, about 10 minutes. Remove and set aside.

2. Add onion and carrots to pan and cook until onion is soft, about 3 minutes. Add tomatoes, mushrooms, thyme, bay leaf, and salt and pepper to taste. Return chicken to pan. Reduce heat to medium-low and simmer 30 minutes, until chicken is tender. Serve in bowls.

266   RON LUCIANO'S EASY TOMATO CHICKEN
Prep: 15 minutes   Cook: 1 hour   Serves: 4

Ron Luciano, the former baseball umpire, is also a passionate eater and an accomplished chef. Here's his recipe for a simple, yet satisfying chicken stew with an Italian accent.

½ cup flour
1 chicken (3 pounds), cut up
   and skinned
2 tablespoons vegetable oil
2 garlic cloves, crushed
1 cup dry white wine
1 can (28 ounces) crushed
   tomatoes
6 carrots, peeled and cut into
   1-inch pieces

1 celery rib, sliced into 1-inch
   pieces
2 tablespoons grated
   Parmesan cheese
1 tablespoon dried basil
½ teaspoon dried oregano
½ teaspoon salt
¼ teaspoon freshly ground
   pepper

1. Place flour in a plastic bag. Add chicken pieces, several at a time, and shake to coat.

2. In a large flameproof casserole, heat vegetable oil over medium heat. Add garlic and cook 2 minutes. Add chicken and cook until golden on all sides, 8 to 10 minutes. Do not brown.

3. Add white wine, tomatoes, carrots, celery, cheese, basil, oregano, salt, and pepper. Mix well, cover, and cook over low heat about 45 minutes, until chicken is tender.

267   CHICKEN KAPAMA
Prep: 10 minutes   Cook: 30 minutes   Serves: 4

Here's a chicken version of a classic Greek lamb dish. The cinnamon in the tomato sauce gives it its distinct flavor. Serve with orzo, tiny pasta that looks like rice.

1 chicken (3 pounds), cut up
   Salt and freshly ground
   pepper
1 tablespoon butter
2 tablespoons olive oil
1 large onion, chopped
1 garlic clove, finely chopped

1 can (14 ounces) Italian peeled
   tomatoes, drained and
   chopped
2 tablespoons tomato paste
½ cup chicken stock or canned
   broth
1 cinnamon stick

1. Season chicken with salt and pepper. In a large frying pan, heat butter and olive oil over medium heat. Add chicken and cook until brown, about 10 minutes. Remove and set aside.

2. Add onion and garlic to pan. Cook until onion is soft, about 3 minutes. Stir in tomatoes, tomato paste, and stock. Add cinnamon stick. Bring to a boil and return chicken to pan. Cover, reduce heat, and simmer 30 minutes, until tender. Season with salt and pepper to taste.

268   CHICKEN CHILI
Prep: 30 minutes   Cook: 50 minutes   Serves: 6 to 8

Chili is one of my favorite party dishes. Nice to know it can be made with chicken instead of red meat, and nice to know this recipe doubles easily and is even better reheated the next day.

1 cup tomato juice	2 cups cooked pinto beans
1 cup raw cracked wheat (bulgur)	3 cups cubed cooked chicken
2 tablespoons vegetable oil	1 can (4 ounces) chopped green chilies
2 medium onions, coarsely chopped	⅓ cup chili powder, mild and/or hot to taste
4 garlic coves, crushed	2 teaspoons ground cumin
3 celery ribs, coarsely chopped	1 teaspoon dried oregano
3 carrots, coarsely chopped	Freshly ground black pepper
1 can (14 ounces) Italian plum tomatoes, with their juices	1 bottle (12 ounces) beer
	Salt

1. In a small saucepan, heat tomato juice over medium heat until it boils. Remove from heat and add cracked wheat. Cover and let stand 15 minutes.

2. In a large Dutch oven, heat oil over medium heat. Add onions and garlic and cook until soft, about 3 minutes. Add celery, carrots, and tomatoes, mashing them with the back of a spoon, with their juices. Cover and cook until celery and carrots are almost tender, about 20 minutes.

3. Add pinto beans, cracked wheat, chicken, green chilies, chili powder, cumin, oregano, black pepper, and beer. Simmer partly covered, for 30 minutes, stirring occasionally to keep cracked wheat from sticking. Season with salt to taste.

269   CHICKEN CURRY WITH APPLE
Prep: 20 minutes   Cook: 40 minutes   Serves: 6 to 8

This is a quick and easy dish for leftover chicken. A variety of toppings will really dress up the simple stew.

2 tablespoons butter or margarine	4 cups chopped cooked chicken
1 cup chopped onion	Garnishes: Toasted coconut, mandarin oranges, chopped peanuts, raisins, crumbled cooked bacon, mango chutney, chopped onion
1 cup chopped peeled apple	
1 can (16 ounces) stewed tomatoes, with their juice	
1 cup chicken broth	
1 teaspoon lemon juice	
1 tablespoon curry powder, or more to taste	

1. Melt butter in a large frying pan over medium heat. Add onion and cook until softened, about 3 minutes. Add apple, tomatoes and their juice, broth, lemon juice, and curry powder. Simmer, uncovered, 35 minutes.

2. Add chicken and heat through, about 5 minutes. Serve with any of the assorted garnishes on the side.

270 CHICKEN PROVENÇAL
Prep: 25 minutes   Cook: 1 hour   Serves: 4

2 chicken bouillon cubes
1 cup boiling water
½ cup flour
½ teaspoon salt
¼ teaspoon freshly ground
    pepper
1 chicken (3 pounds), cut up
2 tablespoons olive oil
½ cup chopped green bell
    pepper
12 small white onions, peeled
¼ cup chopped scallions
3 garlic cloves, minced

½ cup dry white wine
1 bay leaf
6 medium-size tomatoes,
    peeled, seeded, and cut
    into thin strips
½ cup halved black olives
¼ teaspoon dried thyme
¼ teaspoon hot pepper sauce
1 jar (2 ounces) pimientos,
    drained and cut into strips
¼ pound mushrooms, sliced
2 tablespoons chopped parsley

1. Preheat oven to 350°. Dissolve bouillon cubes in boiling water and set aside.

2. In a plastic bag, combine flour, salt, and pepper. Place chicken pieces in bag and shake to coat well. In a large frying pan, heat oil over medium heat. Add chicken and cook, turning, until browned, about 10 minutes. Place chicken in a 2-quart casserole.

3. Add green pepper, onions, scallions, and garlic to frying pan and cook 5 minutes. Add wine, bay leaf, tomatoes, olives, thyme, hot sauce, pimientos, mushrooms, bouillon, and additional salt and pepper to taste. Simmer over low heat for 5 minutes.

4. Pour sauce over chicken. Cover and bake for 45 minutes. Remove bay leaf. Garnish with parsley.

271 CHICKEN, HAM, AND OYSTER STEW
Prep: 10 minutes   Cook: 25 minutes   Serves: 6

3 tablespoons butter
1 onion, chopped
3 tablespoons flour
2 cups canned chicken broth
2 cups canned beef broth
1 cup chopped cooked ham
2 carrots, sliced
¾ cup long-grain white rice

1 bay leaf
1 pint oysters, with their
    liquor
1 cup chopped cooked chicken
Dash of hot pepper sauce
Salt and freshly ground
    pepper
2 tablespoons chopped parsley

1. In a large saucepan, melt butter over medium heat. Add onion and cook 3 minutes, until tender. Add flour and cook 1 minute, stirring constantly.

2. Whisk in chicken and beef broth and bring to a boil. Add ham, carrots, rice, and bay leaf; reduce heat, cover, and simmer about 20 minutes, until rice is tender.

3. Add oysters with their liquor, hot sauce, and salt and pepper to taste. Cook 5 minutes, until oysters begin to curl around the edges. Remove bay leaf and serve in bowls, garnished with parsley.

272 CHICKEN BOUILLABAISSE
Prep: 15 minutes   Cook: 45 minutes   Serves: 6

Tomatoes, olive oil, saffron, and Pernod are the Mediterranean flavors that distinguish this take-off on the classic fish stew. Serve with garlic croutons and a green salad.

2 tablespoons Pernod	6 red ripe tomatoes, peeled
¼ cup olive oil	and chopped, or 1 can
¼ teaspoon ground saffron	(14 ounces), drained and
4 pounds chicken breasts,	chopped
legs, and thighs	½ teaspoon fennel seeds,
Salt and freshly ground	crushed
pepper	2 quarts boiling water
1 large onion, chopped	4 potatoes, peeled and diced
2 garlic cloves, crushed	
through a press	

1. Combine Pernod, 2 tablespoons of the olive oil, and saffron in a small bowl. Season chicken with salt and pepper. Rub Pernod marinade over chicken; let stand 15 minutes.

2. Meanwhile, heat remaining 2 tablespoons olive oil in a large Dutch oven. Add onion and garlic, cook until onion is soft, about 3 minutes. Add tomatoes, fennel seeds, chicken, and marinade. Pour boiling water over all, cover, and simmer 20 minutes. Add potatoes and simmer 20 additional minutes, until chicken and potatoes are tender. Season with additional salt and pepper to taste.

273 CURRIED CHICKEN STEW
Prep: 30 minutes   Cook: 45 minutes   Serves: 6

2 pounds skinless, boneless	1 garlic clove, minced
chicken breasts, cut into	2 teaspoons curry powder
2-inch cubes	1 can (28 ounces) Italian peeled
¾ teaspoon salt	tomatoes, broken up, with
½ teaspoon freshly ground	their juice
pepper	1 tablespoon Kitchen Bouquet
2 tablespoons vegetable oil	2 tablespoons chopped parsley
½ cup chopped onion	¼ cup raisins
½ cup chopped green bell	
pepper	

1. Season chicken with salt and pepper. In a large frying pan, heat oil over medium heat. Add chicken and cook, stirring, until opaque outside, about 10 minutes. Remove chicken from pan with a slotted spoon.

2. Add onion, bell pepper, garlic, and curry powder to pan. Cook, stirring, until onion and pepper are tender, about 3 minutes. Return chicken to pan. Add remaining ingredients and simmer, partly covered, 45 minutes. Serve over rice.

274 CHICKEN WITH GREEN BEANS, ARTICHOKES, AND CARROTS

Prep: 30 minutes   Cook: 1 hour   Serves: 6

Can be prepared ahead and refrigerated. Add 15 to 20 minutes to baking time.

3 tablespoons vegetable oil	1/2 teaspoon dried basil
4 pounds chicken legs, breasts, and thighs	1 bay leaf
1 large onion, chopped	2 tomatoes, peeled and quartered
6 carrots, sliced	3/4 cup chicken broth
3/4 pound green beans, cut into 1-inch pieces	1 can (14 ounces) artichoke hearts, drained and cut into quarters
1/2 teaspoon dried thyme	

1. Preheat oven to 350°. In a large frying pan, heat vegetable oil over medium heat. Add chicken and cook, turning, until lightly browned, about 10 minutes. Transfer to a 13 x 9 x 2-inch baking dish.

2. To same pan, add onion, carrots, and green beans; cook 3 to 5 minutes, until vegetables are crisp-tender. Add thyme, basil, bay leaf, tomatoes, and broth. Bring to a boil and pour over chicken.

3. Spread artichokes over all. Cover with foil and bake 1 hour, until chicken is tender. Serve with rice or pasta.

275 WATERZOOIE OF CHICKEN

Prep: 10 minutes   Cook: 45 minutes   Serves: 4

A rich Belgian soup-stew, traditionally made with a stewing hen. This quicker adaptation uses a standard broiler-fryer. Serve with dark bread and a crisp salad.

3 tablespoons vegetable oil	1/2 teaspoon salt
1 chicken (3 pounds), cut up	1/4 teaspoon freshly ground pepper
1/2 cup dry white wine	
2 leeks (white only), chopped	1 small onion stuck with 2 cloves
2 celery ribs, chopped	3 egg yolks
2 tablespoons finely chopped parsley	1/2 cup heavy cream
1 teaspoon dried thyme	1 lemon, cut into thin slices
6 cups chicken broth	

1. In a large Dutch oven, heat oil over medium heat. Add chicken pieces and cook, turning, until brown, about 10 minutes. Add wine and stir, loosening brown bits from bottom of pan.

2. Add leeks, celery, parsley, thyme, broth, salt, pepper, and onion. Bring to a boil. Reduce heat and simmer, covered, for 30 minutes, until chicken is tender. Skim off fat; remove onion.

3. Beat together egg yolks and cream in a small bowl. Gradually whisk in 1 cup of hot broth. Stir mixture into remaining broth. Heat through, but do not boil. Serve in bowls, garnished with lemon slices.

276 CHICKEN IN BEER WITH TOMATOES
Prep: 10 to 15 minutes   Cook: 1¼ hours   Serves: 4

Beer is a wonderful stewing liquid. You can't really taste it after long cooking, but it leaves behind a trace of bitterness and added depth of flavor. This can be assembled ahead and baked when company arrives; add 15 minutes to cooking time.

⅓ cup flour
1 teaspoon salt
½ teaspoon freshly ground pepper
½ teaspoon paprika
1 chicken (3 pounds), cut up
⅓ cup bacon drippings or vegetable oil
1 garlic clove
¾ chopped onion

¾ cup chopped green bell pepper
1 can (35 ounces) Italian peeled tomatoes, drained and coarsely chopped
1 can (12 ounces) beer
½ can (3 ounces) tomato paste
½ teaspoon dried thyme
½ teaspoon dried marjoram

1. Combine flour, salt, pepper, and paprika in a paper or plastic bag. Add chicken pieces, a few at a time, and shake to coat.

2. In a large frying pan, heat bacon drippings over medium heat. Add whole garlic clove and chicken. Cook, turning, until chicken is brown, about 10 minutes; remove garlic. Transfer chicken to a 13 x 9 x 2-inch baking dish.

3. Preheat oven to 350°. In same frying pan, sauté onion and pepper until tender, 3 to 5 minutes. Sprinkle over chicken.

4. In a large bowl, blend tomatoes, beer, tomato paste, thyme, and marjoram; pour over chicken. Bake, covered, 1 hour, until chicken is tender. Serve with rice.

Chapter 16

Broiled and Barbecued

Recipes for both broiled and grilled chicken are included in one chapter because the techniques are in most cases interchangeable. In general, charcoal grilling produces a higher direct heat—and adds that wonderful smoky flavor. Yet, almost any grilled recipe can be reproduced under the broiler, though cooking time may be a little longer. Conversely, most broiler recipes can be taken outdoors to the grill, though cooking time will probably be a little shorter.

With both barbecues and broilers, cooking times must be taken as approximate, since the heat of either varies so much from home to home. Rely primarily on tests for doneness, and check the meat often to prevent it from drying out.

Because these are hot, dry methods of cooking, savory marinades are often used to add flavor and further tenderize the meat, since it will cook so quickly. Basting with a marinade keeps a grilled meat moist and juicy.

If you are into "gourmet" grilling with mesquite, hickory, or apple wood, be sure to soak the chips in water for at least half an hour. A couple of handfuls is usually enough for a standard 18-inch grill. Toss them on top of the hot coals just before you put the chicken on the grill.

277 GRILLED CHICKEN AND RICE BUNDLES

Prep: 30 minutes   Cook: 40 minutes   Serves: 4

2 cups canned chicken broth
1 cup rice
3 tablespoons butter or
   margarine, melted
1 garlic clove, crushed
½ teaspoon dried tarragon
½ teaspoon salt
¼ teaspoon freshly ground
   pepper

2 small chickens (about 2
   pounds each), cut in half
1 medium-size green bell
   pepper, chopped
1 medium-size tomato,
   chopped
1 medium-size onion,
   chopped

1. In a small saucepan, bring chicken broth to a boil. Add rice, cover, and reduce heat. Simmer 25 minutes, until liquid is absorbed.

2. In a small bowl, combine melted butter, garlic, tarragon, salt, and pepper. Brush chicken halves all over with tarragon butter. Place each half, skin side down, in center of a length of heavy-duty aluminum foil large enough for adequate wrapping.

3. Combine cooked rice with bell pepper, tomato, and onion. Spoon rice mixture over chicken.

4. To form package, bring longer ends of foil together over chicken. Fold down loosely in locked folds, allowing for heat circulation and expansion. Fold up short ends, crimping to seal.

5. Grill over moderate heat for 40 minutes, until chicken is tender. Remove foil package and open carefully. Serve directly out of packets, if desired, or transfer to heated plates.

278 GRILLED CHICKEN WITH SASSY SAUCE

Prep: 20 minutes   Cook: 1½ hours   Serves: 8

2 tablespoons butter or
   margarine
1 medium-size onion,
   chopped
1 garlic clove, chopped
½ cup chopped green bell
   pepper
2 cups ketchup
½ cup (packed) brown sugar

½ cup cider vinegar
2 tablespoons Worcestershire
   sauce
1 tablespoon Liquid Smoke
1 teaspoon dried oregano
1 teaspoon ground cinnamon
2 chickens (3 pounds each),
   quartered

1. In a medium-size saucepan, melt butter over low heat. Add onion, garlic, and green pepper, cook 5 minutes. Add ketchup, brown sugar, vinegar, Worcestershire sauce, Liquid Smoke, oregano, cinnamon, and 1 cup water. Simmer 30 minutes.

2. Light grill. Place chicken skin side down and cook 30 minutes over medium-direct heat. Turn chicken and cook 15 minutes longer. Cook, brushing frequently with sauce, another 15 minutes, until chicken is tender. Chicken can also be broiled about 10 minutes a side until cooked through.

279   HONEY-GARLIC CHICKEN
Prep: 10 minutes   Marinate: 1 hour   Cook: 1 hour   Serves: 4

This recipe originates with Chef Reinhardt Schmidt of the famed Jockey Club of Miami, Florida. The sauce, which can be made ahead of time and refrigerated, is traditionally used on barbecued ribs, but Chef Schmidt has created a grilled chicken version for this book.

1 chicken (about 3 pounds), cut up
1 cup plus ½ cup white vinegar
2 tablespoons butter
1 medium onion, finely chopped
6 cloves garlic, peeled and minced

1 small can (6 ounces) frozen orange juice concentrate
²/₃ cup honey
1 teaspoon salt
1 teaspoon freshly ground pepper
1 teaspoon paprika

1. Place chicken in medium-size bowl, add 1 cup vinegar, and marinate at least 1 hour at room temperature.

2. Meanwhile, melt butter in small frying pan, add onion and garlic, and sauté until tender, about 3 minutes. Transfer onion and garlic to a medium-size saucepan. Place pan over medium heat, stir in orange juice, honey and ½ cup vinegar, and bring to a boil. Reduce heat and simmer, stirring occasionally, for about 10 minutes. Remove from heat and refrigerate to allow sauce to cool and thicken.

3. Remove chicken from vinegar marinade and reserve marinade. Sprinkle both sides of chicken with salt, pepper and paprika.

4. Light grill. Place chicken on grill, skin side up, and cook over medium direct heat for 20 minutes, turning and basting frequently with vinegar marinade only. Cook for additional 20 minutes, turning and basting frequently and liberally with honey-garlic sauce.

---

280   TANDOORI CHICKEN
Prep: 15 minutes   Marinate: at least 4 hours
Cook: 40 minutes   Serves: 4

The flavor and texture of this dish really improves if marinated overnight, so plan ahead if you can.

1 chicken (3 pounds), quartered
2 tablespoons lime juice
1½ teaspoons salt
2½ cups yogurt
2 tablespoons grated fresh ginger
8 garlic cloves, crushed through a press

1½ teaspoons ground cardamom
½ teaspoon cumin
¼ to ½ teaspoon cayenne pepper, to taste
¼ teaspoon freshly ground black pepper
1 teaspoon red food coloring (optional)
Scallions and lime wedges

1. Remove skin from chicken; make two deep gashes in each piece of meat.

Rub chicken all over with 1½ tablespoons of the lime juice and 1 teaspoon salt. Place in a 12 x 8 x 2-inch baking dish.

2. In a medium-size bowl, combine yogurt with ginger, garlic, cardamom, cumin, cayenne, black pepper, remaining lime juice and salt, and food coloring, if desired. Pour over chicken and turn to coat. Cover loosely and refrigerate, turning occasionally, for at least 4 hours or overnight to develop flavors.

4. When ready to cook, light charcoal grill or preheat oven to 400°. Grill over medium-hot coals or bake 40 to 45 minutes, turning and basting frequently with yogurt marinade. Garnish with scallions and lime wedges.

---

281 CHICKEN FAJITAS
Prep: 10 minutes   Marinate: 1 hour   Cook: 10 minutes   Serves: 8

If you've had this dish in your favorite Mexican restaurant, you'll be surprised at how easy it is to prepare at home. Serve with guacamole, refried beans, and lots of cold beer.

½ cup vegetable oil
3 tablespoons white wine vinegar
2 tablespoons fresh lime juice
1 small onion, finely chopped
1 garlic clove, crushed through a press
1 teaspoon hot pepper sauce
½ teaspoon salt

¼ teaspoon freshly ground pepper
8 skinless, boneless chicken breast halves
16 flour tortillas, warmed
Fresh Tomato Salsa (recipe follows)
Sour cream and shredded lettuce

1. In a large bowl, combine oil, vinegar, lime juice, onion, garlic, pepper sauce, salt, and pepper. Add chicken and marinate at least 1 hour at room temperature, or overnight in the refrigerator.

2. Light charcoal grill or preheat broiler. Remove chicken from marinade; reserve marinade. Grill over medium-hot coals or broil, turning and basting with marinade several times, for 10 minutes, until chicken is opaque throughout but still juicy.

3. To serve, spread tortillas with salsa and sour cream. Add chicken and top with lettuce. Wrap up tortilla and pick up to eat.

FRESH TOMATO SALSA

3 medium-size ripe tomatoes, chopped
1 small onion, minced
1 jalapeño pepper, seeded and minced

2 tablespoons vegetable oil
1 tablespoon white wine vinegar
½ teaspoon salt
¼ cup chopped fresh coriander

Mix together all ingredients except coriander. Cover and refrigerate, if desired. Stir in coriander just before serving.

282   CHICKEN SATAYS WITH PEANUT DIPPING SAUCE

Prep: 20 minutes   Marinate: 30 minutes   Cook: 10 minutes
Serves: 8

Sweet-hot and wonderfully savory, these tasty kebabs make popular appetizers or an unusual main course for a barbecue. The same recipe works just as well with chicken livers, beef, and pork, though cooking times will vary.

Satays:
- ¼ cup soy sauce
- ¼ cup lemon juice
- 2 tablespoons vegetable oil
- 1 tablespoon sugar

- 2 pounds skinless, boneless chicken breasts, cut into ½-inch cubes

Peanut Dipping Sauce:
- 2 garlic cloves
- 2 shallots
- 2 tablespoons lime juice
- 1 tablespoon brown sugar
- ½ teaspoon ground coriander

- ¼ teaspoon crushed hot red pepper, or dash of hot pepper sauce
- ¾ cup peanut butter
- ¾ cup cream of coconut milk

1. In a medium-size bowl, combine soy sauce, lemon juice, oil, and sugar. Add chicken cubes. Let marinate at room temperature, tossing occasionally, for 30 minutes.

2. Meanwhile, in a food processor, combine garlic, shallots, lime juice, brown sugar, coriander, and hot pepper. Process until garlic and shallots are finely chopped. Add peanut butter and coconut milk. Process until smooth.

3. Thread chicken on 10-inch wooden picks or skewers. Grill over direct medium-high heat for 10 minutes, until tender and opaque. Baste with peanut butter sauce. Serve remaining sauce for dipping.

283   GRILLED CHICKEN BREASTS WITH DIABLO SAUCE

Prep: 15 minutes   Cook: 40 minutes   Serves: 6

- 6 chicken breast halves with bone
- 4 tablespoons butter or margarine, melted
- 1 tablespoon minced onion
- 1 garlic clove, crushed through a press
- ½ teaspoon dried basil
- ½ teaspoon dried thyme

- ½ teaspoon salt
- ¼ teaspoon freshly ground pepper
- ⅓ cup sour cream, at room temperature
- ⅓ cup mayonnaise
- 1 tablespoon coarse-grain Dijon mustard
- ¼ cup toasted sliced almonds

1. Tear off 6 sheets of heavy-duty aluminum foil 18 x 12 inches. Place chicken breasts, skin side up, on foil.

2. In a small bowl, combine butter, onion, garlic, basil, thyme, salt, and pepper; brush half of butter mixture over chicken. Turn chicken; brush with remaining butter mixture, leaving skin side down. Bring top half of foil over chicken; fold open edges in a series of locked folds to seal.

3. Grill over medium-direct heat for 40 minutes, or bake in a 350° oven for 40 minutes, until tender.

4. While chicken is cooking, combine sour cream, mayonnaise and mustard.

5. To serve, carefully remove chicken from foil package and spoon sauce on top of each breast. Garnish with almonds.

---

284   GRILLED CHICKEN DIJONNAISE

Prep: 15 minutes   Marinate: 30 minutes   Cook: 10 minutes
Serves: 6

¼ cup vegetable oil
¼ cup fresh lemon juice
½ teaspoon freshly ground
   pepper
6 skinless, boneless chicken
   breast halves
3 tablespoons tarragon
   vinegar

2 tablespoons dry white wine
1 teaspoon dried tarragon
4 tablespoons butter or
   margarine
2 tablespoons Dijon-style
   mustard

1. In a shallow dish, combine oil, lemon juice, and pepper. Add chicken and turn to coat with marinade. Marinate, turning occasionally, for 30 minutes.

2. Meanwhile, combine vinegar, wine, and tarragon in a small nonaluminum saucepan; boil until reduced to about 2 tablespoons. Reduce heat to low, add butter and mustard, and stir until butter melts. Set sauce aside; keep warm.

3. Drain chicken well. Grill or broil over medium heat, turning once, and basting frequently with mustard sauce, until just cooked through, about 5 minutes a side. Be careful not to overcook chicken.

---

285   GINGERED CHICKEN WITH YOGURT

Prep: 10 minutes   Marinate: at least 1 hour   Cook: 40 minutes
Serves: 4

1 cup plain yogurt
8 garlic cloves
   1-inch piece peeled fresh
   ginger
1 tablespoon lemon juice

1½ teaspoons chili powder
1 teaspoon salt
1 chicken (3 pounds), cut up
   Lemon slices, for garnish

1. In a blender or food processor, combine all ingredients except chicken and lemon slices. Purée until smooth. Arrange chicken in a large shallow dish. Pour yogurt marinade over chicken. Let stand at room temperature, turning occasionally, for 1 to 3 hours, or cover and refrigerate overnight.

2. On a charcoal grill, cook chicken over medium direct heat, turning occasionally, for 40 minutes, or broil 25 to 30 minutes, until tender. Serve hot or cold. Garnish with lemon slices.

286   CHICKEN AND VEGETABLES IN FOIL PACKET

Prep: 20 minutes   Cook: 40 minutes   Serves: 4

¼ cup olive oil
4 small baking potatoes, scrubbed and sliced
1 green bell pepper, cut into ½-inch strips
1 red bell pepper, cut into ½-inch strips

2 medium-size onions, sliced
1 chicken (about 3 pounds), quartered
1 teaspoon coarse (kosher) salt
¼ teaspoon freshly ground pepper

1. Tear off 4 sheets of heavy-duty aluminum foil 18 x 14 inches. Brush with oil.

2. Divide vegetables evenly among the foil sheets. Brush with more oil. Top with chicken quarters, skin side up, brushing with remaining oil. Season with salt and pepper. Bring the top half of foil over chicken; fold open edges in a series of locked folds.

4. Grill over medium direct heat for 40 minutes, or bake in a 350° oven for 50 minutes, until chicken is tender. Open foil packages carefully and serve.

287   HONEY-LEMON KEBABS

Prep: 20 minutes   Marinate: 2 hours   Cook: 12 minutes   Serves: 6

¼ cup vegetable oil
⅓ cup honey
⅓ cup soy sauce
⅓ cup bourbon
2 garlic cloves, finely chopped
¼ teaspoon freshly ground pepper
2 pounds skinless, boneless chicken breasts, cut into 1-inch cubes

2 whole lemons, cut into wedges, then halved
24 medium-size mushrooms, trimmed
12 small white onions, peeled
2 green bell peppers, cut into 2-inch pieces
1 red bell pepper, cut into 2-inch pieces

1. In a large bowl, combine oil, honey, soy sauce, bourbon, garlic, and pepper. Whisk to blend.

2. Add chicken and remaining ingredients and marinate 2 hours at room temperature or refrigerate overnight, turning chicken occasionally.

3. Soak 12 long wooden skewers in water for 30 minutes to prevent burning when broiling. Drain chicken and vegetables, reserving marinade. Divide chicken and vegetables among skewers.

4. Place kebabs on a foil-lined broiler pan. Broil, turning and brushing with marinade, for 12 minutes, until edges of chicken are brown, but do not overcook. Or grill over a charcoal fire of medium heat for 12 to 15 minutes, until chicken is tender.

288   GRILL-ROASTED CHICKEN WITH HERBS

Prep: 10 minutes   Cook: 1¼ hours   Serves: 4

1 whole chicken, about 3
   pounds
1 large onion, cut into eighths
1 bay leaf
½ teaspoon celery seed
½ teaspoon poultry seasoning

1 stick (½ cup) butter or
   margarine
½ teaspoon dried basil
½ teaspoon dried tarragon
1 garlic clove, finely chopped

1. Wash chicken and pat dry. Place onion, bay leaf, celery seed, and poultry seasoning in cavity of chicken. Tie legs together with string. Insert meat thermometer in thickest part of the breast.

2. Melt butter in a small saucepan. Add basil, tarragon, and garlic.

3. Place chicken on grill over drip pan. Grill over medium indirect heat (see note) in a covered cooker until meat thermometer reads 180° to 185°. Baste every 15 minutes with basil-tarragon butter.

Note: To grill over indirect heat, place coals to one side of the grill; set an aluminum foil drip pan under food.

289   APPLE-TARRAGON BARBECUE

*Prep: 25 minutes   Marinate: at least 1 hour   Cook: 40 minutes
Serves: 4*

1 cup apple cider
⅓ cup cider vinegar
⅓ cup sliced scallions
¼ cup vegetable oil
3 tablespoons honey
2 tablespoons steak sauce

1½ teaspoons dried tarragon
1 teaspoon salt
¼ teaspoon freshly ground
   pepper
1 chicken (3 pounds), cut up

1. In a small saucepan, combine all ingredients except chicken. Bring to a boil, reduce heat, and simmer uncovered 15 minutes. Let cool 5 minutes.

2. Place chicken pieces in a large bowl. Add apple-tarragon marinade. Cover and marinate, turning occasionally, 1 to 3 hours at room temperature, or refrigerate overnight.

3. Grill chicken pieces over medium direct heat, turning, for about 40 minutes, or broil 25 to 30 minutes, until chicken is tender.

290 GRILLED CHICKEN TERIYAKI-STYLE

Prep: 10 minutes   Marinate: at least 3 hours   Cook: 40 minutes
Serves: 4

A tasty low-fat grill that goes beautifully with a variety of vegetables and salads.

½ cup soy sauce	2 tablespoons vegetable oil
⅓ cup dry sherry	1 garlic clove, crushed
½ cup (firmly packed) brown sugar	½ teaspoon ground ginger
¼ cup cider vinegar	3 pounds chicken legs, thighs, and/or breasts

1. In a large bowl, combine all ingredients except chicken. Stir to dissolve the sugar. Add chicken and turn to coat with marinade. Refrigerate, turning occasionally, at least 3 hours, and preferably overnight.

2. Grill chicken over medium heat for about 40 minutes, or broil for about 15 minutes, turning, until chicken is crisp outside and tender.

291 BROILED CHICKEN BREASTS WITH PESTO SAUCE

Prep: 5 minutes   Cook: 20 minutes   Serves: 4

Easy and impressive. Serve with buttered pasta and juicy ripe tomatoes.

4 chicken breast halves with bone	¼ cup minced fresh basil
3 tablespoons fresh lemon juice	¼ cup grated Parmesan cheese
¼ teaspoon salt	1 garlic clove, crushed through a press
⅛ teaspoon freshly ground pepper	2 tablespoons olive oil

1. Preheat broiler. Brush chicken breasts with lemon juice. Season with salt and pepper. Place chicken, skin side down, on broiler pan and broil about 8 inches from heat for 5 minutes. Turn and broil 5 minutes longer.

2. Meanwhile, in a blender, combine basil, cheese, garlic, and oil; mix until well blended. Spread over skin of each chicken breast. Broil 5 to 10 minutes longer, until chicken is opaque throughout but still juicy.

Chapter 17

Chicken and Fruit

I suspect that more people would like to use fruit in their cooking if they only knew what to do with it. Chicken is the answer. Its subtle flavor pairs beautifully with a cornucopia of fruity tastes—bananas, grapefruit, oranges, apples, grapes, pineapple, prunes, peaches, raspberries, cranberries, cherries, tangerines, apricots, and pears, to name a few. And with fresh fruit now available throughout most of the country year-round, it is almost a shame not to take more advantage of nature's tart, sweet bounty.

It is simple to cook with fruit, and fruit also adds color, which can turn a predictable mid-week meal into a festive occasion.

Fragrant spices and sometimes a counterpoint of vinegar add just the right touch to most of these special recipes.

292 STIR-FRIED LEMON CHICKEN WITH PEARS AND GINGER

Prep: 30 minutes   Cook: 6 minutes   Serves: 2

A light, easy, refreshing meal. Ingredients can easily be doubled or tripled.

2 tablespoons soy sauce
1 teaspoon grated lemon peel
2 tablespoons lemon juice
2 teaspoons sugar
2 teaspoons cornstarch
2 garlic cloves, minced
2 teaspoons grated fresh
    ginger
3 tablespoons water

2 tablespoons vegetable oil
¾ pound skinless, boneless
    chicken breasts, cut into
    1-inch cubes
½ pound fresh snow peas
3 scallions, green tops only,
    cut into 1-inch lengths
2 fresh Bartlett pears, cored
    and sliced

1. To make sauce, combine soy sauce, lemon peel, lemon juice, sugar, cornstarch, garlic, ginger, and water.

2. Heat vegetable oil in a large nonstick frying pan or wok. Add chicken and stir-fry over high heat for 2 minutes, until chicken is opaque. Remove to a platter.

3. Add snow peas to pan and stir-fry for 1 minute. Reduce heat to medium. Return chicken to pan. Add scallion greens, pears, and sauce. Cook, stirring, until sauce boils and thickens, about 3 minutes.

293 BAKED CHICKEN WITH PRUNES AND SWEET POTATOES

Prep: 5 minutes   Cook: 1¼ hours   Serves: 4

1 cup prunes
1 chicken (3 pounds), halved
1 tablespoon butter or
    margarine, softened

Salt and freshly ground
    pepper
4 medium sweet potatoes,
    boiled, peeled, quartered

1. In a small saucepan, combine prunes and 1 cup water. Bring to a boil, reduce heat to low, and simmer 15 minutes, until prunes are soft.

2. Drain off liquid, reserving 2 tablespoons. Purée prunes in a blender or food processor with the reserved liquid.

3. Preheat oven to 450°. Place chicken on a large sheet of heavy-duty aluminum foil and rub with butter. Season with salt and pepper. Spread prune purée over chicken. Bring up edges of foil to enclose and fold and crimp edges to seal well. Place in a shallow baking dish and bake 45 minutes.

4. Carefully open foil and arrange sweet potatoes around chicken, basting with purée. Reduce oven to 400°. Return to oven and bake uncovered 15 minutes longer, basting chicken and potatoes every 5 minutes.

294 PRUNES AND PEPPERS CREOLE
Prep: 20 minutes   Cook: 1 hour   Serves: 4

1 cup chopped pitted prunes
1 cup hot chicken broth
2 tablespoons vegetable oil
1 chicken (3 pounds), cut up
2 medium onions, chopped
1 medium green bell pepper,
    cut into 1-inch squares
1 garlic clove, chopped

1 can (16 ounces) whole
    tomatoes, broken up
½ teaspoon salt
½ teaspoon dried basil
¼ teaspoon freshly ground
    pepper
¼ teaspoon dried thyme

1. In a small bowl, combine prunes and chicken broth. Set aside.

2. Heat oil in a large frying pan over medium heat. Add chicken and cook, turning, until brown, about 10 minutes. Transfer chicken to a 13 x 9 x 2-inch baking dish.

3. Preheat oven to 375°. Drain all but 2 tablespoons fat from pan. Add onions, green pepper, and garlic. Cook, stirring, 5 minutes, until vegetables soften. Stir in tomatoes, salt, basil, pepper, and thyme. Bring to a boil and pour over chicken. Bake for 30 minutes.

4. Pour prunes and broth over chicken, stirring to combine. Bake 15 minutes, until chicken is tender.

295 FRUITED CHICKEN THIGHS
Prep: 30 minutes   Cook: 1 hour   Serves: 4

6 tablespoons butter or
    margarine
1 medium onion, chopped
¼ cup finely chopped celery
1 garlic clove, minced
1 cup seasoned croutons

2 medium apples, cored and
    chopped
¼ cup raisins
¼ cup chopped walnuts
1 egg, beaten
8 large chicken thighs
1 teaspoon dried tarragon

1. In a medium-size frying pan, melt 2 tablespoons of the butter. Add onion, celery, and garlic. Sauté about 3 minutes, until onion and celery are tender. Remove from heat and add croutons, apples, raisins, walnuts, and eggs; mix well.

2. Preheat oven to 350°. Prepare chicken thighs by pulling the skin away from the meat without removing it. Stuff apple mixture between skin and meat. Arrange chicken in a foil-lined 13 x 9 x 2-inch baking dish.

3. Melt remaining 4 tablespoons butter. In a small bowl, combine melted butter and tarragon. Brush over chicken thighs. Bake, uncovered, basting every 15 minutes, for 1 hour, until chicken is tender.

296   BOMBAY CHICKEN
Prep: 15 minutes   Cook: 1 hour   Serves: 6

1 chicken (3 pounds), cut up
  Salt and freshly ground
    pepper
1 cup rice
1 package (6 ounces) mixed
    dried fruit

1 medium onion, chopped
4 teaspoons curry powder
2 cups chicken broth
2 tablespoons butter or
    margarine, melted
½ teaspoon paprika

1. Preheat oven to 375°. Season chicken with salt and pepper.

2. Combine rice, fruit, onion, 2 teaspoons of the curry powder, and chicken broth in a 13 x 9 x 2-inch baking dish; stir well. Arrange chicken over rice mixture.

3. In a small bowl, combine melted butter, paprika, and remaining 2 teaspoons curry powder; brush over chicken. Cover with aluminum foil and bake 1 hour, until chicken is tender and liquid is absorbed.

297   CHICKEN AND PEACHES ORIENTALE
Prep: 15 minutes   Cook: 1¼ hours   Serves: 4

1 chicken (3 pounds), cut up
  Salt and freshly ground
    pepper
1 large onion, sliced
1 cup ketchup
1 tablespoon honey

2 tablespoons soy sauce
1 large green bell pepper, cut
    into 1-inch pieces
2 peaches, peeled and sliced
    into eighths

1. Preheat oven to 450°. Sprinkle chicken with salt and pepper. Place skin side up in a lightly greased 2½-quart baking dish. Bake 20 minutes.

2. Remove from oven and place onion slices on top. Blend ketchup, honey, soy sauce, and 1 cup water. Pour over chicken. Cover and bake 30 minutes.

3. Add green pepper and peaches. Spoon sauce over chicken, peppers, and peaches. Cover and bake 15 minutes.

298   SPICED CHICKEN WITH PEACHES AND PINEAPPLE SAUCE
Prep: 15 minutes   Cook: 1 hour   Serves: 4

The nutty flavor of couscous goes nicely with this sweetly spiced fruity chicken. Use instant boxed couscous for a quick, delicious dinner.

1 chicken (3 pounds), cut up
1 can (8 ounces) crushed
    pineapple
1 cup orange juice
½ cup raisins
½ cup sliced almonds

¼ teaspoon ground cinnamon
¼ teaspoon ground cloves
1 can (16 ounces) cling peaches,
    drained and puréed
  Salt and freshly ground
    pepper

1. In a large frying pan, combine chicken, pineapple, orange juice, raisins,

almonds, cinnamon, and cloves. Simmer, partly covered, 45 minutes, turning chicken occasionally.

2. Add peach purée to pan and stir until well blended. Simmer uncovered 15 minutes longer, until chicken is tender and sauce is slightly thickened. Season with salt and pepper to taste.

---

299   SUNSHINE CHICKEN
Prep: 25 minutes   Cook: 1 hour   Serves: 4

3 **pounds chicken thighs**	2 **tablespoons brandy**
½ **teaspoon salt**	2 **teaspoons cider vinegar**
¼ **teaspoon freshly ground pepper**	1 **teaspoon grated orange peel**
5 **teaspoons cornstarch**	½ **teaspoon dried tarragon**
2 **teaspoons sugar**	1 **navel orange, peeled and sectioned**
1 **cup chicken broth**	½ **seedless grapefruit, peeled and sectioned**
½ **cup orange juice**	

1. Preheat oven to 350°. Arrange chicken skin side up in a 12 x 8 x 2-inch baking dish. Season with salt and pepper. Bake for 45 minutes.

2. In a medium-size saucepan, mix cornstarch and sugar. Stir in broth, orange juice, brandy, vinegar, orange peel, and tarragon. Cook, stirring, over medium heat until sauce boils and thickens, about 3 minutes. Stir in orange and grapefruit sections.

3. Spoon sauce and fruit over chicken. Return to oven for 15 minutes longer, until chicken is fork tender.

---

300   ORANGE CHICKEN WITH GREEN GRAPES
Prep: 10 minutes   Cook: 1 hour   Serves: 4

1 **chicken (3 pounds), cut up**	1½ **teaspoons instant chicken bouillon granules**
½ **teaspoon salt**	½ **teaspoon finely grated orange peel**
¼ **teaspoon freshly ground pepper**	1 **tablespoon cornstarch dissolved in 1 tablespoon cold water**
¾ **teaspoon paprika**	
½ **cup orange juice**	
1 **tablespoon chopped scallions**	⅔ **cup seedless green grapes, halved**

1. Preheat oven to 350°. Arrange chicken in a 13 x 9 x 2-inch baking pan. Season with salt, pepper, and ¼ teaspoon of the paprika.

2. In a small bowl, mix together orange juice, scallion, bouillon granules, and orange peel. Pour over chicken. Bake 1 hour, until chicken is brown and tender. Remove chicken to a serving platter and keep warm. Reserve ¾ cup pan drippings.

3. In a medium-size saucepan, mix together dissolved cornstarch and remaining ½ teaspoon paprika. Stir in reserved ¾ cup pan drippings; bring to a boil. Cook until thick and bubbly, stirring constantly. Add grapes and cook 2 minutes, until hot.

301 CHICKEN NORMANDE WITH APPLES AND CREAM
Prep: 20 minutes   Cook: 35 minutes   Serves: 4

Cream and apples are two of the major products and cooking ingredients of Normandy, on the northwest coast of France. This pairing of flavors, homey and rich at the same time, is typical of the region.

1 chicken (3 pounds), cut up
Salt and freshly ground pepper
3 tablespoons butter or margarine
2 shallots, chopped
1 garlic clove, finely chopped

½ cup dry white wine
¼ teaspoon dried thyme
2 tart-sweet apples, peeled, cored, and cut into wedges
½ cup heavy cream
4 ounces shredded Gruyère or Swiss cheese (about 1 cup)

1. Season chicken with salt and pepper. In a large frying pan, melt butter over medium heat. Add shallots and garlic and sauté until soft but not brown, 1 to 2 minutes. Add chicken and sauté for about 5 minutes a side, until lightly browned. Add wine and thyme. Cover and simmer 20 minutes. Add apples and simmer 10 minutes.

2. Preheat oven to broil. Transfer apples and chicken to a flameproof serving dish.

3. Pour cream into frying pan, stirring constantly until mixture comes to a boil. Pour over chicken. Sprinkle cheese over chicken. Broil until cheese is melted and bubbly.

302 SAUTÉED ORANGE CHICKEN WITH GINGER
Prep: 20 minutes   Cook: 30 minutes   Serves: 4

Fresh ginger can be found in many supermarkets these days, as well as in Oriental groceries. Buy a large, firm "hand." Store wrapped in a paper towel inside a plastic bag.

3 pounds chicken legs and/or thighs
Salt and freshly ground pepper
2 tablespoons vegetable oil
2 garlic cloves, finely chopped
1 cup orange juice

2 navel oranges, peeled and sectioned
2 tablespoons minced fresh ginger
4 teaspoons white vinegar
1 teaspoon dried basil

1. Season chicken with salt and pepper. In a large frying pan, heat oil over medium heat. Add chicken and cook, turning, until brown all over, about 10 minutes. Add garlic and cook for 1 minute.

2. Pour orange juice over chicken. Add orange sections, ginger, vinegar, and basil; stir well. Cover and simmer for about 30 minutes, until chicken is tender.

303   APRICOT CHICKEN ROLLS
Prep: 30 minutes   Cook: 30 minutes   Serves: 6

6 skinless, boneless chicken breast halves, pounded to ¼-inch thickness
Salt and freshly ground pepper
8 tablespoons butter or margarine, softened
¼ teaspoon dried basil
18 dried apricot halves, cut into thin strips

¼ cup flour
1 cup bread crumbs
1 can (16 ounces) apricot halves, drained, or 4 fresh apricots, peeled and halved
¼ cup chili sauce
2 teaspoons brown sugar
½ teaspoon prepared white horseradish

1. Place chicken on wax paper and season with salt and pepper. In a small bowl, mix 4 tablespoons of the butter with basil. Spread over chicken breasts. Sprinkle dried apricot strips over butter. Starting at a small end, roll up chicken breasts, jelly-roll style; secure with wooden toothpicks.

2. Preheat oven to 350°. Melt remaining 4 tablespoons butter. Place flour, melted butter, and bread crumbs in separate shallow dishes. Roll chicken breasts in flour, dip in butter, then roll in bread crumbs.

3. Arrange chicken in a 13 x 9 x 2-inch baking dish. Cover with aluminum foil. Bake for 20 minutes. Uncover and bake for 10 minutes more, until chicken is lightly browned and tender.

4. While chicken is cooking, place apricot halves, chili sauce, brown sugar, horseradish, and ¼ teaspoon salt in a blender or food processor. Blend until smooth. Place in a small saucepan and heat through. Serve over chicken.

304   WALNUT, APPLE BRANDY CHICKEN
Prep: 25 minutes   Cook: 15 to 20 minutes   Serves: 6

3 tablespoons butter or margarine
½ cup finely chopped walnuts
2 shallots, minced
2 pounds skinless boneless chicken breasts, cut into ½-inch strips
2 apples, peeled, cored, and sliced

¼ cup apple brandy (applejack or Calvados)
1 cup heavy cream
1 teaspoon Dijon mustard
¼ teaspoon salt
⅛ teaspoon freshly ground pepper
2 tablespoons chopped parsley

1. In a small frying pan, melt 1 tablespoon of the butter over medium heat. Add walnuts and cook until lightly toasted, 1 or 2 minutes.

2. In a large frying pan, melt remaining 2 tablespoons butter over medium heat. Add shallots and cook until softened, 1 to 2 minutes. Add chicken strips and cook 3 to 5 minutes, tossing, until chicken turns white.

3. Add apples and brandy. Ignite brandy. Stir in cream, mustard, salt, and pepper. Simmer 5 minutes. Remove to a warm serving platter and garnish with parsley.

305   TANGERINE CHICKEN
Prep: 5 minutes   Cook: 20 minutes   Serves: 4

3 tablespoons butter or
    margarine
4 skinless, boneless chicken
    breast halves
    Salt and freshly ground
    pepper
2 tablespoons flour

1 cup frozen orange juice
    concentrate reconstituted
    with ½ cup water
¼ teaspoon cinnamon
3 tangerines, peeled and
    sectioned
1 tablespoon grated tangerine
    peel

1. In a large frying pan, melt butter over medium heat. Add chicken and season with salt and pepper. Cook, turning once, until chicken is cooked through, 8 to 10 minutes. Remove chicken.

2. Add flour to fat in pan. Cook, stirring, for 1 to 2 minutes without coloring. Whisk in orange juice. Bring to a boil, reduce heat, and simmer, stirring, until sauce is smooth and thick, about 2 minutes. Season with cinnamon and salt and pepper to taste. Return chicken to pan and turn to coat with sauce. Mix in tangerine sections and peel and serve.

306   MANDARIN CHICKEN IN APPLE MADEIRA SAUCE
Prep: 10 minutes   Cook: 45 minutes   Serves: 6

3 tablespoons butter or
    margarine
6 chicken breasts or whole legs
1 large onion, finely chopped
1 garlic clove, finely chopped
1 apple, peeled, cored, and
    chopped
¼ cup Madeira

1 cup orange juice
1 teaspoon cornstarch
    dissolved in 1 tablespoon
    water
    Salt and freshly ground
    pepper
1 can (11 ounces) mandarin
    oranges, drained

1. In a large frying pan, melt butter over medium heat. Add chicken; cook until lightly browned, about 10 minutes a side. Remove and set aside.

2. Add onion, garlic, and apple to pan; sauté 3 to 5 minutes, until onion is soft. Return chicken to pan, add orange juice and simmer, covered, about 20 minutes, until cooked through.

3. Remove chicken to a platter. Stir dissolved cornstarch into pan. Bring to a boil, reduce heat, simmer, stirring, until smooth and thickened. Pour over chicken. Garnish with mandarin oranges.

307   CRANBERRY ORANGE CHICKEN
Prep: 10 minutes   Cook: 20 minutes   Serves: 4

2 tablespoons butter or
  margarine
4 chicken breast halves with
  bone
⅔ cup fresh orange juice
⅔ cup fresh or frozen
  cranberries

1 tablespoon honey
2 tablespoons grated orange
  peel
2 teaspoons cornstarch
⅛ teaspoon ground cloves

1. In a large frying pan, melt butter over medium heat. Add chicken breasts and cook about 10 minutes on each side, until juices run clear.

2. In a medium-size nonaluminum saucepan, combine orange juice, cranberries, honey, orange peel, cornstarch, and cloves. Cook over medium heat, stirring occasionally, until thickened. Spoon sauce over chicken breasts.

308   CURRIED CHICKEN CARIBE
Prep: 20 minutes   Cook: 50 minutes   Serves: 4

¼ cup flour
1½ teaspoons salt
1 teaspoon curry powder
½ teaspoon paprika
1 chicken (3 pounds), cut up
3 tablespoons vegetable oil
1 can (8 ounces) unsweetened
  pineapple chunks,
  drained, juice reserved

1 can (11 ounces) mandarin
  orange sections, drained,
  juice reserved
¼ cup brown sugar
2 teaspoons cornstarch
¼ cup cider vinegar
8 maraschino cherries
  (optional)

1. Combine flour, 1 teaspoon of the salt, ½ teaspoon of the curry powder, and paprika in a plastic or paper bag; shake to mix. Add chicken pieces, a few at a time, and shake to coat.

2. In a large frying pan, heat oil over medium heat. Add chicken and cook, turning, until browned, about 5 minutes a side. Transfer to a 13 x 9 x 2-inch baking dish.

3. Preheat oven to 350°. In a 1 cup measure, combine reserved pineapple and orange juice; add water to make 1 cup.

4. In a medium-size saucepan, combine brown sugar, cornstarch, remaining ½ teaspoon salt, and remaining ½ teaspoon curry powder. Stir in fruit juice and vinegar. Heat to boiling, stirring constantly; cook until mixture thickens, about 3 minutes.

5. Pour sauce over chicken. Cover with foil and bake for 30 minutes. Add pineapple chunks, oranges, and cherries. Bake uncovered for 20 minutes, until chicken is tender.

309   BANANA COCONUT CHICKEN
Prep: 20 minutes   Marinate: 2 hours   Cook: 1 hour   Serves: 4

1 chicken (3 pounds), cut up
2 garlic cloves, finely chopped
1 tablespoon soy sauce
1 can (15 ounces) cream of coconut
2 tablespoons cider vinegar
1/3 cup finely chopped celery with leaves

1/4 teaspoon freshly ground pepper
2 tablespoons cornstarch
1 tablespoon rum
4 bananas, sliced
1 teaspoon thinly sliced orange peel

1. Arrange chicken pieces in a 13 x 9 x 2-inch baking dish. In a small bowl, combine garlic, soy sauce, 3/4 cup of the coconut cream, vinegar, celery, and pepper. Mix well. Pour over chicken, cover, and marinate at room temperature for 2 hours, turning occasionally.

2. Preheat oven to 350°. Turn chicken skin side up and bake for 1 hour, until tender and browned. Transfer to a platter and cover to keep warm.

3. Pour drippings into a measuring cup; skim off fat. Add additional coconut cream to measure 1 cup. Stir in cornstarch. Pour into a small saucepan, add rum, bring to a boil, and cook, stirring constantly, until thickened. Add bananas and orange peel. Pour over chicken.

310   FIG, NUT, AND APRICOT CHICKEN
Prep: 25 minutes   Marinate: overnight   Cook: 1 hour   Serves: 8

2 chickens (3 pounds each), cut up
1/2 cup red wine vinegar
1/4 cup olive oil
1 1/2 cups dried apricots (about 8 ounces)
1 cup chopped dried figs
6 garlic cloves, finely chopped

1 teaspoon dried thyme
1 teaspoon cumin
1/2 teaspoon ground ginger
1 teaspoon salt
1/2 cup Madeira
1 cup chopped pecans (about 4 ounces)

1. Place chicken in a 14 x 12 x 2 1/2-inch roasting pan. In a bowl, combine vinegar, oil, apricots, figs, garlic, thyme, cumin, ginger, and salt; mix well. Pour over chicken, cover, and marinate overnight in refrigerator, turning chicken occasionally. Remove 1 hour before cooking.

2. Preheat oven to 350°. Arrange chicken in a single layer in two 13 x 9 x 2-inch baking dishes. Pour marinade and wine over chicken, distributing evenly. Bake uncovered for 1 hour, until chicken is tender. Serve garnished with pecans.

311   CHICKEN BREASTS WITH RASPBERRIES
Prep: 5 minutes   Cook: 20 minutes   Serves: 4

A gorgeous, elegant dish for very special guests. Be sure you use a raspberry brandy and not a sweetened liqueur.

8 skinless, boneless chicken breast halves, pounded to ¼-inch thickness
Salt and freshly ground pepper
4 tablespoons butter
¼ teaspoon raspberry or red wine vinegar

1 cup unsalted chicken stock, or ½ cup canned broth diluted with ½ cup water
3 tablespoons raspberry brandy (framboise)
½ pint fresh raspberries

1. Season chicken with salt and pepper. In a large frying pan, melt 2 tablespoons of the butter over medium heat. Add chicken breasts and cook 3 minutes a side, until tender and opaque; do not brown. Remove to a serving platter and cover with foil to keep warm.

2. Add vinegar to pan drippings and boil about 2 minutes, until reduced to about 1½ tablespoons. Add stock and raspberry brandy; boil until reduced by half, about 5 minutes.

3. Remove from heat and swirl in remaining 2 tablespoons butter. Gently stir raspberries into sauce. Pour over chicken and serve.

312   SKILLET CHERRY CHICKEN
Prep: 10 minutes   Cook: 40 minutes   Serves: 6

1 tablespoon cornstarch
2 tablespoons lemon juice
1 can (16 ounces) bing cherries
¼ teaspoon ground cloves
¼ teaspoon allspice
½ cup flour
1 teaspoon salt

½ teaspoon freshly ground pepper
6 chicken breast halves with bone, or 6 whole chicken legs
¼ cup vegetable oil

1. In a small bowl, dissolve cornstarch in lemon juice. Add cherries, cloves, and allspice. Mix well and set aside.

2. In a large plastic or paper bag, combine flour, salt, and pepper. Add chicken pieces, a few at a time, and shake to coat.

3. In a large frying pan, preferably nonstick, heat oil over medium heat. Add chicken and fry, turning, until brown all over, about 10 minutes. Reduce heat, cover, and simmer for 20 minutes, until tender. Remove to a serving platter and cover with foil to keep warm.

4. Remove all but 1 tablespoon of fat from frying pan. Add cherry mixture. Bring to a boil, stirring constantly until sauce thickens and mixture is heated through. Pour over chicken and serve.

313   CHICKEN CHERRIES FLAMBÉ

Prep: 20 minutes   Cook: 15 minutes   Serves: 8

4 tablespoons butter or margarine
¼ cup slivered almonds
¼ cup sliced scallions
1 package (3 ounces) cream cheese, softened
¼ teaspoon salt
⅛ teaspoon freshly ground pepper
8 chicken breast halves with bone

2 tablespoons vegetable oil
1 can (16 ounces) pitted dark sweet cherries, drained, liquid reserved
¼ teaspoon grated orange peel
1 tablespoon cornstarch dissolved in 2 tablespoons water
¼ cup brandy

1. Melt 2 tablespoons of the butter in a medium-size frying pan. Add almonds and scallions and cook about 3 minutes, until scallions are soft and nuts are lightly browned. Remove to a small bowl; add cream cheese, salt, and pepper; mix until well blended.

2. Slit a pocket in each chicken breast. Stuff each with a portion of cream cheese mixture and secure with wooden toothpicks. Season with additional salt and pepper.

3. In a large frying pan, heat remaining 2 tablespoons butter in the oil. Brown chicken on all sides over medium-high heat, about 8 minutes. Add cherries with juice and orange peel to chicken and cook, covered, for 10 to 15 minutes, until cooked through. Arrange chicken and cherries on a serving dish and cover with foil to keep warm.

4. Bring liquid in pan to a boil and boil until reduced to about ⅔ cup. Stir dissolved cornstarch into juices in pan. Cook, stirring constantly, until sauce boils and thickens. Season with salt and pepper to taste. Pour half the sauce over chicken.

5. Warm brandy in a large ladle or small saucepan, but do not boil. Ignite carefully and pour flaming brandy over chicken. Pass remaining cherry sauce separately.

314 SWEET-AND-SOUR CHICKEN WITH PINEAPPLE

Prep: 20 minutes   Cook: 1 hour   Serves: 4

1 chicken (3 pounds), cut up
   Salt and freshly ground
   pepper
2 tablespoons cider vinegar
2 tablespoons tomato paste
1 can (16 ounces) pineapple
   chunks, syrup reserved
2 tablespoons soy sauce

½ teaspoon ground ginger
1 large onion, chopped
1 large green bell pepper, cut
   into 1-inch squares
1 tablespoon cornstarch
   dissolved in 2 tablespoons
   water

1. Preheat oven to 450°. Season chicken with salt and pepper. Arrange skin side up in a lightly greased 13 x 9 x 2-inch baking dish. Bake in oven for 20 minutes, until browned.

2. Combine vinegar, tomato paste, and pineapple syrup with enough water to make 2 cups liquid; pour into a large bowl. Add soy sauce and ginger; stir until well blended. Add onion and bell pepper and set aside.

3. Lower oven to 325°. Pour syrup mixture over chicken, cover with foil, and bake for 30 minutes.

4. Add pineapple to chicken, cover, and return to oven for 10 minutes, until chicken is tender and fruit is heated through. Remove chicken to a platter. Pour sauce into a small saucepan. Stir in dissolved cornstarch. Bring to a boil, stirring until thickened. Pour over chicken.

315 SAUTÉED CHICKEN WALDORF

Prep: 15 minutes   Cook: 45 minutes   Serves: 6

6 chicken breast halves with
   bone
   Salt and freshly ground
   pepper
3 tablespoons vegetable oil
1 onion, sliced
3 celery ribs, sliced

3 apples, peeled, cored, and
   chopped
2 tablespoons flour
1½ cups beef stock
½ cup heavy cream
   Toasted walnuts, for garnish

1. Season chicken breasts with salt and pepper. In large frying pan, heat oil over medium heat. Add chicken and cook, turning once, until browned, about 10 minutes. Remove chicken and set aside.

2. Add onion, celery, and apples to pan. Cook until vegetables are tender, 3 to 5 minutes. Stir in flour and cook for 1 to 2 minutes without browning. Slowly whisk in stock. Return chicken to pan, cover, simmer 40 minutes, until chicken is tender.

3. Remove chicken to a serving platter. Add cream to sauce and simmer 3 minutes. Serve over chicken and garnish with walnuts.

316   HAWAIIAN CHICKEN BREASTS

Prep: 30 minutes   Chill: 1 hour   Cook: 20 minutes   Serves: 6

3 tablespoons butter or
   margarine, softened
2 teaspoons chili powder
¼ cup flaked coconut
6 skinless, boneless chicken
   breast halves, pounded to
   ¼-inch thickness
4 tablespoons vegetable oil
¼ cup chopped onion
½ cup ketchup
½ cup apricot preserves
1 tablespoon brown sugar
1 tablespoon cider vinegar

1 teaspoon curry powder
1 can (8 ounces) unsweetened
   pineapple chunks
1 can (16 ounces) sweet
   potatoes, drained and
   quartered
3 firm bananas, peeled and cut
   in half lengthwise
1 egg, beaten
¾ cup bread crumbs
½ teaspoon salt
¼ teaspoon freshly ground
   pepper

1. In a small bowl, combine butter, chili powder, and coconut. Spread over chicken breasts. Roll up jelly-roll style and secure with wooden toothpicks. Refrigerate 1 hour. (The recipe can be prepared to this point up to a day ahead.)

2. In a large saucepan, heat 1 tablespoon of the oil over medium heat. Add onion and cook until soft, about 2 minutes. Add ketchup, apricot preserves, brown sugar, vinegar, and curry powder; blend well. Add pineapple, sweet potatoes, and bananas and cook gently until heated through, about 5 minutes. Keep warm over low heat.

3. Place beaten egg in a shallow dish, and bread crumbs with salt and pepper in another. Dip chicken rolls into egg, then dredge in bread crumbs to coat.

3. In a large frying pan, heat remaining 3 tablespoons oil over medium heat. Add chicken rolls and brown evenly all over until just cooked through, about 10 minutes. Remove chicken to a platter. Remove pineapple, sweet potatoes, and bananas from sauce and arrange around chicken. Pour sauce over all and serve.

Chapter 18

Chicken and Pasta

Chicken and pasta are, of course, a natural duo. Both share sound nutritional qualities and cook in almost no time at all. And there's no doubt about it—America has discovered pasta. True, we've been eating spaghetti and noodles for a long time, but the availability of good-quality hard durum wheat pasta in all its various forms, the recognition of the nutritional benefits of a high-carbohydrate diet, and a growing awareness of the many ways pasta can be served has boosted it to new heights of popularity.

To cook pasta properly, use a very large pot with 5 or 6 quarts of boiling salted water. Special pots, with built-in colanders that can be lifted out, make the pasta easy to drain. Cook it at a rolling boil until it is tender but still slightly resistant to the bite, *al dente,* not soft and mushy. Begin tasting after 10 minutes to test. Check every 30 seconds after that. When perfectly cooked, drain immediately into a colander and rinse briefly under running water to rinse off the surface starch so the pasta won't stick or clump together.

317   CHICKEN SPAGHETTI SAUCE
Prep: 15 minutes   Cook: 1 hour   Serves: 4

Here's a white meat version of everyone's favorite. Garlic, herbs, and red wine give this sauce a zesty taste. Serve over spaghetti, linguine, or pasta shells. Pass a bowl of freshly grated Parmesan cheese on the side.

2 tablespoons vegetable oil
1 large onion, chopped
3 garlic cloves, finely chopped
1 pound chicken meat, finely chopped
1 can (28 ounces) plum tomatoes, chopped, with their juices
1 can (6 ounces) tomato paste

1 teaspoon dried oregano
1 teaspoon dried basil
1 bay leaf
1 cup dry red wine
¼ teaspoon freshly ground black pepper
Dash of cayenne pepper
Salt

1. In a large saucepan, heat oil over medium heat. Add onion and cook until soft, about 3 minutes. Add garlic and cook 1 minute longer. Add chicken and cook until white, about 4 minutes.

2. Add tomatoes, tomato paste, oregano, basil, bay leaf, wine, black pepper, and cayenne. Reduce heat and simmer 1 hour, until mixture thickens. Season with salt to taste.

318   CHICKEN IN A NEST
Prep: 20 minutes   Cook: 40 minutes   Serves: 4

8 ounces spinach fettuccine
8 chicken thighs, boned
   Salt and freshly ground pepper
1 tablespoon olive oil
1 tablespoon butter or margarine

½ cup cottage cheese
1 cup chopped scallions
1 cup chopped red bell pepper
⅓ cup flour
3 cups chicken broth
3 tablespoons dry white wine

1. In a large pot of boiling salted water, cook fettuccine until just tender, 10 to 12 minutes; drain.

2. Season chicken with salt and pepper. In a large frying pan, heat oil and butter over medium heat. Add chicken and cook until browned, about 5 minutes a side.

3. Arrange fettuccine in eight individual nest-shaped circles in a 13 x 9 x 2-inch baking dish. Place 1 tablespoon cottage cheese in each nest; top each with a chicken thigh.

4. Preheat oven to 350°. Remove and discard all but 4 tablespoons of pan drippings from frying pan. Add scallions and bell pepper. Cook over medium heat for 2 minutes. Stir in flour and cook 2 minutes more, until mixture just begins to color.

5. Slowly whisk in chicken broth. Cook, stirring constantly, until thick and smooth. Stir in wine and bring to a boil. Pour sauce over chicken nests. Bake, uncovered, for 20 minutes, until chicken is tender.

319 SPINACH AND PASTA TARRAGON DINNER
Prep: 25 Minutes   Cook: 10 minutes   Serves: 6

This entire dish can be assembled ahead and popped into the oven to heat through 10 to 15 minutes before serving.

1 **pound fettuccine**	1 **container (15 ounces) ricotta**
6 **tablespoons butter or**	**cheese**
margarine	½ **cup dry white wine**
1 **cup sliced leeks (white part**	½ **teaspoon dried tarragon**
only)	2 **packages (10 ounces each)**
¼ **pound mushrooms, sliced**	**frozen spinach, thawed**
¾ **pound skinless, boneless**	**and drained**
chicken breasts, cut into	¼ **cup heavy cream**
1-inch cubes	¾ **cup grated Parmesan cheese**

1. In a large pot of boiling salted water, cook fettuccine until just tender; drain. In a large bowl, toss pasta with 3 tablespoons of the butter.

2. In a large frying pan, melt remaining 3 tablespoons butter over medium-high heat. Add leeks and mushrooms; cook for 3 minutes. Add chicken pieces; cook, stirring constantly, until chicken turns white. Add ricotta cheese, wine, and tarragon. Blend well and cook until heated through.

3. Preheat oven to 400°. Combine spinach with fettuccine; toss until spinach is well mixed with pasta. Add cream and ½ cup of the Parmesan cheese. Toss again.

4. In a 13 x 9 x 2-inch baking dish or on a large ovenproof platter, arrange fettuccine mixture around the edges, pour chicken mixture in center. Sprinkle remaining ¼ cup of Parmesan cheese over top. Bake for 10 minutes, until heated through.

320 BAKED CHICKEN ROMANESQUE
Prep: 20 minutes   Cook: 45 minutes   Serves: 4

½ **pound spaghetti**	1 **garlic clove, finely chopped**
1 **chicken (3 pounds), cut up**	1 **can (16 ounces) tomato sauce**
Salt and freshly ground	1 **teaspoon Worcestershire**
pepper	**sauce**
2 **tablespoons vegetable oil**	½ **teaspoon dried oregano**
1 **cup chopped onion**	¼ **cup grated Parmesan cheese**
1 **cup chopped green pepper**	

1. In a large pot of boiling salted water, cook spaghetti until just tender, 10 to 12 minutes; drain. Put in a buttered 13 x 9 x 2-inch baking dish.

2. Preheat oven to 350°. Season chicken with salt and pepper. In a large frying pan, heat oil over medium heat. Add chicken; cook until browned, about 5 minutes a side. Arrange on top of spaghetti.

3. Add onion, pepper, and garlic to pan. Cook for 5 minutes, until onion is tender. Add tomato sauce, Worcestershire, and oregano. Cook 1 minute. Pour over chicken and spaghetti. Sprinkle with Parmesan cheese.

4. Cover and bake for 45 minutes until chicken is tender.

321 CHICKEN À LA SAMPION
Prep: 20 minutes   Cook: 1¼ hours   Serves: 8

1 pound small pasta shells
1 pound sliced bacon
8 skinless, boneless chicken breast halves, pounded to ¼-inch thickness
2 containers (16 ounces each) sour cream

2 cans (10¾ ounces each) cream of mushroom soup
1 can (8 ounces) quartered artichokes, drained
½ teaspoon dried marjoram
½ teaspoon dried tarragon
½ teaspoon salt

1. In a large pot of boiling, salted water, cook pasta until barely tender, 10 to 12 minutes; drain.

2. Cook bacon in a large frying pan over low heat until the fat is translucent but soft, not crisp; drain on paper towels. Remove all but ¼ cup of bacon drippings.

3. Raise heat to medium, add chicken to pan, and cook about 4 minutes a side, until lightly browned. Remove from pan. Wrap a strip of bacon around each chicken breast and secure with wooden toothpicks.

4. Preheat oven to 350°. In a medium-size saucepan, mix sour cream, soup, mushrooms, artichokes, marjoram, tarragon, and salt. Cook over low heat, stirring, until well blended.

5. Place drained pasta in a 14 x 12 x 2½-inch disposable foil roasting pan. Add ⅓ of the sour cream mixture and stir. Place chicken on top and cover with remaining sauce. Cover with foil and bake 45 minutes, until chicken is tender.

322 CHICKEN TETRAZZINI
Prep: 15 minutes   Cook: 30 minutes   Serves: 4

A good winter one-pot dinner. Served with a tossed salad and garlic bread.

8 ounces spaghetti, broken in half
5 tablespoons butter or margarine
1 onion, chopped
1 garlic clove, finely chopped
1 cup sliced mushrooms
¼ cup flour
2½ cups milk

Salt and cayenne pepper
1 can (8 ounces) water chestnuts, sliced and drained
2 cups chopped cooked chicken
2 tablespoons dry sherry
½ cup grated Parmesan cheese
Paprika

1. In a large pot of boiling salted water, cook spaghetti until *al dente*, about 10 minutes. Drain and set aside.

2. Meanwhile, melt 1 tablespoon of the butter in a large frying pan over medium-low heat. Add onion, garlic, and mushrooms; cook until tender, about 3 minutes. Remove from pan and set aside.

3. Melt remaining 4 tablespoons butter in pan. Using a whisk, blend in flour and cook, stirring, for 2 to 3 minutes without browning. Whisk in the milk and season to taste with salt and cayenne pepper. Cook until slightly thickened. Add sautéed mushroom mixture, water chestnuts, chicken, and sherry.

4. Preheat oven to 400°. In a greased 2-quart baking dish, arrange a layer of spaghetti, then a layer of creamed chicken. Sprinkle with grated cheese and paprika. Repeat layering procedure until dish is full. Bake 30 minutes.

---

323 CREOLE CHICKEN AND SHRIMP WITH LINGUINE
Prep: 10 minutes   Cook: 15 minutes   Serves: 6

Tomatoes, peppers, Worcestershire, and lemon juice give this dish its distinctive Creole flavor. For a change of pace, try the sauce over fluffy white rice.

4 tablespoons butter or margarine
2 tablespoons vegetable oil
1¼ to 1½ pounds skinless, boneless chicken breasts, cut into ½-inch cubes
1 pound shrimp, peeled and deveined
1 teaspoon dried oregano
½ teaspoon salt
¼ teaspoon freshly ground black pepper
¼ teaspoon cayenne pepper
1 onion, chopped
1 green bell pepper, chopped
2 garlic cloves, crushed
1 tomato, peeled and chopped
2 tablespoons Worcestershire sauce
2 tablespoons lemon juice
1 pound linguine, cooked and drained

1. In a large frying pan, melt 2 tablespoons of the butter in 1 tablespoon of the oil over medium-high heat. Add chicken and shrimp. Sprinkle with oregano, salt, black pepper, and cayenne. Sauté about 3 minutes, until chicken turns opaque and shrimp turns pink. Remove and set aside.

2. Reduce heat to medium and add remaining 2 tablespoons butter and 1 tablespoon oil. Add onion and sauté until softened, about 3 minutes. Add green pepper and garlic and cook until pepper is crisp-tender, 3 to 5 minutes. Add tomato, Worcestershire sauce, and lemon juice.

3. Return shrimp and chicken to pan, mix well, and simmer for 5 minutes. Serve over linguine.

324 SHERRIED CHICKEN WITH PEAS
Prep: 15 minutes   Cook: 30 minutes   Serves: 4

1¼ pounds skinless, boneless
   chicken breasts, cut into
   ¼-inch strips
½ teaspoon salt
¼ teaspoon freshly ground
   pepper
3½ tablespoons butter or
   margarine
1 cup sliced scallions

½ pound mushrooms, sliced
½ cup dry sherry
1 package (10 ounces) frozen
   peas
2 cups chicken broth
¾ pound egg noodles
3 tomatoes, peeled and cut in
   eighths
2 tablespoons cornstarch

1. Season chicken with salt and pepper. In a large frying pan, melt 2 tablespoons of the butter over medium heat. Add chicken and cook, stirring constantly, until opaque, about 3 minutes. Add scallions and mushrooms and cook 2 minutes. Add sherry, peas, and broth. Cover, reduce heat, and cook 20 minutes.

2. Meanwhile, in a large pot of boiling salted water, cook noodles until tender but still firm, 10 to 12 minutes; drain. Toss noodles with remaining 1½ tablespoons butter.

3. Add tomatoes to frying pan. Dissolve cornstarch in 3 tablespoons of cooking liquid; stir into chicken mixture. Bring to a boil and cook, stirring constantly, until mixture thickens, about 5 minutes. Serve over buttered egg noodles.

325 CHICKEN WITH ARTICHOKES AND PISTACHIO NUTS
Prep: 15 minutes   Cook: 15 minutes   Serves: 4

2 tablespoons butter or
   margarine
1 tablespoon olive oil
1 garlic clove, finely chopped
2 shallots, finely chopped
¼ pound mushrooms, sliced
1 can (14 ounces) quartered
   artichoke hearts, drained

1½ pounds skinless, boneless
   chicken breasts, cut into
   1-inch pieces
½ cup dry vermouth
1 teaspoon dried basil
½ pound pasta shells, cooked
   and drained
¼ cup shelled pistachio nuts
2 tablespoons grated
   Parmesan cheese

1. In a large frying pan, melt butter and oil over medium heat. Add garlic and shallots; cook, stirring, for 1 minute, until tender. Add mushrooms and artichokes; cook about 3 minutes, until mushrooms are lightly browned. Add chicken pieces. Cook about 3 minutes, stirring constantly, until chicken turns opaque.

2. Add vermouth and basil. Bring to a boil. Reduce heat and simmer for 5 minutes. Serve over pasta. Sprinkle with pistachio nuts and Parmesan cheese.

Chapter 19

Casseroles

Casseroles have long been an American favorite. I like them because they provide such an excellent way to use leftovers, and as often as not, they can be prepared ahead and popped into the oven at the last moment.

A good casserole dish should be heavy, to provide even cooking. Ovenproof ceramic and enameled cast-iron are excellent materials, though even a heatproof glass baking dish can be used.

326   CHICKEN STROGANOFF CASSEROLE
Prep: 10 minutes   Cook: 45 minutes   Serves: 4

Here's a light-meat version of the traditional beef dish. The chicken can also be sliced into ½-inch strips and served over noodles for a more classic Stroganoff.

3 tablespoons butter or margarine
4 skinless, boneless chicken breast halves
3 tablespoons flour
2 cups sour cream

Freshly ground pepper
1 cup sliced mushrooms
2 tablespoons chopped parsley
4 scallions, chopped
Grated rind of 1 lemon
3 teaspoons lemon juice

1. Preheat oven to 350°. Melt butter in a large frying pan and brown chicken breasts lightly, about 4 minutes. Remove breasts from skillet to an 8 x 8 x 2-inch baking dish.

2. Stir flour into pan; cook 1 minute. Add sour cream and pepper; simmer for 4 minutes. Add mushrooms, parsley, and scallions. Stir in lemon rind and lemon juice.

3. Pour sauce over chicken breasts, cover dish with foil, and bake for 45 minutes.

327   CHICKEN-RICE FLORENTINE
Prep: 20 minutes   Cook: 1 hour 5 minutes   Serves: 6

6 skinless, boneless chicken breast halves
Salt and freshly ground pepper
2 tablespoons vegetable oil
2 tablespoons butter
2 cups homemade or prepared tomato sauce
½ cup dry red wine
1½ cups chicken broth
1 cup rice

½ cup sliced black olives
2 packages (10 ounces each) frozen chopped spinach, thawed, drained, and squeezed dry
1 cup ricotta cheese
2 eggs, beaten
½ teaspoon salt
½ teaspoon nutmeg
¼ cup grated Parmesan cheese

1. Preheat oven to 350°. Season chicken breasts with salt and pepper.

2. In a large frying pan, heat oil and butter over medium heat. Add chicken; cook until browned, about 4 minutes a side.

3. In a small bowl, combine tomato sauce and wine. Spoon 1 cup into bottom of a greased 13 x 9 x 2-inch baking dish. Add chicken broth, rice, and olives. Mix well.

4. Arrange chicken, skin side up, over rice mixture. Cover tightly with foil. Bake 50 minutes, until rice absorbs liquid.

5. In a large bowl, combine spinach, ricotta cheese, eggs, salt, and nutmeg. Mix well. Spoon spinach mixture around the edge of the baking dish. Pour remaining sauce-wine mixture over chicken. Sprinkle with Parmesan cheese. Bake uncovered 15 minutes, until spinach mixture is heated through.

328 OVEN-BAKED BARBECUED CHICKEN
Prep: 25 minutes   Cook: 45 minutes   Serves: 6

How to feed a hungry family from one pan.

1 chicken (3 pounds), cut up
    Salt and freshly ground
    pepper
2 tablespoons vegetable oil
1 can (8 ounces) tomato sauce
2 tablespoons molasses
½ teaspoon Liquid Smoke
2 cans (16 ounces each) baked
    beans

1 can (12 ounces) whole kernel
    corn with red and green
    sweet peppers, drained
1 can (4 ounces) chopped green
    chilies
1 package (8½ ounces) corn
    muffin mix

1. Preheat oven to 400°. Season chicken lightly with salt and pepper. In a large frying pan, heat oil over medium heat. Add chicken and cook, turning, until brown, about 5 minutes a side.

2. In a small bowl, combine tomato sauce, molasses, and liquid smoke. In another bowl, mix together baked beans, corn, and green chilies.

3. Spoon baked bean mixture around rim of bottom of a large roasting pan. Brush chicken pieces with half the barbecue sauce and arrange in a double layer in center of pan. Bake uncovered for 30 minutes.

4. Prepare muffin mix according to package directions. Drop by spoonfuls over beans. Pour remaining barbecue sauce over chicken. Bake for 20 minutes, until muffins are light brown.

329 WILD RICE AND CHICKEN BREASTS WITH MUSHROOM SAUCE
Prep: 40 minutes   Cook: 1 hour   Serves: 6

1 package (6 ounces) wild rice
3 whole chicken breasts, split
6 tablespoons butter or
    margarine
1 teaspoon salt
¼ teaspoon paprika
¼ teaspoon freshly ground
    pepper

½ cup chopped onion
½ pound mushrooms, sliced
1 can (10¾ ounces) cream of
    mushroom soup
¼ cup dry white wine
¼ cup currant jelly
½ teaspoon hot pepper sauce

1. Preheat oven to 350°. Cook wild rice according to package directions. Arrange in bottom of a 13 x 9 x 2-inch baking dish. Arrange chicken, skin side up, on top of rice.

2. Melt 4 tablespoons of the butter in a small saucepan. Add salt, paprika, and pepper. Baste chicken with butter mixture. Bake for 1 hour, until chicken is tender, basting every 15 minutes.

3. In a large frying pan, melt remaining 2 tablespoons butter over medium heat. Add onion and mushrooms. Cook until onions are soft and mushrooms lightly browned, about 5 minutes. Add soup, wine, jelly, and hot sauce; mix well. Heat through and serve with chicken.

330 CHICKEN DIVAN
Prep: 30 minutes   Cook: 20 minutes   Serves: 8

This casserole classic can also be made with sliced cooked turkey.

1 large bunch of broccoli, cut into spears, or 2 packages (10 ounces each) frozen broccoli spears	2 tablespoons dry sherry Salt and freshly ground pepper
4 tablespoons butter	1 cup (4 ounces) shredded Cheddar cheese
½ pound mushrooms, sliced	8 skinless, boneless chicken breast halves, poached
¼ cup flour	
2 cups milk, heated	½ cup bread crumbs

1. Preheat oven to 350°. Steam broccoli spears until barely tender, 3 to 5 minutes; arrange in bottom of a buttered 13 x 9 x 2-inch baking dish.

2. Meanwhile, in a medium-size saucepan, melt butter over moderate heat. Add mushrooms and cook until lightly browned, 3 to 5 minutes. Stir in flour and cook 1 to 2 minutes without browning. Gradually whisk in milk and cook, stirring constantly, until sauce thickens. Stir in sherry. Season with salt and pepper to taste.

3. Pour half the sauce over broccoli. Sprinkle half the Cheddar cheese over sauce. Cover with chicken breasts. Pour remaining sauce over chicken, sprinkle with remaining cheese, and top with bread crumbs. Bake 20 minutes, until hot and bubbly.

331 CHICKEN AND VEGETABLE SCALLOP
Prep: 20 minutes   Cook: 30 minutes   Serves: 6

2 cups cubed cooked chicken	½ teaspoon salt
1 package (10 ounces) frozen corn, thawed	¼ teaspoon freshly ground pepper
1 package (10 ounces) frozen peas, thawed	1 cup chicken broth
	½ cup milk
2 tablespoons butter or margarine	2 eggs, beaten
	¼ cup seasoned bread crumbs
2 tablespoons chopped onion	¼ cup grated Cheddar cheese
3 tablespoons flour	

1. Preheat oven to 350°. Combine chicken, corn, and peas in a 13 x 9 x 2-inch greased baking dish.

2. In a medium-size saucepan, melt butter over medium heat. Add onion and cook until soft, about 3 minutes. Blend in flour, salt, and pepper. Cook 1 to 2 minutes without browning. Gradually whisk in broth and milk. Bring to a boil and cook, stirring constantly, until thick and smooth.

3. Remove from heat and stir in eggs. Pour sauce over chicken mixture.

4. Combine bread crumbs and cheese in a small bowl and sprinkle on top of casserole. Cover with foil. Bake 20 minutes. Uncover and bake 10 minutes, until lightly browned on top.

332 CHICKEN AND SAUSAGE
Prep: 20 minutes   Cook: 40 minutes   Serves: 6

1 **pound sweet Italian sausage**
3 **tablespoons flour**
½ **teaspoon freshly ground pepper**
½ **teaspoon paprika**
1 **chicken (3 pounds), cut up**
¼ **cup oil**
1 **medium onion, sliced**

½ **pound mushrooms, sliced**
1 **can (16 ounces) whole or crushed tomatoes, with their juices**
¼ **teaspoon caraway seeds**
1 **package (10 ounces) frozen peas**

1. Pierce sausage with a fork several times. Place sausage in a small frying pan; cook over low about 20 minutes to render fat. Drain on paper towels. Slice into 1-inch chunks.

2. Place flour, pepper, and paprika in a plastic or paper bag. Add chicken pieces, a few at a time, and shake to coat. Reserve flour mixture.

3. In a Dutch oven, heat oil over medium heat. Add chicken and cook until brown, 5 minutes a side. Remove and drain on paper towels.

4. Add onions and mushrooms; cook until tender. Stir in the remaining seasoned flour. Return chicken to the pan. Add ½ cup water, the tomatoes with their juices, and caraway seeds. Cover and simmer for 20 minutes.

5. Stir in sausages and peas to cook 10 minutes longer, or until heated through.

333 KING RANCH CASSEROLE
Prep: 1 hour 10 minutes   Cook: 1 hour   Serves: 6

An authentic Western recipe, from the world-famous Texas ranch. For a spicier dish, add sliced or minced jalapeño peppers to the soup and tomato mixture.

1 **chicken (3 pounds), cut up**
2 **cans (10¾ ounces each) condensed cream of mushroom soup**
1 **can (15 ounces) tomatoes with green chilies**
2 **cups (½ pound) grated Cheddar cheese**

12 **ounces tortilla chips, or 1 package (1 dozen) corn tortillas, torn into 2-inch pieces**
Sliced black olives, chopped tomato, and shredded lettuce

1. Place chicken in a Dutch oven with enough water to cover. Cover tightly with lid and simmer 40 minutes, until meat falls from bone. Remove chicken: let cool. Discard skin and bone; shred meat.

2. In a large bowl, mix soup concentrates and tomatoes.

3. Preheat oven to 350°. In a buttered 13 x 9 x 2-inch baking dish, layer a third of the tortilla chips, a third of the cooked chicken, a third of the grated cheese, and a third of the soup mixture. Repeat layers, reserving a little cheese and crushed chips for the top. Bake 1 hour, until hot and bubbly. Serve with olives, tomatoes, and lettuce.

334   CHICKEN RICE LOAF WITH MUSHROOM SAUCE

Prep: 15 minutes   Cook: 1 hour   Serves: 6

Chicken Loaf:

2 cups cooked rice	2 tablespoons chopped pimiento
1 cup bread crumbs	½ teaspoon salt
1 cup milk	¼ teaspoon freshly ground pepper
1 cup chicken broth	
3 eggs, beaten	3 cups chopped cooked chicken
2 tablespoons chopped parsley	

Mushroom Sauce:

2 tablespoons butter	½ cup milk
½ pound mushrooms, sliced	¼ teaspoon nutmeg
2 tablespoons flour	Dash of cayenne pepper
1 cup beef broth	

1. Preheat oven to 350°. Combine rice and bread crumbs in bottom of a greased 9 x 5 x 3-inch loaf pan. Press tightly.

2. In a large bowl, combine milk, broth, eggs, parsley, pimiento, salt, and pepper. Mix well. Add cooked chicken. Pour into loaf pan. Bake 1 hour, until set. Let cool 10 minutes and unmold onto a serving platter.

3. Meanwhile, prepare mushroom sauce. In a medium-size saucepan, melt butter over medium heat. Add mushrooms and cook 3 minutes. Stir in flour and cook 1 to 2 minutes without browning.

4. Stir in broth and milk. Bring to a boil, reduce heat, and cook, stirring, until thick and smooth, about 3 minutes. Season with nutmeg and cayenne.

335   CHICKEN AND RICE CASSEROLE

Prep: 10 minutes   Cook: 1¼ hours   Serves: 4

3 slices of bacon, cut into thirds	1 chicken (3 pounds), cut up
1¼ cups rice	Salt and freshly ground pepper
1 package onion soup mix	¼ pound mushrooms, sliced
1 can (10¾ ounces) condensed cream of mushroom soup	2 tablespoons chopped pimientos

1. Preheat oven to 350°. Arrange bacon pieces on bottom of a 23 x 9 x 2-inch baking dish. Sprinkle rice over bacon.

2. In a medium-size bowl, combine onion soup mix, mushroom soup, and 1½ cups water. Mix well. Pour one third of soup mixture over rice.

3. Arrange chicken pieces in dish on top of soup and rice mixture. Sprinkle with salt and pepper. Scatter mushrooms around chicken pieces. Pour remaining soup mixture over chicken. Top with pimientos.

4. Cover with foil. Bake 1 hour 15 minutes, until chicken is tender and rice is cooked.

336   CHICKEN AND BROCCOLI CURRY
Prep: 20 minutes   Cook: 1 hour   Serves: 4

A very easy meal-in-one for guests as well as family. It can be prepared a day in advance and stored in the refrigerator. Add 15 to 30 minutes to cooking time.

1 can (10¾ ounces) cream of
  celery soup
1 can (10¾ ounces) cream of
  mushroom soup
1 cup mayonnaise
½ cup chopped onion
2 tablespoons curry powder
1 cup rice

½ cup dry white wine
2 packages (10 ounces each)
  frozen broccoli spears,
  thawed
1½ pounds skinless, boneless
  chicken breasts, cut into
  2-inch cubes
¼ cup slivered almonds

1. Preheat oven to 350°. In a medium-size saucepan, combine celery and mushroom soups, mayonnaise, onion, and curry. Cook, stirring, over medium heat, until blended.

2. Pour rice into a 13 x 9 x 2-inch baking dish. Stir in wine and one-third of soup mixture. Arrange broccoli around outside edges of baking dish, over-lapping stems to form a decorative border. Reserve several spears.

3. Add chicken pieces to remaining soup mixture. Pour into center of baking dish. Top with remaining broccoli spears. Garnish with slivered almonds. Cover with foil. Bake 1 hour, until chicken is tender and rice is cooked.

337   CELERIED CHICKEN CASSEROLE
Prep: 20 minutes   Cook: 30 minutes   Serves: 6

2 tablespoons vegetable oil
3 celery ribs, chopped
2 medium carrots, finely sliced
1 small onion, finely chopped
1 teaspoon salt
1 teaspoon dried tarragon
3 cups chopped cooked
  chicken

1 cup sour cream
1 cup mayonnaise
¼ cup dry white wine or water
1 cup sliced almonds, toasted
¼ cup bread crumbs
¼ cup grated Parmesan cheese

1. Preheat oven to 350°. In a medium-size frying pan, heat oil over medium heat. Add celery, carrots, onion, salt, and tarragon. Cook about 5 minutes, until carrots are crisp-tender.

2. In a large bowl, combine chicken, sour cream, mayonnaise, wine, almonds, and sautéed vegetables. Mix well and spoon into a 2-quart but-tered casserole.

3. Combine bread crumbs and Parmesan cheese and sprinkle over top. Bake 30 minutes, until heated through and lightly browned on top.

338 FIN AND FEATHERS
Prep: 30 minutes   Cook: 25 minutes   Serves: 6

4 tablespoons butter or
   margarine
1 shallot, chopped
1 garlic clove, crushed
3 tablespoons flour
2 cups chicken broth
¼ pound mushrooms, sliced
2 egg yolks
½ cup cream

Salt and freshly ground
   pepper
3 cups chopped cooked
   chicken
1 cup chopped cooked lobster
   or crab meat
1 package (10 ounces) frozen
   peas, thawed

1. In a medium-size saucepan, melt 2 tablespoons of the butter over moderate heat. Add shallot and garlic and cook until softened but not brown, 2 to 3 minutes. Stir in flour and cook for 1 to 2 minutes without browning. Slowly whisk in broth, bring to a boil, and cook, stirring, until sauce thickens, about 3 minutes. Reduce heat and simmer for 10 minutes, stirring occasionally. Remove from heat. Preheat oven to 400°.

2. Meanwhile, in a small frying pan, melt remaining 2 tablespoons butter. Add mushrooms and cook until lightly browned, about 3 minutes. Set aside.

3. In a small bowl, beat egg yolks and cream. Whisk in about ½ cup of hot sauce. Whisk the egg-cream mixture into the remaining sauce in the pan. Add the mushrooms. Season with salt and pepper.

4. In a 2-quart casserole or 13 x 9 x 2-inch baking dish, arrange chicken, lobster, and peas. Pour sauce over all. Bake for 25 to 30 minutes, until lightly browned on top.

339 BAYOU CASSEROLE
Prep: 20 minutes   Cook: 45 minutes   Serves: 8

This casserole can be made up to a day ahead through Step 3. Cover with foil and refrigerate. Simply add an extra 15 to 30 minutes to the baking time.

1 package (7 ounces) seasoned
   stuffing
2½ cups chicken broth
3 tablespoons bacon drippings
3 garlic cloves, finely chopped
1 cup sliced carrots
1 cup chopped green bell
   pepper
½ cup chopped onion
½ cup chopped celery
½ pound mushrooms, sliced
1 tablespoon Worcestershire
   sauce

½ teaspoon salt
½ teaspoon freshly ground
   pepper
½ teaspoon dried oregano
½ teaspoon dried basil
¼ teaspoon hot pepper sauce
¾ cup chopped parsley
2 eggs, beaten
4 cups coarsely chopped
   cooked chicken
¾ cup cracker crumbs
1 teaspoon paprika

1. Place stuffing in a large bowl; add 2 cups of the chicken broth. Stir to mix and set aside.

2. In a large Dutch oven, heat bacon drippings over medium-high heat. Add garlic and carrots; cook 2 minutes. Add pepper, onion, celery, and mushrooms. Cook 5 minutes, until onion is tender.

3. Preheat oven to 350°. Reduce heat under the Dutch oven to medium. Add Worcestershire sauce, salt, pepper, oregano, basil, and hot sauce. Stir to mix. Add softened stuffing, parsley, remaining ½ cup broth, and eggs. Blend well. Add chicken, blend thoroughly and turn into a 13 x 9 x 2-inch baking dish.

4. Sprinkle with cracker crumbs and paprika. Bake 45 minutes, until heated through.

---

340 TED'S FAMOUS CHICKEN
Prep: 20 minutes   Cook: 30 minutes   Serves: 8

Ted Giannoulas, a.k.a. "The Famous Chicken," formerly known as "The San Diego Chicken," but usually referred to as "that guy who dresses up in a chicken suit," has entertained millions of sports fans with his inspired silliness and slapstick routines. How could anyone do a chicken cookbook without going to at least one "chicken"? Here is the result:

2 tablespoons butter
¾ pound fresh mushrooms, sliced
2 tablespoons dry white wine
1 teaspoon lemon juice
8 skinless, boneless chicken breast halves poached, cut into strips

2 cans (10¾ ounces each) cream of mushroom soup
2 cups sour cream
1 pound spaghetti, cooked and drained
Salt and white pepper
¼ cup grated Parmesan cheese

1. Preheat oven to 325°. In a large frying pan, melt butter over medium heat. Add mushrooms and cook until tender, 3 to 5 minutes. Add white wine and lemon juice. Cook until liquid evaporates.

2. In a large mixing bowl, combine chicken, mushrooms, soup, and sour cream. Add spaghetti and mix well. Season with salt and white pepper to taste.

3. Arrange in a 13 x 9 x 2-inch dish. Top with parmesan cheese. Bake 30 minutes, until hot and bubbly.

341   CHICKEN BREAD PUDDING
Prep: 20 minutes   Cook: 1¼ hours   Serves: 8

This makes a great brunch dish. The entire casserole can be made ahead through Step 3. Cover and refrigerate overnight before baking, if desired.

6 slices firm-textured white bread, crusts removed
2 cups chopped cooked chicken
4 tablespoons butter or margarine
¼ pound fresh mushrooms, sliced
1 can (8 ounces) water chestnuts, drained and sliced
¼ cup mayonnaise

1 cup shredded Cheddar cheese
1 cup milk
1 can (10¾ ounces) cream of celery soup
2 eggs, beaten
2 tablespoons chopped pimiento
1 teaspoon salt
¼ teaspoon freshly ground pepper
½ cup bread crumbs

1. Preheat oven to 350°. Line bottom of a 13 x 9 x 2-inch buttered baking dish with bread, cutting slices to fit. Top with chopped chicken.

2. In a small frying pan, melt 2 tablespoons of the butter over medium heat. Add mushrooms and sauté until browned, 3 to 5 minutes. Remove from heat. Add water chestnuts and mayonnaise. Mix well and spoon over chicken. Sprinkle cheese over all.

3. In a large bowl, combine milk, soup, eggs, pimiento, salt, and pepper. Mix until well blended. Pour over chicken.

4. Bake 1 hour, until a toothpick comes out clean. Sprinkle on bread crumbs; dot with slivers of remaining 2 tablespoons butter. Bake for 10 minutes, until crumbs are lightly browned.

342   WILD CHICKEN
Prep: 30 minutes   Cook: 1 hour   Serves: 6

1 package (6 ounces) wild and white rice with seasonings
1 cup chicken broth
1 package (10 ounces) frozen French-style green beans, thawed and drained
2 cups chopped cooked chicken

1 can (10¾ ounces) cream of celery soup
½ cup mayonnaise
1 can (8 ounces) water chestnuts, drained and sliced
1 can (2.8 ounces) French-fried onions

1. In a medium-size saucepan, prepare rice mixture according to package directions, substituting 1 cup chicken broth for 1 cup of the required amount of water.

2. Preheat oven to 350°. In a large mixing bowl, combine all ingredients, except French-fried onions. Pour mixture into a lightly greased 12 x 8 x 2-inch baking dish. Sprinkle onions on top and bake 45 minutes, until hot and bubbly.

343   CHICKEN-BEEF TAMALE PIE
Prep: 20 minutes   Cook: 3 hours   Serves: 8

2 pounds ground beef
1 cup chopped onion
2 garlic cloves, finely chopped
3 to 4 tablespoons chili powder, or to taste
2 cans (16 ounces each) tomatoes, with their juice
2 jalapeño peppers, minced (optional)
  Salt and freshly ground pepper
2 cans (16 ounces each) pinto beans, drained
1 tablespoon minced fresh coriander
4 cups canned chicken broth
1 cup yellow cornmeal
2 cups fresh or frozen corn kernels
3 cups chopped cooked chicken
1 cup grated Monterey Jack or Cheddar cheese

1. Brown beef in a Dutch oven over medium heat. Remove meat with a slotted spoon and drain on paper towels. Remove all but 1 tablespoon pan drippings; add onion and garlic and cook until soft, about 3 minutes. Return meat to pan and sprinkle with 2 to 3 tablespoons of the chili powder. Add canned tomatoes and jalapeños. Simmer uncovered over low heat for 1 to 2 hours. Season with additional chili powder and salt and pepper to taste. Stir in beans and coriander.

2. Preheat oven to 350°. In large saucepan, bring 3 cups of the broth to a boil. In a small bowl, combine cornmeal and remaining 1 cup chicken broth; blend until smooth. Stir into boiling chicken stock. Cook, stirring constantly (to avoid lumps), over low heat, until mixture thickens, about 30 minutes.

3. Line the bottom and sides of a 12 x 8 x 2-inch baking dish with cornmeal mush. Bake for 15 minutes. Remove from oven and place a layer of corn, then chicken, a layer of corn, and a layer of the meat mixture on top. Cover with cheese. Bake 30 minutes.

344   APRICOT CHICKEN CASSEROLE
Prep: 40 minutes   Cook: 1 hour   Serves: 4

1 chicken (3 pounds), cut up
  Salt and freshly ground
  pepper
2 tablespoons vegetable oil
1 cup chopped celery
1 can (8 ounces) water
  chestnuts, drained and
  sliced

½ teaspoon dried rosemary
2 cups cooked long-grain rice
¾ cup dry white wine
1 can (16 ounces) apricot halves
  in syrup
4 teaspoons cornstarch

1. Preheat oven to 350°. Season chicken with salt and pepper. In a large frying pan, heat oil over medium heat. Add chicken and cook until brown, about 5 minutes a side. Remove and set aside.

2. To the same pan, add celery, water chestnuts, and rosemary. Cook until celery is tender, about 3 minutes. Remove from heat. Add cooked rice and ½ cup of the wine. Pour rice mixture into a 13 x 9 x 2-inch baking dish. Top with chicken and cover with foil. Bake for 35 minutes.

3. Meanwhile, drain apricots, reserving syrup. In a small saucepan, combine syrup and cornstarch. Cook over medium heat until thickened and sauce turns clear. Add remaining ¼ wine.

4. Arrange apricots around chicken. Pour apricot sauce over all. Bake uncovered for 10 to 15 minutes, until chicken is tender.

345   ALMOND CHICKEN CASSEROLE
Prep: 20 minutes   Cook: 30 minutes   Serves: 6

1 tablespoon vegetable oil
½ cup chopped onion
1 garlic clove, finely chopped
¼ pound fresh mushrooms,
  sliced
⅓ cup flour
2½ cups milk
¾ cup mayonnaise
1 teaspoon dried basil
  Freshly ground pepper
1 cup shredded Swiss cheese

⅓ cup dry white wine
1 cup sliced almonds
¼ cup chopped pimiento
2 cups chopped cooked
  chicken
8 ounces small pasta shells,
  cooked and drained
1 package (10 ounces) frozen
  chopped broccoli, thawed
  and drained
¼ cup grated Parmesan cheese

1. In medium-size frying pan, heat oil over medium heat. Add onion, garlic, and mushrooms. Cook 3 minutes, until onion is tender. Stir in flour; cook 1 minute without browning. Gradually add milk, stirring constantly, until thickened. Add mayonnaise, basil, pepper, Swiss cheese, and wine. Stir until mayonnaise is smooth and cheese melts. Remove from heat. Add ¾ cup of the sliced almonds and the pimiento; stir. Set sauce aside.

2. Preheat oven to 350°. Arrange chicken, pasta, and broccoli in a 13 x 9 x 2-inch baking dish. Pour sauce over the top; mix gently. Sprinkle with remaining ¼ cup sliced almonds. Bake for 30 minutes, until heated through. Sprinkle with Parmesan cheese and serve.

Chapter 20

Crêpes and Pastries

Chicken goes a long way by itself, but when paired with flaky pastry crust or wrapped inside a tender crêpe, it can be stretched even further. Some of these recipes start from scratch, but the majority are tailored to chopped or diced cooked chicken. With a few vegetables, seasonings, and some sauce, a little leftover cooked chicken can be transformed into an entirely new dish.

Use any unsauced leftovers—white or dark meat—from a roast or baked or poached chicken. If one of these dishes appeals to you and you have no leftover chicken in the house, follow the instructions for poaching chicken breasts on page 37.

BASIC CREPES

These are so easy to make and great to have in the freezer to pull out for a quick, elegant meal. To freeze, prepare crêpes as directed and place between sheets of wax paper. Completely wrap with heavy-duty aluminum foil and freeze. Take out several hours before filling to defrost.

1 cup flour	2/3 cup milk
2 tablespoons butter or margarine, melted	Pinch of salt
3 eggs	Vegetable oil

1. In a blender or food processor, blend the flour, butter, eggs, milk, salt, and 2/3 cup water. Refrigerate for at least 1 hour.

2. Heat a 7-inch crêpe or frying pan over medium heat; brush lightly with vegetable oil. Add slightly less than 1/4 cup of batter. Quickly tilt and rotate pan so batter covers bottom in a thin even layer. Cook until bottom of crêpe is lightly browned and edges lift easily, about 30 seconds. Turn and brown lightly on the other side, 10 to 15 seconds. Remove crêpe to a platter, brush pan with oil and repeat. Makes 16 to 20 crêpes.

346   SHERRIED CHICKEN CRÊPES
Prep: 10 minutes   Cook: 10 minutes   Serves: 6

Any leftover green vegetable—broccoli, asparagus, peas—can be added for variety to this basic chicken crêpe recipe. Chop into bite-size pieces before adding.

4 tablespoons butter or
   margarine
2 tablespoons flour
2 cups milk
¼ teaspoon salt
¼ teaspoon dry mustard
¼ teaspoon freshly ground
   pepper
  Dash of hot pepper sauce

1 tablespoon dry sherry
½ pound fresh mushrooms,
   sliced
3 scallions, finely chopped
2 cups chopped cooked
   chicken
12 crêpes (p. 205)
¾ cup shredded Swiss cheese

1. In a medium-size saucepan, melt 2 tablespoons of the butter over low heat. Add flour and cook, stirring constantly, for about 2 minutes without browning. Whisk in milk, raise heat to medium, and stir vigorously until the sauce boils and thickens. Season with salt, mustard, pepper, hot sauce, and sherry.

2. Preheat oven to broil. In a large frying pan, melt remaining 2 tablespoons butter over medium heat. Add mushrooms and scallions; sauté for about 5 minutes, until mushrooms are tender. Add chicken.

3. Stir chicken-mushroom mixture into cream sauce. Spoon filling onto crêpes, dividing evenly. Roll crêpes and arrange side by side, seam side down, in a buttered 12 x 8 x 2-inch baking dish. Sprinkle with Swiss cheese, broil 3 to 5 minutes, until crêpes are heated through and cheese is melted and lightly browned.

347   QUICK CHICKEN CRÊPE FILLING
Prep: 5 minutes   Cook: 10 minutes   Serves: 4

A quick-and-easy convenience-food variation on the above, cooked in one pan.

2 tablespoons butter or
   margarine
½ pound fresh mushrooms,
   sliced
⅛ teaspoon freshly ground
   pepper

1 can (10¾ ounces) condensed
   cream of mushroom soup
½ cup milk
3 tablespoons dry Marsala
2 cups chopped cooked
   chicken
2 tablespoons chopped parsley
8 crêpes (p. 205)

1. Preheat oven to 250°. In a medium-size frying pan, melt butter over medium heat. Add mushrooms, season with pepper, and sauté 3 to 5 minutes, until tender.

2. Stir in condensed soup, milk, and Marsala. Heat, stirring until boiling. Reduce heat, add chicken, and simmer 5 minutes. Stir in parsley. Fill crêpes and warm in oven until time to serve.

348   ENCHILADA CHICKEN CRÊPES
Prep: 25 minutes   Cook: 5 minutes   Serves: 6

2 cups chopped cooked
  chicken
1 can (7 ounces) mild chopped
  green chilies
1 can (10 ¾ ounces) condensed
  cream of chicken soup
½ teaspoon garlic salt
¼ teaspoon freshly ground
  pepper

2 ripe avocados, peeled and
  pitted
12 crêpes (p. 205)
¼ cup grated Monterey Jack
  cheese
¼ cup grated sharp Cheddar
  cheese
  Chopped tomatoes and
  shredded lettuce

1. In a large frying pan, combine chicken, chilies, soup, garlic salt, and pepper. Cook over medium-high heat 5 to 10 minutes, until boiling. Meanwhile, chop 1 of the avocados; add to chicken mixture.

2. Preheat broiler. Divide the filling among the crêpes. Roll and place seam side down in a large flameproof gratin dish. Slice remaining avocado lengthwise and arrange on top of crêpes. Sprinkle with cheese. Place under broiler and heat until cheese melts, about 5 minutes. Garnish with tomatoes and lettuce.

349   CRÊPES DE POLLO
Prep: 20 minutes   Cook: 30 minutes   Serves: 4

2 cups chopped cooked
  chicken
1½ cups shredded Swiss cheese
  (about 6 ounces)
2 pickled jalapeño peppers,
  seeded and minced
1 jar (2 ounces) pimientos

1 tablespoon minced onion
¼ teaspoon salt
¼ teaspoon freshly ground
  pepper
8 crêpes (p. 205)
1 cup heavy cream

1. Preheat oven to 350°. In a large bowl, combine chicken, 1¼ cups of the cheese, jalapeño peppers, pimientos, onion, salt, and pepper. Divide filling among crêpes and roll up. Arrange seam side down in a 12 x 8 x 2-inch baking dish.

2. Sprinkle remaining ¼ cup cheese on top of crêpes and pour cream evenly over all. Bake 25 to 30 minutes, until hot and bubbly.

350   CHICKEN AND ZUCCHINI CRÊPE CAKE
Prep: 30 minutes   Cook: 30 minutes   Serves: 6

This is an impressive dish for a brunch or luncheon. It can be prepared several hours ahead and kept refrigerated. Allow 5 to 20 minutes to heat through.

7 tablespoons butter or margarine	¾ teaspoon salt
2 large onions, sliced	¼ teaspoon freshly ground pepper
4 medium-size zucchini, coarsely shredded	3 tablespoons flour
2 cups chopped cooked chicken	1½ cups milk
2 tablespoons chopped parsley	2 eggs
½ teaspoon dried oregano	¼ cup grated Parmesan cheese
	10 crêpes (p. 205)

1. In a large frying pan, melt 2 tablespoons of the butter over medium heat. Add onions and sauté until tender, stirring often, about 5 minutes. Remove with a slotted spoon to a large bowl.

2. Melt 2 tablespoons of the butter in the frying pan over high heat. Add zucchini and cook, stirring often, until zucchini is tender and juices evaporate, 5 to 10 minutes; do not brown. Add zucchini and chicken to onions and mix well. Stir in parsley, oregano, ¼ teaspoon of the salt, and pepper.

3. Preheat oven to 350°. Melt remaining 3 tablespoons butter in a medium-size saucepan over medium heat. Stir in flour and remaining ½ teaspoon salt. Gradually whisk in milk. Cook, stirring constantly, until sauce thickens and boils, about 1 minute. Beat eggs in a small bowl. Gradually beat in ½ cup hot white sauce. Stir back into saucepan. Stir in all but 1 tablespoon of the cheese. Measure out and reserve 1 cup of sauce.

4. Place 1 crêpe in a buttered 10-inch pie plate or shallow baking dish; spread with generous ⅓ cup chicken filling and about 2 tablespoons sauce. Continue stacking and filling, ending with a plain crêpe on top. Pour reserved 1 cup sauce over top. Sprinkle with reserved 1 tablespoon cheese. Bake for 25 to 30 minutes, until heated through and brown on top. Cut in wedges to serve.

351   EASY CHICKEN AND ASPARAGUS PIE
Prep: 25 minutes   Cook: 20 minutes   Serves: 6

1 can (10¾ ounces) condensed cream of celery soup	½ cup finely chopped celery
1 package (10¾ ounces) frozen asparagus, thawed and cut into 1-inch pieces	2 tablespoons chopped pimientos
1 cup chopped cooked chicken	⅓ cup dry sherry
2 hard-cooked eggs, chopped	Dash of mace
	Pastry for 9-inch pie shell (p. 209)

1. Preheat oven to 450°. In a medium-size bowl, combine soup, asparagus, chicken, eggs, celery, pimientos, sherry, and mace. Place mixture in a 9-inch pie plate.

2. Roll out pastry about 11 inches in diameter. Lay on top of pie plate. Trim edge. Cut several slits on top with a sharp knife. Bake 20 minutes, until pastry is golden brown.

352   SOUR CREAM CHICKEN QUICHE
Prep: 35 minutes   Cook: 50 minutes   Serves: 6

Two kinds of cheese—Cheddar and Swiss—and the tang of sour cream give this quiche a richness and depth of flavor.

Pastry for 9-inch pie shell (recipe follows)	**¼ teaspoon nutmeg**
1 tablespoon olive oil	**¼ teaspoon freshly ground pepper**
2 tablespoons chopped onion	**½ cup shredded sharp Cheddar cheese**
2 tablespoons chopped green bell pepper	**¼ cup shredded Swiss cheese**
1 tablespoon flour	**2 eggs, slightly beaten**
1 cup chopped cooked chicken	**¾ cup milk**
¼ teaspoon salt	**¾ cup sour cream**

1. Line a 9-inch pie plate with pastry; set in refrigerator until ready to fill. Preheat oven to 400°.

2. In a medium-size frying pan, heat olive oil over medium-high heat. Add onion and green pepper. Cook 3 minutes, stirring frequently, until onion is tender. Add flour; cook and stir for 2 minutes. Stir in chicken, salt, nutmeg, and pepper.

3. Spread chicken mixture over bottom of unbaked pie shell. Top with Cheddar and Swiss cheeses. In a small bowl, combine eggs, milk, and sour cream; mix until smooth. Pour over chicken mixture. Bake for 20 minutes.

4. Reduce oven temperature to 350° and bake an additional 30 to 35 minutes, until a knife inserted near center comes out clean. Let cool for 10 minutes before cutting into wedges.

BASIC PASTRY

1 cup all-purpose flour	**⅓ cup plus 1 tablespoon chilled shortening**
½ teaspoon salt	**1 to 2 tablespoons ice water**

1. In a medium-size bowl, combine flour and salt. Cut in shortening until mixture resembles cornmeal.

2. Sprinkle water onto flour mixture, 1 tablespoon at a time. Toss lightly with a fork after each tablespoon of water is added until flour is moistened. Gather dough together with hands and press firmly into a ball. If dough does not hold together, add 1 to 2 teaspoons more water.

3. To roll pastry, use a pastry cloth and cloth-covered rolling pin into which flour has been rubbed. Flatten dough into a disk. Roll from center to outside in all directions. For even thickness, lift rolling pin toward edge. Roll to a ⅛- to ¼-inch thickness, 1½ inches larger all around than inverted pie plate. Transfer to pie plate; crimp edges. Makes one 9-inch pie crust.

353   PAT'S GREEN CHILE–CHICKEN QUICHE
Prep: 30 minutes   Cook: 45 minutes   Serves: 6

Pastry for 9-inch pie shell
    (p. 209)
2 cups shredded Monterey
    Jack cheese (about
    ½ pound)
1½ cups shredded sharp
    Cheddar cheese (about
    6 ounces)
1 cup chopped cooked chicken

1 can (7 ounces) chopped green
    chilies
1½ cups half-and-half or light
    cream
4 eggs
¼ teaspoon salt
¼ teaspoon freshly ground
    pepper
1 teaspoon hot pepper sauce

1. Preheat oven to 400°. Roll out pastry and line 9-inch pie plate. Bake 5 minutes.

2. Reduce oven to 375°. Spread Monterey Jack cheese, ¾ cup of the Cheddar cheese, and chicken on bottom of pie shell. Sprinkle chopped chilies over all.

3. In a small bowl, beat together half-and-half, eggs, salt, pepper, and hot sauce; pour over all. Sprinkle remaining Cheddar cheese on top. Bake for 45 minutes. Let stand 15 minutes before cutting.

354   CHICKEN-RICE PIE
Prep: 35 minutes   Cook: 1 hour   Serves: 8

Pastry for 9-inch double-
    crust pie shell (p. 209)
2 tablespoons butter or
    margarine
½ cup sliced onion
½ cup sliced celery
1 medium garlic clove, minced
1 can (10¾ ounces) condensed
    cream of mushroom soup

½ cup half-and-half or light
    cream
½ cup chopped cooked chicken
⅓ cup chopped parsley
1 tablespoon lemon juice
⅛ teaspoon ground nutmeg
    Freshly ground pepper
1½ cups cooked rice
4 hard-cooked eggs, sliced
1 egg, slightly beaten

1. Prepare pastry. Line a 9-inch pie plate with bottom crust.

2. Preheat oven to 375°. In a medium-size saucepan, melt butter over medium heat. Add onion, celery, and garlic; cook until onion is tender, about 3 minutes. Add soup, half-and-half, chicken, parsley, lemon juice, nutmeg, and pepper. Cook, stirring, until blended.

3. Spread alternate layers of rice, hard-cooked eggs, and chicken mixture in pastry-lined pie plate. Top with remaining pastry; seal and trim edges. Cut slits in pastry; brush with beaten egg. Bake for 1 hour, until golden brown.

355   CHICKEN IN PHYLLO
Prep: 30 minutes   Cook: 30 minutes   Serves: 6

Phyllo, or strudel leaves, which can be substituted, are found in the refrigerated or frozen section of your supermarket or in Middle Eastern groceries.

8 tablespoons (1 stick) butter
   or margarine
2 medium onions, finely
   chopped
2 celery ribs, finely chopped
½ cup finely chopped carrot
2 tablespoons flour
1 cup chicken broth

2 cups chopped cooked
   chicken
1 teaspoon salt
¼ teaspoon ground nutmeg
2 tablespoons finely chopped
   parsley
2 eggs, beaten
12 phyllo or strudel leaves

1. In a large frying pan, melt 4 tablespoons of the butter over medium heat. Add onion, celery, and carrot. Cook until onion is tender, about 2 minutes. Stir in flour; cook 1 minute without browning. Gradually whisk in broth; cook, stirring constantly, until thickened and smooth. Add chicken, salt, nutmeg, and parsley; let cool 10 minutes. Stir in eggs.

2. Preheat oven to 350°. Melt remaining 4 tablespoons butter. Stack 6 phyllo leaves, brushing each sheet with butter as stacked. Repeat with second stack.

3. Place half the chicken mixture in the center of each phyllo stack. Roll jelly-roll style, tucking in the ends.

4. Place rolls seam side down on a lightly buttered baking sheet. Brush with remaining melted butter. Bake 30 minutes, until golden brown. Cut into thick slices and serve.

356   YORKSHIRE CHICKEN
Prep: 10 minutes   Cook: 1 hour   Serves: 4

¼ cup vegetable oil
1⅓ cups flour
2 teaspoons salt
¼ teaspoon freshly ground
   pepper
¾ teaspoon crumbled sage
1 chicken (3 pounds), cut up

1 teaspoon baking powder
1½ cups milk
3 eggs, beaten
4 ounces Cheddar cheese,
   shredded (1 cup)
2 tablespoons minced parsley

1. Preheat oven to 350°. Place oil in a 13 x 9 x 2-inch baking dish. In a plastic or paper bag, combine ⅓ cup of the flour, 1 teaspoon salt, pepper, and sage; add chicken and shake to coat. Arrange in baking dish. Bake 40 minutes.

2. In a medium-size bowl, combine remaining 1 cup flour, baking powder, and 1 teaspoon salt. Add milk, stirring until smooth. Add eggs, cheese, and parsley; blend well.

3. Pour batter over chicken and bake 20 minutes, until Yorkshire pudding is puffed and brown and chicken is tender.

357   BETTY GROFF'S CHICKEN STOLTZFUS™
Prep: 20 minutes   Cook: 1 hour   Serves: 6 to 8

Betty Groff and her husband, Abe, own Groff's Farm Restaurant on Mount Joy, Pennsylvania. This was their wedding chicken recipe, which they served over pastry squares (basic pastry [p. 209] cut into squares and prebaked). I also love it over frozen pastry shells.

1 chicken (about 5 pounds), cut up	1 cup light cream, or ½ cup each milk and evaporated milk
1 tablespoon salt	
⅓ teaspoon freshly ground pepper	¼ cup finely chopped parsley
Pinch of saffron	Pastry squares
12 tablespoons butter	Parsley sprigs, for garnish
12 tablespoons flour	

1. Place chicken in a large kettle, and cover with water. Add salt, pepper, and saffron and bring to a boil. Reduce heat to medium and simmer partly covered for 1 hour. Remove the chicken and cool enough to debone.

2. Reduce the stock to 4 cups, strain, and set aside. Remove the skin and bones from the chicken and cut the meat into bite-size pieces. Melt butter in kettle over medium heat, add flour, mix, and cook, stirring, for 3 minutes. Pour in chicken stock and cream, stirring constantly. Cook over medium-high heat until the sauce comes to a boil. Simmer until thickened and smooth. Reduce heat and add the chicken pieces and chopped parsley. Serve hot over pastry squares. Garnish with parsley sprigs.

358   QUICK CHICKEN PIROSHKI
Prep: 35 minutes   Cook: 15 minutes   Serves: 4

2 tablespoons butter or margarine	½ cup chopped cooked ham
	½ cup cooked rice
¼ cup chopped shallots	2 tablespoons chopped parsley
1 medium garlic clove, minced	⅛ teaspoon dried thyme
1½ cups chopped fresh mushrooms (about 6 ounces)	Salt and freshly ground pepper
	1 can (8 ounces) crescent rolls
1 cup chopped cooked chicken	1 egg, beaten

1. Preheat oven to 350°. In a large frying pan, melt butter over medium heat. Add shallots and garlic and cook until tender but not brown, about 2 minutes. Add mushrooms and cook, stirring, until moisture is evaporated. Stir in chicken, ham, rice, parsley, thyme, and salt and pepper to taste.

2. Separate crescent rolls into 4 squares; seal line in each square. Divide chicken mixture equally among squares; fold to make a triangle and seal edges. Prick tops of pastry with fork and brush with egg. Bake on an ungreased baking sheet 15 minutes, until golden brown. Remove to a serving platter and keep warm until ready to serve.

359   CHICKEN BREASTS EN CROÛTE
Prep: 45 minutes   Cook: 35 minutes   Serves: 6

4 **tablespoons butter or**
  margarine
6 **skinless, boneless chicken**
  breast halves
½ **teaspoon dried tarragon**
¼ **teaspoon freshly ground**
  pepper
1 **package (10 ounces) frozen**
  patty shells, thawed
  Dijon mustard
6 **thin slices boiled ham**

1 **package (10 ounces) frozen**
  broccoli spears, cooked,
  drained, and coarsely
  chopped
6 **slices Swiss cheese**
1 **egg, lightly beaten with**
  1 tablespoon water
2 **tablespoons flour**
½ **cup chicken broth**
½ **cup dry vermouth**

1. In a large frying pan, melt 2 tablespoons of the butter over medium heat. Cook chicken breasts 4 minutes on each side. Remove and sprinkle with tarragon and pepper.

2. Preheat oven to 400°. On a pastry cloth, roll out patty shells into 7-inch circles. Place one breast half on the lower half of each pastry. Brush a thin coat of mustard on a ham slice and fit over chicken; top with a small amount of broccoli and a slice of cheese. Moisten pastry edges with water. Press edges together; crimp edges with a fork to seal. Place on ungreased baking sheet. Brush each pastry with egg glaze. Bake 35 minutes, until golden brown.

3. For sauce, melt remaining 2 tablespoons butter in a small saucepan over medium heat. Whisk in flour; cook, stirring, 1 minute. Blend in chicken broth and vermouth. Heat to a boil; lower heat and simmer 3 minutes. Pass with chicken breasts en croûte.

360   CHICKEN-CHEESE PASTRIES WITH SWEET-AND-SOUR SAUCE
Prep: 30 minutes   Cook: 10 minutes   Serves: 4

4 **skinless, boneless chicken**
  breast halves
1 **can (8 ounces) crescent**
  dinner rolls
4 **ounces Rondele cheese with**
  pepper or Alouette cheese

1 **egg, beaten**
½ **teaspoon dry mustard**
1 **tablespoon brown sugar**
2 **tablespoons white wine**
  vinegar
2 **tablespoons vegetable oil**

1. Place chicken breasts in a medium-size saucepan with enough water to cover. Bring to a boil, reduce heat, and simmer 20 minutes. Drain and cool.

2. Preheat oven to 400°. Separate crescent rolls into 4 squares; seal line in each square. Place chicken breast on each square. Spread 1 ounce of cheese on each breast and completely wrap breast with the dough. Place seam side down on an ungreased baking sheet and brush with beaten egg. Bake 10 to 12 minutes, until golden brown. Transfer to a serving platter.

4. For sauce, blend together dry mustard, brown sugar, vinegar, and oil in a small saucepan. Simmer 5 minutes. Drizzle over chicken breasts and serve.

361 CHICKEN PIE SUPREME
Prep: 30 minutes   Cook: 25 minutes   Serves: 6

½ cup chopped onion
5 tablespoons butter or
   margarine
2 cups flour
3 cups chicken broth
2 cups chopped cooked
   chicken
½ cup sliced cooked carrots
½ cup cooked peas

½ teaspoon salt
¼ teaspoon freshly ground
   pepper
1 teaspoon dried tarragon
¼ teaspoon cayenne pepper
2 teaspoons baking powder
3 eggs, separated
¾ cup milk

1. Preheat oven to 375°. In a large frying pan, cook onion in 4 tablespoons butter over medium heat until tender, about 3 minutes. Add ½ cup of the flour and cook, stirring, for 1 to 2 minutes without browning. Gradually whisk in broth and cook, stirring constantly, until thick and very smooth.

2. Add chicken, carrots, and peas. Season with ¼ teaspoon salt and the pepper. Add tarragon and cayenne. Pour into a 2-quart baking dish.

3. In a medium-size bowl, stir together remaining 1½ cups flour, baking powder, and ¼ teaspoon salt. With a pastry blender, cut in remaining 1 tablespoon butter until mixture resembles cornmeal. Beat egg yolks slightly and add milk. Add to flour mixture and blend well. Beat egg whites until stiff but not dry. Fold into batter. Spread over top of casserole. Bake for 25 to 30 minutes, until lightly browned.

362 EASY EMPANADAS
Prep: 30 minutes   Cook: 15 minutes   Serves: 4

Empanadas are small pastries filled with meat, fish, or vegetables. They are good hot or cold.

2 tablespoons olive oil
¼ cup chopped onion
½ cup chopped green bell
   pepper
2 garlic cloves, finely chopped
1 can (14 ounces) Italian peeled
   tomatoes, drained,
   seeded, and chopped

½ cup chopped prosciutto
2 cups chopped cooked
   chicken
2 cans (10 ounces each)
   buttermilk biscuits,
   refrigerated
1 egg, slightly beaten

1. Preheat oven to 375°. In a medium-size saucepan, heat oil over medium heat. Add onion and green pepper and cook until onion is tender, about 3 minutes. Add tomatoes and prosciutto and cook 5 minutes.

2. In a medium-size bowl, combine ½ cup sauce and chicken; set filling aside.

3. Roll each biscuit into 3½-inch circles. To make empanadas, spoon about 2 tablespoons filling on half the pastry circles; top with remaining circles. Seal edges. Arrange on a baking sheet; brush with egg. Bake for 15 minutes, until brown.

4. Meanwhile, blend ¼ cup water with remaining sauce. Heat, stirring occasionally. Serve with turnovers.

363 CHONITAS
Prep: 30 minutes   Cook: 30 minutes   Serves: 6

Chonitas are a corn flour variation of the classic (wheat flour) Spanish empanadas.

FILLING
- 2 tablespoons butter or margarine
- ½ cup chopped onion
- 1 cup chopped cooked chicken
- ¼ cup grated Parmesan cheese
- 2 tablespoons chopped pimiento

PATTIES
- 1½ cups masa harina (corn flour)
- ⅔ cup cracked wheat
- ½ cup grated Parmesan cheese
- ¼ teaspoon salt
- 4 tablespoons butter or margarine, softened
- 1¼ cups warm water
- Vegetable oil, for frying

SAUCE
- 1 can (8 ounces) tomato sauce
- ½ cup chopped onion
- 1 can (7 ounces) chopped green chilies
- ½ teaspoon dried oregano

1. For filling, melt butter over medium heat in a small saucepan. Add onion and cook until tender, about 3 minutes. Add chicken, cheese, and pimiento; remove from heat and set aside.

2. For sauce, in a small saucepan, combine tomato sauce, ½ cup water, onion, chilies, and oregano. Simmer for 10 minutes over low heat.

3. In a large bowl, mix together masa harina, cracked wheat, Parmesan cheese, and salt. Work in butter and gradually stir in warm water, using your hands. Immediately form 5-inch round patties, ¼ inch thick. Place 2 tablespoons filling in center of each patty. Fold over; seal edges well.

4. In a large saucepan or deep-fat fryer, heat 2 inches of oil to 375°. Fry chonitas in batches without crowding, turning once, until golden brown, 5 to 7 minutes a side. Drain on paper towels. Serve sauce over chonitas.

364 CHICKEN POT PIE WITH SWEET POTATO CRUST

Prep: 30 minutes   Cook: 35 minutes   Serves: 6

Sweet potatoes create a lovely orange color in the crust and add a different flavor to a chicken pot pie.

3 cups chopped cooked chicken	1 cup half-and-half or light cream
1 cup chopped cooked carrots	2 cups chicken broth
12 small whole white onions, cooked	¾ teaspoon salt
½ cup chopped cooked celery	¼ teaspoon freshly ground pepper
1 cup cooked peas	1 teaspoon baking powder
1 tablespoon chopped parsley	1 cup cold mashed sweet potatoes
6 tablespoons butter or margarine	⅓ cup vegetable oil
1 cup plus 6 tablespoons flour	1 egg, well beaten

1. Preheat oven to 350°. In a 2½-quart baking dish, arrange chicken, carrots, onions, celery, peas, and parsley.

2. In a medium-size saucepan, melt butter over medium heat. Stir in the 6 tablespoons flour. Cook, stirring, for 1 minute. Whisk in half-and-half and chicken broth slowly. Season with ½ teaspoon salt and the pepper. Continue cooking and stirring until sauce boils and thickens. Pour sauce over chicken and vegetables.

3. In a medium-size bowl, mix remaining 1 cup flour, baking powder, and ¼ teaspoon salt. With a fork, work in sweet potatoes with oil and egg. Roll out dough on lightly floured board to about ¼-inch thickness.

4. Cover baking dish with dough and pinch edges all around. Make a small slit in dough. Bake for 35 minutes, until crust is golden brown.

365   CHICKEN BREASTS WELLINGTON
Prep: 40 minutes   Cook: 50 minutes   Serves: 6

Frozen patty shells are used to create an elegant dish that would take much longer to make from scratch. The recipe can easily be prepared early in the day and kept in the refrigerator until ready to bake and serve.

1 package (6 ounces) long grain and wild rice	2 eggs, separated
2 tablespoons grated orange peel	1 package (10 ounces) frozen patty shells, thawed and rolled out to six 7-inch rounds
3 tablespoons butter or margarine	
6 skinless, boneless chicken breast halves	1 can (16 ounces) whole berry cranberry sauce
Freshly ground pepper	2 tablespoons orange liqueur
1/4 pound mushrooms, sliced	2 tablespoons lemon juice
	1/4 teaspoon dry mustard

1. Cook rice according to instructions on package for firmer rice. Add orange peel and let cool.

2. Preheat oven to 400°. In a large frying pan, melt butter over medium heat. Add chicken breasts and cook until browned, about 4 minutes a side. Remove with tongs and season with pepper. Add mushrooms to remaining butter and cook until tender, about 3 minutes.

3. Beat egg whites until soft peaks form. Add cooked rice and mushrooms; mix well.

4. On each pastry circle, place 1/3 cup rice mixture and top with chicken. Moisten edge with water; press to seal edges together. Place seam side down on a large ungreased baking sheet.

5. In a small bowl, beat egg yolks lightly with 1 tablespoon water; brush over dough. Bake uncovered for 35 minutes.

6. For sauce, combine cranberry sauce, orange liqueur, lemon juice, and mustard in a small saucepan. Heat over low heat until warmed. Serve over chicken.

Index